Terrence O'Keeffe

High Treason and Low Comedy

Egon Erwin Kisch's Cabaret Plays as History and Art

Terrence O'Keeffe

HIGH TREASON
AND
LOW COMEDY

Egon Erwin Kisch's Cabaret Plays as History and Art

ibidem Verlag

Bibliografische Information der Deutschen Nationalbibliothek

Die Deutsche Nationalbibliothek verzeichnet diese Publikation in der Deutschen Nationalbibliografie; detaillierte bibliografische Daten sind im Internet über http://dnb.d-nb.de abrufbar.

Bibliographic information published by the Deutsche Nationalbibliothek

Die Deutsche Nationalbibliothek lists this publication in the Deutsche Nationalbibliografie; detailed bibliographic data are available in the Internet at http://dnb.d-nb.de.

ISBN-13: 978-3-8382-1379-8

© *ibidem*-Verlag, Stuttgart 2020

Alle Rechte vorbehalten

Printed in the EU

Table of Contents

Preface and Acknowledgments...7

Chapter 1.
Introducing Egon Erwin Kisch, the Raging Reporter.................11

Chapter 2.
Notes on the Plays: Sources and Translation 37

Chapter 3.
The Pursuit...45

Chapter 4.
Kisch and the Redl Case: Reportage into Melodrama................83

Chapter 5.
The Ascension of Toni Gallows to Heaven...................................111

Chapter 6.
Toni Gallows, a Real Prague Legend: Feuilleton into
Comic Fantasy 141

Chapter 7.
Kisch's Career as Playwright...161

Chapter 8.
Theatrical Context: German Playwrights and Weimar
Comedy and Cabaret...193

Chapter 9.
Afterlife of the Redl Story: Films, on the English Stage,
a Slovak Novel 207

Chapter 10.
The Toni Gallows Story on Film, the Prague Stage Again,
and Television..249

Chapter 11.
Transformations: History, Historical Fiction, and Fantasy 265

Notes 275

Bibliographical Note on earlier Kisch editions and
the Kisch *Gesammelte Werke* 297

Bibliography 303

Index 311

Preface and Acknowledgments

This book is the offspring of an earlier unfinished manuscript to which I had given the provisional title *The Posthumous Lives of Colonel Redl*. I came to the topic of Egon Erwin Kisch and the role he played in 'breaking the Redl espionage case' in 1913 (and continuing to write about it throughout his colorful career as a journalist) after seeing István Szabó's film, *Oberst Redl*. "Excellent film," I thought, but, as I began to read biographies of Redl and Kisch and the works of historians interested in the Redl affair, I realized the film was almost entirely fictitious, even fantastic, in its treatment of a scandal that had rocked the Habsburg military and political leaderships on the eve of World War One. From there my research spread into the many different social, political and cultural streams that wound their way through Kisch's life. And I discovered that the Redl story continued to interest not just Szabó (70 years after the event) but a number of artists, right up to the present day.

The wave of First World War histories that began to appear in 2013 (many of which were 'revisionist' in their framing) usually mentioned the Redl case, sometimes in garbled fashion. So, Kisch and the espionage affair were still known and discussed in certain quarters, though, in English, much of this discussion was superficial or misleading. Although he had been well-known during the interwar years, Kisch's reputation receded into an undeserved obscurity in the English-speaking world after his death in 1948. However, there are serious works that explain this trend and try to counter it. Kisch's most recent major biographers (who published their books in 1997, one in German, the other in English) suggested that his earlier international renown had diminished in Western Europe, the UK, and the US as a result of the polarized opinions of the Cold War era (Kisch had been a prominent leftist activist during the last three decades of his life). The exception to this was Germany, where his works are still a subject of literary and historical discourse.

My research into the espionage affair led me to read Kisch's 1920s play about Redl's last day and then look at his other plays, none of which had come over into English. Among these works for the stage one stood out immediately. This was his comedic treatment of the story of a rowdy Prague prostitute (nicknamed 'Toni Gallows') who argues her way into heaven. I translated the two plays and began to build the present book around themes the plays address and the role this 'theatrical' phase of Kisch's life played in his writing as he soon became 'the raging reporter' and the star of international reportage during the years between the two world wars. As the reader can see, these are diverse topics, but I have tried to tie them together in a sensible fashion. Remote from Kisch's day and concerns, but culturally significant as a gloss on his work, is the present book's examining the long afterlives of both of these stories in several media over the last century, a topic that informs my ideas of what happens when historical events become the basis of artistic transformations.

The preceding is the specific background of how my interest in Kisch and his writing evolved. This had a 'prehistory' of many years of reading Central European history and literature, supplemented by numerous trips to that part of the world, which led me to write essays about the region's writers, history and culture that were published in small magazines, starting in 2011. For these earliest opportunities to publish I owe thanks to Dr. Ewa Thompson, editor of *The Sarmatian Review*, who accepted long pieces about Andrzej Stasiuk. Similar gratitude is due Zsófia Zachár, who opened the pages of the *The Hungarian Quarterly* to an essay about Hungary's beloved Gyula Krudy. Regarding the Redl affair, my personal experience as a sergeant in the US army's military intelligence branch during 1968–1969 whetted my curiosity about the once-famous espionage case. But, in order to write the present book, I had to expand my reading to include a large number of specialized historical works, critical writing about Kisch, and a variety of Central European novels in translation. I also needed directional guidance and practical help.

Over the years I received advice, encouragement, and assistance from numerous people who took an interest in my writing about Kisch in general or the Redl espionage affair and the 'Toni Gallows' play in particular. Here is where I thank them. My earliest advisor and supporter was the talented linguist, translator, and writer about Central European culture, the late Harold B. Segel. In the course of doing research about John Osborne's Redl play I received similar support from Osborne's biographer, Luc Gilleman, also sadly deceased before his time. I thank Charles Sabatos as well—he is the skilled translator of two novellas and one short story written by the inventive Pavel Vilikovský, and he was happy to correspond with me about Vilikovký's writing. In discussing the complexities and unresolved details of the historical Redl case I received sound advice from Dr. Ian Armour, who has written about Central European history and military intelligence matters in the old Dual Monarchy. In acknowledging help with matters pertaining to the complicated Czech-German-Jewish nexus, I thank Dr. Gary Cohen for useful suggestions, and similarly, with respect to Weimar-era theater, Dr. William Grange. I owe a debt of gratitude to James Walker of Camden House, who read an early draft of the manuscript and gave me useful advice about rewriting and reorganization of the text. For their enthusiastic and encouraging responses to a late draft of the manuscript, which elevated my mood, I thank Dr. Leslie Morris of the University of Minnesota and Dr. Todd Herzog of the University of Cincinnati.

Researchers and staff members of several institutes in Germany, Austria, and the Czech Republic also assisted me by sending documents and downloads of old films and television plays that are often difficult to locate. Dr. Viera Glosiková, of Prague's Charles University faculty, was invaluable, sending me her articles on Kisch as a dramatist and remarking on this part of his life. With regard to old plays, films, and contemporaneous critical reactions to them, I thank the following for bibliographical guidance and help in securing hard-to-get materials: Karolina Košťálová of the National Library of the Czech Republic; Matěj Strnad of the Czech Film Archive; Susanne Rocca of the Filmarchiv Austria; and Juliane Riedel and Martina Seidel of the German Radio Archive (dRA). For a long-term conversation about Kisch's adventures in Australia that made him a "hot news item" in the English-speaking world during 1934-35, I owe thanks to Dr. Carolyn Rasmussen of Melbourne University, who also steered me to Australian authors who wrote about his impact on that nation's culture. And, of course, I express my gratitude to those at the *ibidem*-Verlag who assisted me administratively and editorially, especially Valerie Lange and Jessica Haunschild. Back in the US, I owe thanks to Stuart Moss of the Nathan Kline Institute for bibliographical help and to Jan Hrabě for translating the dialogue of a Czech television play for me. I hope I haven't left anyone out, but it's possible that I have. I close this with a salute to the memory of Harold B. Segel, a distinguished professor whose knowledge of Central European writing and culture was broad and deep and who was an enthusiastic partisan of E. E. Kisch's writing.

Some notes on the text are advisable here. Unless otherwise indicated in the text or footnotes, translations are mine. Square brackets indicate my clarifying notes within quotes or translated passages. Footnotes are grouped by the chapter as book end-notes; some contain important supplementary information about historical matters. Citations are in 'short form', while full publication information on each work cited or discussed is in the Bibliography. A Bibliographical Note supplies detailed information about the main contemporary repository of Kisch's writing, the Kisch *Gesammelte Werke* (Collected Works). In the main text, footnotes, and bibliography my citations and other references to the Collected Works use the later edition, referred to as *GW (1992)* or *GW (1993)*. The first appearance of the German title of a book, article, play or film has its English translation in parentheses. Where the English translation of a title is not italicized, this indicates that the book was never published in translation, e.g., *Wagnisse in aller Welt* (Worldwide Exploits). Truncated German and English titles are used in passages with multiple references to a work under discussion (e.g., *Die Abenteuer in Prag* becomes *Abenteuer*, while *A Patriot for Me* becomes *Patriot*).

Chapter 1.
Introducing Egon Erwin Kisch,
the Raging Reporter

Egon Erwin Kisch (1885–1948) became a professional journalist in 1906. During his first two decades as a writer he was well-known in Austria, Germany and Czechoslovakia. As his reputation spread throughout and beyond Europe during the interwar years, he acquired the sobriquet 'the raging reporter'.[1] The nickname stems from the critical success and large sales of his 1925 book, *Der rasende Reporter*, a collection of his reportage and other short pieces published in Berlin. In terms of 'identity' (using categorizations common to his own period) he was Jewish (by family religious affiliation, not 'nationality'), a citizen of the Austrian half of the Dual Monarchy, a 'real Praguer', and a man who thought and wrote in German but had a good command of Czech. After World War I he was a citizen of the new Czechoslovakian First Republic. From 1921 on he lived in Berlin until his exile in 1933, moving first to Paris, then to Mexico City during World War II. He returned from exile to Prague in 1946, old, tired, and somewhat disillusioned, yet managed to revise earlier works and write new pieces up until the time of his death.

Kisch undertook long journeys abroad during the 1920s and 1930s to observe and investigate contemporary political events and their historical and cultural milieus, which he reported on in a series of thematic books.[2] These travels included trips to France, England, Spain, Russia, the USA, North Africa, China, Japan, Ceylon, and Australia. As a man he was gregarious, ebullient, and broadly curious about the world he lived in. As a journalist he was an inventive stylist. He was also active in left-wing political movements after 1918 (his communist affiliations will be discussed below). Most importantly, he was a prolific writer of both short and long nonfiction works, most of which are deemed to be 'reportage' by later critics and students of his *oeuvre* (the pigeonholing of his writing into this elastic genre is somewhat misleading). At the age of 29 he wrote a novel that was well-received, and during the first half of the 1920s he developed an ancillary career as a playwright, a phase of his life and work that will be examined in detail for the first time in English in the present book.

Translations of Kisch's two most successful works for the stage are in Chapters 3 and 5 below. The first of the plays is a historical melodrama that deals with the last day on earth of an infamous, high-ranking Austro-Hungarian traitor, Colonel Alfred Redl, whose story played an important role in Kisch's career as a journalist. The second play is entirely different in origins and atmosphere. It is the story of 'Toni Gallows', a rowdy Prague prostitute whose earthly travails unfold in slang as she tries to argue her way into heaven; here Kisch turned a short feuilleton into a cabaret fantasy-comedy with a strong streak of pathos. These two plays are treated in the present book as portals into a wider world. Inclusion of the translated plays is a necessary basis for discussions placing them in several overlapping contexts: biographical, historical, and cultural. Each of these plays enjoyed a long afterlife in several different media. Chapters 9 and 10 examine these various adaptations in the context of what happens when artists (including Kisch himself) transform history into art. Treating them in both intensive and expansive fashion allows discussion of the plays to ramify out in space and time, and takes the reader down informative and eventful pathways through history. But before reading the plays and the commentaries on them, the reader should learn more about their author and his career.

The English-language reader has three available sources of information about Kisch and his writing. First there is a fair sampling of his work in English translation: five of his books and a smattering of his magazine articles were translated into English during his lifetime. This sample is not fully representative of his interests or his approach to writing. Second is a 1997 "Bio-Anthology" written and edited by Harold Segel, an American scholar whose concise critical biography of Kisch is followed by his translations of 26 of Kisch's outstanding pieces. (In German there are at least three major biographies of Kisch, several minor ones, and two 'illustrated miscellanies'.) And, third, there are re-

views of Kisch's translated books and articles that critically ana-
lyze his work. This last body of writing in English is small, a mere
trickle in comparison to the large number of such pieces about
Kisch in German. In terms of significance, however, an exception
to this is Scott Spector's book (*Prague Territories*) about the unique
'identity problems' of German-Jewish writers in Prague during
the years between ca. 1890 and 1920. Spector presents an in-depth
analysis of Kisch's chosen path (journalism and the evolution of
his politics from typical German liberalism to secular-socialist activism) as exemplary of one of a complex of ideological and practical choices open to him and his Jewish peers in the 'Prague circle' in their attempts to reconcile the differences between Czechs
and Germans.[3] This will be discussed in more detail when dealing
with Kisch's 'readership problems' in Chapter 7 below.

During his lifetime Kisch had a presence in the English-
speaking world that depended originally on newspaper and magazine publicity about his activities. In Europe his reputation as a
journalist with a distinct voice and leftist perspective depended on
his prolific writing of vivid newspaper and magazine articles and
essays, often republished in book form as collections of reportage,
and six or seven topical books based on his far-ranging travels. Between 1912 and 1948 twenty-four books by Kisch were published
in German; this count does not include his juvenilia, co-written or
co-edited works, pamphlet-sized publications, or several of his
short plays. Many of his books were reissued during his lifetime,
and equally many were translated into a variety of European languages (Czech, Polish, Romanian, Serbian, French, Dutch, Spanish, Russian, English, Swedish, and Italian).

Kisch is often credited with being the founder, foremost advocate, and best-known interwar practitioner of reportage, a form
of journalism and essay-writing that will be discussed in more detail below. Posthumously his name and reputation have diminished outside the German-speaking lands, with the exception of
the Czech Republic (and former Czechoslovakia), where he is one
of the few 'Prague Germans' honored as 'native sons and daughters' of the city. In contrast to the normal fate of fading interest in
all but the most famous men and women of any particular era, his

name and writing are kept alive in recent German editions. In Germany (and, to a lesser extent, Austria) his status as the 'master of reportage' remains a subject of critical literary discourse. Film and television adaptations of his pieces continue to flourish.

In the English-speaking world Kisch has more or less fallen into oblivion since his death in 1948 (excepting Australia, for reasons explained below). Several of his pieces appeared in American magazines during the late 1920s and early 1930s,[4] followed in the years 1935-1937 by English translations of three topical books that reported on his travels and direct observations. These were: *Changing Asia* (1935), *Secret China* (1935), and *Australian Landfall* (1937). Based on his 1931 travels through the peripheral Muslim lands of the USSR, *Changing Asia* conveyed a good deal of statistical (and bureaucratic) information and made the argument that 'de-feudalization' and vast improvements in the quality of life had been accomplished through Soviet economic programs; in addition to his political and social observations the book contains several colorful 'adventure chapters'. The German title of the 1932 book, *Asien gründlich verändert* (Asia Fundamentally Changed) is more definitive of Kisch's judgment that this modernization program had succeeded than the translated title used by his English publisher.

Secret China recorded Kisch's illegal entry into the country and his travels between March and July, 1932, when he visited Shanghai, Peking, and Nanking. His trip took place at a time when a Japanese military incursion in Shanghai was in progress and when there was armed strife between Chiang Kai-Shek's nationalist government, local warlords, and communist insurgents. In addition to his usual leftist-internationalist interpretation of these events (which led him to create an idealized picture of the Red Chinese enclave, based on the verbal reports of his contacts), Kisch wrote vivid chapters on Shanghai crime-lords and their corrupt police abettors and on his visit to an establishment housing retired Chinese Imperial harem officials, all of whom had been castrated. In comparison to the publisher's translation, the German title of his 1933 China book captures the immediacy of his reporting on current affairs: *Egon Erwin Kisch berichtet: China geheim* (Egon Erwin Kisch Reports: Secret China).

This surge of translations of Kisch's writing into English occurred toward the end of the period when his international renown peaked. His exploits in Australia in 1934–1935 also resulted in widespread publicity in the English-speaking world (and defamatory press coverage in Nazi Germany). Selected by Henri Barbusse, Kisch had gone there as the sole European delegate to a pacifist and anti-Fascist congress. Based on confidential intelligence reports from the UK, the Australian government had forbidden his entry. Attempting to bypass the ban, Kisch broke a leg when jumping from ship to dock in Melbourne. His legal case wound its way through the courts while he roamed the country on crutches, attending meetings and rallies as the government continued its efforts to deport him. Pro- and anti-government newspaper coverage of his case swelled into a floodtide of publicity.[5] The trip yielded a book, *Landung in Australien*, published in Amsterdam in 1937. Its long opening chapter covered his political travails, with a good deal of facetious writing about the ineptitude of the government; it concluded with hortatory socialist rhetoric. Its second half comprised ten local color sketches about the history of the Australian labor movement and 'exotic' topics such as variants in the game of cricket and a famous horseracing murder case (of the horse, that is); it also included a rather misguided polemical chapter on "Lenin and Australia". Noted above, its English translation, *Australian Landfall*, was published in London in the same year.

While both the original and the English translation of his book about his trip were banned in Australia between 1937 and 1969,[6] Australians had a full report of his activities in their nation available in *On the Pacific Front: The Adventures of Egon Kisch in Australia*, a 1936 book written by one of their own, "Julian Smith", the pen-name of a seasoned leftist journalist, Tom Fitzgerald.[7] Smith recounted Kisch's perambulations and painted a portrait of a witty, combative, risk-taking man whose character appealed to many Australians. His reportorial style was a direct tribute to Kisch's, its author being an admirer and advocate of reportage as practiced by the master. Julie Wells has given readers an account and analysis of Kisch's long-lasting influence on Australian journalism and liberal-leftist perspectives in the arts in general (e.g., he was a founding member of the Australian Writers' League, which, though short-lived, had a significant local impact).[8]

Though the most widely publicized of Kisch's long trips abroad, this was not his last. His on-the-scene reporting on the Spanish civil war was to follow, resulting in only one piece translated into English at the time, "The Three Cows",[9] while his other pieces about the war were published in German exile magazines and newsletters. Decades later they were gathered into a posthumous collection, *Unter Spaniens Himmel* (Under Spanish Skies), published in East Germany in 1961.[10] His ten-month internment in New York in 1940 was followed by his 1940–1945 exile in Mexico, resulting in a book about historical matters and current life there, *Entdeckungen in Mexiko* (Mexican Discoveries). One of its reportages, "An Indian Village under the Star of David" has come over into English in two different translations, one as part of *Tales from Seven Ghettos*,[11] the other in Segel's Kisch Bio–Anthology.[12] Both books are discussed in more detail below.

In late 1941 the English translation of his memoirs, *Sensation Fair*, came out ahead of the German version, *Marktplatz der Sensationen*, released in Mexico City in July, 1942.[13] While the memoirs were critically praised in the US,[14] they could only make a small impression, given the magnitude of recent events and the flood of reportorial and partisan writing about the unfolding of World War II. Their publication in New York coincided with the entry of the US into the Asian and European wars, the stalled German offensive on the outskirts of Moscow after six months of vast conquests in Russia, and a period of menacingly successful German U–boat activity in an attempted blockade of England. *Sensation Fair* recounts Kisch's childhood and pre-World War I days as an enterprising reporter in Prague, with chapters that bring in events from his 1914–1918 life as a soldier and his 1920s research into the 1913 espionage case and major public scandal known as 'the Redl affair',[15] which is the subject of one of the two plays presented below. Later additions to the memoirs during and after his lifetime are discussed in a Bibliographical Note that follows the main text of the present book. The memoirs present feuilletons, reportages, and articles that had appeared elsewhere in print as reminiscences, while also weaving essayistic connections between topics and between the different phases and perspectives of a long life as an adventurous and controversial professional journalist. Nowhere in Kisch's memoirs does he mention that he had been a member of the Communist Party since 1919. His evasiveness on this point and what his Party membership meant for his writing will be discussed below.

The last of his books to come over into English was *Tales from Seven Ghettos*, a 1948 translation and augmentation of his 1934 book, *Geschichten aus sieben Ghettos*.[16] The translator, Edith Bone, added chapters based on Kisch's post-1934 writing about Jewish matters. *Tales* gives us the ruminations of Kisch, a thoroughly assimilated, non-practicing Jew, on Jewish lives and topics around the world in which he and they lived; it also includes essays about 'exotic' and legendary Jewish stories from across several centuries.

After Kisch's death in 1948 there were no new translations of his work into English until 1997, when Harold Segel's *Egon Erwin Kisch, The Raging Reporter: A Bio-Anthology* was published. Segel's compact biography of Kisch also has translations of a wide variety of his reportages and essays, most of which had not been translated before. This yielded a virtual 'sixth book' of Kisch in English. Its concise bibliographical and critical discussions make it an ideal starting point for English-language readers to become acquainted with Kisch's life and work, while its translations offer a wide sampling of his writing from over a period of four decades. Of relevance for the present book, Segel included a translation of Kisch's small but influential 1924 book about the Redl espionage case.[17] In the same year the most recent large-scale critical biography of Kisch in German was also published, Marcus Patka's *Egon Erwin Kisch: Stationen im Leben eines streitbaren Autors* (Egon Erwin Kisch: Way-Stations in the Life of a Militant Writer). Patka's exhaustive bibliography of writing by and about Kisch is the most comprehensive source of information for any and all research on the man, his works, and critical evaluation of his writing.[18]

Patka followed this in 1998 by compiling, editing, and contributing a summary critical essay to a profusely illustrated 'Kisch biographical miscellany', *Der rasende Reporter Egon Erwin Kisch: Eine Biographie in Bildern* (The Raging Reporter Egon Erwin Kisch: A Pictorial Biography). In addition to numerous quotations from Kisch's works, including letters, the book contains reminiscences of friends, reviews of and commentary on Kisch's writing by other writers and colleagues, and amusing anecdotes about the colorful, energetic, and congenial man himself. Illustrations are in the form of photographs (often of 'Kisch among the famous' of his era) and reproductions of sketches, finished drawings, paintings, postcards and posters that show Kisch in a variety of settings: his domiciles and favorite haunts in Prague, Berlin, Paris and elsewhere; meetings with colleagues and friends on political and informal occasions; and, important documents that chronicle aspects of his life. Patka's essay, *"Facetten rasender Zeit: Der Schriftsteller Egon Erwin Kisch hinter der Maske des Reporters"*,[19] was, in slightly edited form, translated as "The Writer behind the Reporter's Mask" by Heidi Zogbaum. This is the Afterword to her informative 2004 book, *Kisch in Australia: The Untold Story*.[20] Here Patka makes his case for Kisch as a "poet of everyday life", also arguing that the Manichean polarities of Cold War-era opinion resulted in Kisch being arbitrarily and incorrectly dismissed as a merely "communist reporter" (or even a propagandist) in the West, including England and the US. The exception to this dismissal was continued and more nuanced interest in Kisch in both halves of the divided Germany. The present author believes that the available translations of Kisch in English support Patka's contentions in this respect and give the reader an idea of his wide range of interests and his literary strengths (and occasional weaknesses as well).

Two more English translations of Kisch pieces came out in 2003 and 2015, respectively. The first was a chapter about "Fordism in Detroit" from Kisch's 1929 book, *Paradies Amerika* (American Paradise), followed by Sheila Skaff's analysis of Kisch's rhetorical techniques, which show his literary gifts and convey his leftist political outlook on life.[21] The full title of Kisch's American travelogue is *Egon Erwin Kisch Beehrt Sich Darzubieten: Paradies*

Amerika (Egon Erwin Kisch Has the Honor to Present You: American Paradise), showing his ironical attitude toward the 'paradisical' aspects of the USA. The second piece is "Elliptical Treadmill", a vivid snapshot of the crowd at Berlin's immensely popular six-day bicycle races, taken from 1925's *Der rasende Reporter*.[22] Graham Davis's translation captures the excitement of Kisch's sketch of the fervid atmosphere of a form of urban entertainment patronized by people from all walks of life, from prostitutes and gamblers to families with children, workingmen, and wealthy men-about-town, all in search of diversion through intoxication, sexual opportunities, and the thrill of thousands cheering on their favorites. Kisch's gifts as a feuilletonist portraying a popular social phenomenon (with sociological implications) can be compared here with those of Joseph Roth, who covered the same event in his piece, "The Twelfth Berlin Six-Day Races", available in a translation by Michael Hofmann.[23]

The preceding summary account of 'Kisch in English' takes the reader through representative Kisch pieces from the pre-World War I era (as recounted in his memoirs and stories in *Tales from Seven Ghettos*) up until the mid-1940s. Though amounting to about seven volumes of prose, it is small and somewhat selective in comparison to Kisch's total output, at least half which deals with matters in Central Europe (if we extend that appellation to interwar Germany as well as to the successor states of the vanished Austro-Hungarian Empire). The English-language reader with some command of German has to go to linked compare-and-contrast books, like *Paradies Amerika* and *Zaren, Popen, Bolschewiken* (Czars, Priests, Bolsheviks) in order to get the full flavor of Kisch's writing about contemporary social and political phenomena of intrinsic interest to Kisch's wide readership during his heyday; or to books like *Der rasende Reporter*, with its 53 short, graphic pieces, to see why Germans and Austrians considered Kisch to be a master of *Kleinkunst* ("the small art form")[24] with a specifically modern cast.

As with all authors, it is necessary to take the facts of Kisch's life into account when evaluating his writing—he lived in several cultural milieus that changed over time and had an impact on his responses to the world around him. Therefore a biographical sketch is given here.

Born in 1885 in Prague, Egon was the third of Hermann and Ernestine Kisch's five sons. His family was middle-class and Jewish. His father owned a draper's-clothier's fabric shop, and many of his uncles and cousins were also small businessmen or professional men in Prague. Kisches, originally from the Eger (Pilsen) area of Bohemia, had lived in Prague for many generations and branched out into a variety of trades and professions, including medicine and law. Like the vast majority of Prague's Jews, the family's primary language and cultural affiliation was German, though Kisch himself was fluent in Czech and, in general, supported the aspirations of Czechs for more political autonomy within the Dual Monarchy. Eventually this turned into support for the new Czechoslovakian First Republic established as the Habsburg dynasty collapsed at the end of World War I and its holdings became reborn, new, or expanded nations.

Kisch attended the same Catholic elementary school (staffed by Piarists) where Franz Kafka, two years older, had been a student, followed by completion of the *Staatsrealschule* course of studies. Upon graduation he went to a technical school for journalism but did not complete the program. In 1904 he went through the one-year voluntary military program designed to advance its trainees to Second Lieutenant rank within the Austro-Hungarian reserve army. Having problems with discipline, he spent much of his time on guardhouse duty and finished the program as a corporal in the reserves, a status that would have an impact on his fate when World War I broke out. He was shifting about and dabbling with literature, having a volume of verse published in 1905; his always-supportive mother subsidized the publisher's small edition. In the following year he had a collection of short stories published, *Der freche Franz und andere Geschichten* (Cheeky Frank and Other Stories). He later dismissed his poetry as sentimental juvenilia, while avoiding judgmental remarks on the quality of his stories.

In 1906 Kisch also began his career as a journalist, first interning for *Prager Tagblatt*, where his assignment was to attend the large number of public lectures on politics, science, and cultural topics given in Prague and then submit short, summary reports on them. After six weeks of this unsatisfying (and unpaid) employment he obtained a starting position with another Prague German-language newspaper, *Bohemia*, where he began as a daily-beat reporter covering fires, accidents, other mishaps, and any aspect of street-life that had 'local-color' value to the paper's readers. He soon became a 'specialist in crime', reporting on Prague's criminal underworld, police courts, associated seedy venues, and its demi-monde of prostitutes, pimps, and assorted low-level thugs who lived in the legal twilight zones common to all large cities. As he continued as a reporter he acquired editorial duties and wrote a Sunday feuilleton column, "Roaming through Prague"—he used the opportunity to live briefly with the homeless and to take a variety of proletarian jobs in order report on the abysmal living and working conditions of Prague's large 'underclass', which had few tribunes speaking publicly on their behalf.[25] Edited and rewritten material from his newspaper reports came out in book form as well, beginning with 1912's *Aus Prager Gassen und Nächten* (From Prague's Alleyways and Nights) and 1913's *Prager Kinder* (Children of Prague — with "children" meaning the city's native sons and daughters).

In his last two weeks at *Bohemia* Kisch was involved in breaking the story behind the suicide of Colonel Alfred Redl during the early morning hours of May 25th, 1913. Within two days of the event, Kisch, based on his journalistic experience and intuition, had acquired enough information from unnamed 'inside sources' to contradict the benign story put out by the General Staff of the Austro-Hungarian army that Redl had taken his own life because he was suffering from "insomnia and nervous exhaustion" related to his diligence in the performance of his military duties as the General Staff Chief of Prague's VIIIth Army Corps. Redl, well known to the Viennese public, had spent most of the previous decade as the leading military intelligence expert within the General Staff's *Evidenzbüro*, which managed both espionage and counterespionage matters. He proved to be the highest-ranking traitor within the army, having sold large amounts of sensitive military information to Russia and Italy for a decade or more. Kisch's un-signed reports on the scandal led to a press, parliamentary, and dynastic furor directed at the General Staff and its Chief, Lieuten-ant Field Marshall Baron F. X. Conrad von Hötzendorf (usually re-ferred to by historians as "Conrad"). The details of the scandal and how Kisch wrote about it in a 1924 book of investigative jour-nalism will be discussed in Chapter 4 below, because portions of it are the basis of his 1920s play about Redl, *Die Hetzjagd*. Addition-ally, the book is illustrative of the theme of what happens to a nar-rative when historical material is used for subsequent transfor-mations into works of art.

In mid-June, 1913, Kisch moved to Berlin in search of other writing opportunities and a broader reading public. During his year in Berlin he wrote a novel, *Der Mädchenhirt* (The Shepherd of Young Women, a colloquial expression for a pimp — in English the book is usually referred to as "The Pimp"). It drew upon his ob-servations of Prague's underworld during the preceding years and was hailed as a "return to naturalism"[26] at a time when vari-ous forms of modernism, especially Expressionism, were ascend-ant (at least in critical opinion) in all of the arts.[27] As some critics pointed out, the main virtue of Kisch's novel, regardless of its po-sition in the ongoing debates about appropriately 'modern styles' and about German vs. Czech strife in Prague, was its bringing to the attention of the public the pressing issue of social inequality as manifested through the struggles of 'little people' in the new ur-ban jungles of the era.[28] Spector noted that Kisch had craftily es-caped the rhetoric of 'biological' and cultural arguments regarding 'nature vs. nurture' as the determinants of character and behavior (advanced by 'race theorists', including German nationalists). In-stead Kisch redefined the Czech–German contest as part of the un-folding class conflict of modernity, in other words, as a type of raw power struggle in which 'national character traits' were irrel-evant. In addition his protagonist, the illegitimate offspring of a sexual liaison between a German father and Czech mother, sub-verted the old Bohemian-German trope of masculine Aryans sub-duing and stewarding hyperemotional, culturally primitive, 'fem-inine' Czechs (who here represent Slavs in general, all in need of 'good German management').[29] While writing his novel in Berlin Kisch patronized bohemian cafés and circles, looking for an entrée into writing for the stage. In June 1914 he was appointed Dramaturge of a small theater and troupe that presented 'socially conscious' plays (*Sozietätsbühne*). This prospective career came to a sudden halt with the outbreak of World War I—as a reservist in the VIIIth Army Corps, Kisch was summoned to Prague and activated as an infantryman with the rank of corporal.

Kisch served in the Austro-Hungarian army for the duration of the war. As a footslogging rifleman he participated in one of the war's earliest battles, an offensive launched into a salient between the Sava and Drina Rivers in Serbia. His graphic description of this battle, in which the Austro-Hungarian army, a victim of its own haphazard planning and incompetent leadership, suffered large losses of men and equipment to withering Serbian machine-gun and artillery fire, was translated by Harold Segel as "Episodes from the Serbian Front".[30] The piece comes from Kisch's war diary, which appeared in 1922 as *Soldat im Prager Korps* (A Soldier in the Prague Corps) and was reissued in edited and augmented form in 1930 as *Schreib das auf, Kisch!* (Write It Down, Kisch!). The diary was not published at the time of its creation on account of Austria's strict censorship of any and all realistic reporting about the war (a policy most notably belittled by Karl Kraus in his 'monster play', *Die letzte Tagen der Menschheit*, or "Mankind's Last Days"). A hundred years later the historian Max Hastings, in *Catastrophe 1914*, cited passages from Kisch's diary in order to vivify his accounts of battles fought on the Serbian and Russian fronts.[31] Kisch's unit was transferred to participate in the grim 1914–1915 winter fighting along the line of the Carpathian mountains, where he was promoted to lieutenant, wounded by a grenade, and, after hospitalization, assigned to the army's press corps. In this job he re-established contact with Franz Werfel and met Joseph Roth and Robert Musil, who was his editor for a while; he maintained contact with both of these colleagues and rivals over the decades.[32]

The loss of the war, the collapse of the Habsburg dynasty, and the rapid disintegration of Austria-Hungary in October, 1918, led Kisch into a new phase of life and a new set of political commitments. Like those of many soldiers on both sides of the conflict, his beliefs about society and politics had been radicalized by his experience of the war. During his last year of service he illegally attended various leftist conferences and 'soldiers councils' meetings. At the war's end Kiich was on the scene in Vienna in uniform, becoming an agitator and leader of the Red Guard, a paramilitary force that threw its support to communists and other leftists in an abortive coup attempt against the conservative government of rump Austria.[33] Soon thereafter he joined the Communist Party.[34] Kisch remained evasive about his Party membership throughout his life. In situations that held the prospect of negative consequences (e.g., his status in Australia in 1934–1935 or in New York in 1939–1940), Kisch lied outright and denied any affiliation with the Communist Party.[35] In contrast, Istvan Deak's prosopography of Germany's leftist, radical, and revolutionary intellectuals associated with the journal *Die Weltbühne* supplies a concise biography of Kisch that emphasizes his Party connections and various left-wing committees and organizations he either founded or belonged to.[36]

Kisch remained in Vienna throughout 1919, took part in the press wars between the left- and right-wing factions of Austrian political life, and experienced discouragement about the political situation and his diminishing opportunities to publish in Austria. He returned to Prague in 1920, worked for *Prager Tagblatt*, and reestablished connections with his numerous friends and acquaintances who were active in both German and Czech literary and theatrical circles. He wrote *Die Abenteuer in Prag* (Prague Adventures) during 1920. It was a synthesis of reminiscences about his family and its history with colorful episodes recounting the city's political and cultural life; it included versions of some of the work he had published in 1912 and 1913 and has been called by some "his first memoir".

In 1921 he resettled in Berlin, which became his home base until his expulsion from Germany in 1933. Throughout the 1920s he traveled whenever necessary to Prague and Vienna in connection with his theatrical efforts and other publishing projects. In 1923 he compiled and edited an anthology of "classical journalism". Kisch's book about the Redl affair appeared in 1924. Though involved in theatrical projects during these years, he was obviously busy in writing to his main strength, reportage. In 1925 the book that spread his reputation as a master of reportage, *Der rasende Reporter*, sold well, was widely reviewed,[37] and went into numerous reissues.[38] Late in the same year he took his first trip to the Soviet Union, beginning his series of world-wide travels that resulted in thematic books of reportage.

Because Kisch and 'reportage' were almost synonymous for many of his readers, it is necessary to characterize this form of writing. What was it and what was it believed to be, especially with regard to Kisch's career? The first hint can be seen in the materials that Kisch chose for his compilation *Klassischer Journalismus*, which gathered pieces by venerable ancestors of reportage as Kisch came to see it. Though many of the selected authors (e.g., Pliny, Luther, Napoleon, Bismarck) had not been journalists, he grouped them with writers from the late 18th century forward who had practiced journalism at one time or another in their lives, much of it adversarial. Vivid writing based on direct observation influenced his selections, so he was amenable to including short pieces by Viennese feuilletonists whose work he admired (e.g., Peter Altenberg). In his Introduction to the collection Kisch stated his belief that there was such a thing as totally objective or impartial journalism.[39] Within a few years he was to change his mind about this, influenced by his leftist political beliefs and impressed by John Reed's *Ten Days That Shook the World*, which gave an enthusiastic, approving portrait of the Bolshevik leadership in the USSR (he wrote an Introduction to a 1927 German translation of Reed's book).[40] In Kisch's mind, reportage acquired a leftist political impetus and political goals, which, if skillfully woven into the narrative of a report, would persuade the reader that the implicit sociopolitical framework of his writing was the correct one.

Using Kisch's own criteria for writing 'legitimate reportage', a working definition would include the following elements. It is fact-based reporting that also investigates deeper social and political causes behind the facts. It uses what Kisch called "logical fantasy", which he defined as the most plausible and effective narrative means to connect and explain a series of related facts. It is open to literary devices such as metaphor, irony, sarcasm, taking an indirect path to a revelation, and fashioning an authorial narrative persona who observes and reports, but it should use everyday language and avoid literary flourishes based on purely aesthetic standards ('art for art's sake'). It is often impressionistic in its attempt to vividly re-create a situation or event, using fragments of reality in the manner of photographic montage. It is partial to a 'you-are-there' recounting of events, emphasizing the reporter's direct observation and the human factor, i.e., how events affect the common man and woman *as they perceive them*. In the right hands (e.g., Kisch's) it can be used to address historical topics as well as current events.

As to its political component, reportage is adversarial toward the conservative forces of society and those in power. It advances the causes of progressivism and improvements in the lives of workers and anyone else excluded from social and political influence. And, through militancy and exhortations, it aims to change society as well as to observe and describe it. Thus, Kisch's 1935 piece, "Reportage als Kunstform und Kampfform" ("Reportage as Art-Form and Combat Style") highlights militant advocacy as a basic component of reportage.[41] In an analysis of *Der rasende Reporter*, Keith Williams noted that although the book's Foreword hewed to the principle that the ideal journalist should be neutral, the actual writing implied just the opposite, i.e., there are no simple 'facts' in economic and social life—the reader needs information about prevailing political structures and ideologies that underlie the facts in order to understand how and why they exist as they do. Williams calls the interlocked set of techniques Kisch used to indicate these underlying structures "defamiliarizing the familiar". For Kisch this meant, as Williams puts it, "demystifying the alienated appearances sponsored by capitalism."[42]

None of the foregoing constitutes a theory of reportage, but is rather a set of journalistic guidelines or standards. During the Weimar Republic years, when Kisch advocated this kind of writing, he was not alone in his turn away from the recent achievements and stylistic approaches of other forms of modernism (e.g.,

Symbolism, Expressionism, 'stream of consciousness' writing). In Weimar-era Germany the term *die neue Sachlichkeit* ("new objectivity" or "new matter-of-factness") described the period's turn toward more 'factually engaged' works in the realms of literature, painting, architecture, film, theater, and music. The extent of this stance can be seen in the subtitle of John Willett's survey of Weimar-era art and politics, *The New Sobriety 1917–1933*, wherein "sobriety" is an alternate interpretation of *Sachlichkeit*. Willett writes that Kisch's contemporaries saw him as an able representative of the era and its concerns, to the point that in their minds his name was synonymous with reportage, a form of writing they perceived as parallel to experimental ventures in film, drama, and the visual arts.[43]

The foregoing account of reportage's ideal constituent elements can be challenged when considering any particular piece that claims to adhere to its standards. Political tendentiousness might undermine accuracy, and imputed motives and causes might be incorrect. Contextualizing one's gathering of facts ('raw data') within a political-philosophical ideology, Marxism-Leninism, already points to ways in which the meaning of facts might be distorted, while inconvenient facts might be ignored. Needless to say, this applies to all ideological frameworks through which facts are selected and interpreted (e.g., reporting that assumes the 'natural' or 'inevitable' status of capitalism, as in our own time). In addition to these commonplace provisos about the nature of journalistic objectivity, Kisch's desire to make his reporting interesting and entertaining points to other ways in which fictional devices (story arcs, clear contrasts between villains and heroes, the invented persona of an 'objective narrator', reconstructed dialogues, etc.) penetrate literary nonfiction. There are no firm criteria for deciding when the already vague boundary between objectivity and the reporter's subjectivity drifts too far to the subjective or interpretive side. Another way to put this is that the boundary between fiction and nonfiction is often not clear. Whether Kisch pondered such matters in any depth is unknown.

In English-language writing the problem has reared its head several times in the recent past. Debates about the relative merits of tabloid journalism *versus* writing published by august newspapers with stricter fact-checking criteria have been running for more than a century. The American 'New Journalism' of the 1960s–1980s yielded extended interpretive reportages (by Tom Wolfe, Gay Talese, Jimmy Breslin, Janet Malcolm, Norman Mailer and others) and even 'nonfiction novels' (e.g., by Truman Capote and Mailer); these blurred previous journalistic boundaries. The advent of round-the-clock cable television news programs, internet news blogs and tendentious websites, including those that dispense 'fake-news', has exacerbated competing standards of 'what is fit to print'. Were he alive today, Kisch might relish some of these contentious battles while being mystified or horrified by others.

During his pre-1914 years as a Prague journalist Kisch made no specific pleas for parties on the left. He was vaguely aligned with the old liberal Bohemian-German values that had been adopted by many of Prague's Jewish families. After the war, when his political beliefs took a definite shape, he used wry suggestiveness rather than blatant didacticism to convey his ideology to the reader; occasionally he shifted into outright propaganda. He was, in principle, a communist, but he did not allow his topical interests or his writing style to be dictated by the rigid Party line. It seems that the cultural bureaucrats of the Party never attempted to force Kisch into this mold; perhaps, with his celebrity and his broad network of moderate, liberal, and non-communist leftist contacts, he was too valuable an asset to be bullied or tampered with. In the terminology of Russian and Comintern intelligence and Western counterintelligence he was an 'agent of influence', putting him on a plane with non-communist 'fellow travelers', though he was far better informed and more purposeful than they were. Whatever influence his communist affiliations had on his writing, Kisch wandered away from reportage with political implications whenever opportunities to do so occurred, indicating his broad, eclectic curiosity about human life. However, during the post-World War II years, Kisch's East German biographers emphasized his credentials as a communist writer who often advanced the Party's goals—at times this is a fair evaluation, but

Kisch was much more (and perceived to be much more) than a writer who stuck to the Party line or had his writing pre-approved by Party officials.

An interesting light on Kisch's status as an iconic socialist (or communist) journalist in post-1948 East Germany is shed by passages in Maxim Leo's 'family biography', *Red Love*, published in translation in 2013 and critically discussed by the present author elsewhere.[44] Leo remarked that his mother and her father (a well-known foreign-affairs journalist who served the DDR's press agency, with intelligence duties as well) were admirers of Kisch. But they lamented the fact that they would never be allowed to write like Kisch, i.e., they could not apply their powers of observation and literary skills to an examination of the underlying power politics of the Soviet bloc and the grim realities of social and cultural life in the DDR. Like Kisch, they were uneasy about the trend of socialism in the Soviet world, but maintained a public silence. Here Kisch assumes the typical lineaments of an official icon honored in word, but not deed.

A glimpse into Kisch's attitude toward the new communist state in the Soviet Union can be had by considering his trip there in 1925-1926. Michael Horowitz quoted a brief, starry-eyed letter that Kisch wrote to his mother soon after his arrival:

> Dearest Mom—So I've been in Moscow and have been really lucky, for this city, both in appearance and in its inner essence, is the most beautiful in all the world. A thousand good wishes and kisses from yours, Egonek.[45]

Following up on this, Horowitz wrote that in his letters Kisch also noted the lack of housing, overcrowding in all public institutions, large numbers of homeless children living on the streets, decrepit public transport, and every other person appearing to be a newly minted bureaucrat. Here the reader sees enthusiasm, even awe, tempered by objectivity about persistent social and economic problems in the USSR. This objectivity was probably why Kisch's book *Zaren, Popen, Bolschewiken*, the fruit of his observations during his first trip to Russia, was not translated into Russian, though earlier and later collections of his reportage were.

Both concise and more expansive definitions and discussions of reportage can be found in Kisch's works,[46] in the analyses by Kisch's major East German biographers, Dieter Schlenstedt[47] and Fritz Hofmann,[48] in the 1997 biographies by Segel[49] and Patka,[50] in Spector's parsing of Kisch's reportage as a "cultural re-mapping of Prague",[51] in Peter Monteath's article on Kisch's Australian adventures[52] and in pieces about Kisch written by his contemporary admirers[53] and imitators.[54] Looking at pitfalls inherent in accepting at face value an idealized form of reportage as presented by its practitioners and advocates, Peter Steiner undertook a critique of the most famous post-World War II piece of reportage, Julius Fučik's *Reportage: Notes from the Gallows*, first published in Czech five years after Fučik was guillotined in 1943.[55] Steiner's analysis makes plain the book's religious-mythical ('Christological') framing of the story of Fučik's captivity and execution by the Nazis and how it became a propaganda tool of the Czech communist leadership during the post-war years (as it was caustically depicted in Milan Kundera's novel, *The Joke*). In such a case of hortatory, partisan political writing it is difficult for an author to escape using the devices of fiction, sometimes drifting into poetic and rhetorically driven representation of crass realities, as Fučik often did.

In its glory years, when the claims of reportage were being advanced as an alternative to conventional journalism ('just the facts' articles and the printing of officially released information without challenge or comment), Kisch and others also argued for reportage's superiority over fiction as a mirror of the world. They presumed it was the wave of the future, with literary fiction itself on the verge of death due to trends in current political and literary life; obviously this was a mistaken judgment. Reportage did not disappear with Kisch's death in 1948. In the West the term denominates social and political reporting that exhibits the author's literary skills and analyzes current events in terms of deeper, yet explicable causes that may not be immediately apparent to the reader; it often has an implicit political message. Large anthologies of reportage have been published in the US and Great Britain between the 1950s and the present, yet none of them includes articles by Kisch or even mentions him as a major, influential interwar practitioner of the form.[56] As Patka surmised, this reluctance in the West to deal with Kisch as a master of reportage is an artifact of the fixed attitudes that accompanied Cold-War polarization of opinion. Kisch's reputation in Germany and Austria, built almost entirely upon an assessment of him as the founder and cynosure of modern reportage, remains strong. However, in the US and the UK (but not Australia) he has gone missing from the genealogy of reportage in the minds of contemporary editors and compilers of anthologies.

While continuing to practice journalism in this mode, Kisch encountered major impediments in reaching his German-speaking readership after the Nazis ascended to power in early 1933. After the Reichstag fire he was rounded up as a target for internment by the new authorities; his account of his captivity has been translated by Harold Segel.[57] The possession of a Czech passport facilitated his release from jail, but from March, 1933, until the end of the Second World War his books were banned (and burned) in Germany. Kisch made Paris his next home base, soon moving to the town of Versailles, where, in 1938, he married his secretary of many years, Gisela Lyner (he had a reputation as a 'charmer' and womanizer in his earlier years). During his exile from Germany his new volumes of reportage, numerous newspaper articles, and reports of his anti-Nazi and anti-Fascist activities could only reach a vastly reduced audience of German readers, i.e., fellow-exiles and emigrants from Germany predisposed to sharing his ideas and ideals.

Kisch's travels continued—England, Australia, Spain during its civil war—as did translations of his work, but the growing tide of partisan journalism associated with political turbulence and the likelihood of a major war tended to drown out his voice. This was especially true in the English-speaking lands, which had their own prominent overseas journalists, for instance Hemingway, Orwell, and John Gunther; the first two of these were 'literary journalists', while Gunther's practice of writing countrywide socio-political surveys was similar to Kisch's approach to international reportage. He stayed one step ahead of the Nazis, leaving France in 1939. Quarantined in New York for ten months, he was denied entry into the US on political grounds (as a known leftist and 'trouble-maker'), resulting in his spending the World War II years in Mexico, where he completed two books discussed above.

It was in Mexico that the allegation that Kisch was a communist propagandist (or 'Party hack') received some ammunition. Kisch wrote a slanderous diatribe against Gustav Regler, an old colleague who had left the Party and denounced the sins and crimes of Stalin and his abettors. Regler, to use the stilted jargon of the era, was now accused by pro-Russian intellectuals and writers of being 'objectively Fascist', because he did not give the USSR carte-blanche in its internal political life or manipulative machinations abroad (he was also accused of collaboration with the Vichy authorities). Kisch praised Stalin's 1937–1938 lethal purge of military men on trumped-up charges as necessary and useful in bolstering the USSR's military capacity—a nonsensical and factually false interpretation of events that also ignored the inconvenient fact that the Hitler-Stalin pact of 1939 had facilitated Nazi aggression. The offending article was published in the *New Masses* in March, 1942 and became the focus of an ongoing war of words between Party hard-liners and the non-communist, anti-Stalinist left in the US.[58] This unseemly controversy and the political and personal reasons behind Kisch's behavior in the case have been analyzed and interpreted by Patka,[59] Heidi Zogbaum,[60] and Jonathan Miles, Otto Katz's biographer.[61] Zogbaum remarked that Kisch's writing about Regler may have been motivated by his desire to protect Katz (a well-known organizer who used the alias André Simone) from expulsion from Mexico, while his collapse into mendacity and implausible reverence for Stalin was probably motivated by uncertainty over his own prospective post-war status and livelihood. Separation from the Party at this point in his life would have meant social isolation and anxiety about what would happen to him and his wife in the near future. His role in the affair did, in fact, isolate him from a variety of American liberals and leftists who had previously admired him.

In April 1945, during the final weeks of the war in Europe, Kisch celebrated his 60th birthday in Mexico City. The festivities put together by the exile community went on for a week, and there were gifts and tributes to him from abroad as well.[62] Of relevance to the present work it is notable that his friends put on a revival of his play about Colonel Redl as part of the celebrations.[63] Rather than nostalgia or recognition of how the case had contributed to the demise of the Old Regime, perhaps what they were marking with this choice was the fact that Kisch's reporting on the case had spread his reputation as a tenacious investigative reporter. The specific controversies of the late Habsburg world were now, or seemed to be, in the distant past, given the events of 1933–1945.[64] This distancing was the product of an optical illusion, although it was not clear at the time. These old (pre-1914) controversies have not yet totally subsided, as can be seen in the rampant chauvinism, irredentism, and anti-Semitism within Central and Eastern Europe in the present day. Four decades of Moscow-enforced 'fraternal socialism' in the Soviet bloc of satellite states collapsed into civil wars and ethnic-supremacy campaigns after the dissolution of the bloc in 1989–1992.[65] Once again nationalist autocrats ('strongmen') of the 1930s ilk[66] accrued power in the region.[67] The interwar strongmen were an outgrowth of widespread economic problems and nationalistic dissatisfaction with the peace treaties of 1918–1920. Today's strongmen also reflect economic and ethnic dissatisfactions brought into the open by the collapse of communism, the social inequities and environmental damage caused by a form of global capitalism that seems beyond local political control, and perceived impingements on national sovereignty (and 'national culture') by the European Union.

In 1946 Kisch returned to Prague, where he was one of the few 'Prague Germans' allowed to resettle in Czechoslovakia (in 1945–1946 a thorough and often violent expulsion of approximately three million Germans from the reconstituted Czechoslovakia took place). His health was not good, putting an end to his days a roving reporter, though he wrote fresh pieces and revised older works. Kisch returned to a city that no longer had a vibrant, multicultural life, and he felt isolated and depressed on account of the death of family members and friends in the Holocaust. As Erhard Schütz wrote in an essay in the literary journal *Text + Kritik*, Kisch's misgivings about how communism had developed in the

USSR, his distress about the systematic anti-Germanism of the Czechoslovakian state, and a growing emotional bond with his fellow Jews characterized his postwar years in Prague.[68] A series of strokes culminated in his death in March 1948, soon after the take-over of Czechoslovakia by a communist coup that had a high level of popular support. As some of his biographers and commentators point out, had Kisch survived until the time of the hysterical, anti-Semitic Slánský show-trial in 1952, it is probable that he would have been among the indicted.[69] Given his broad web of non-communist contacts in the West, charges of 'cosmopolitanism' and espionage could have been levied against him. In fact, the all-purpose 'Trotskyite' slur was aimed at him even after his death.[70] Like his old friend Katz (André Simone) he might have gone to the gallows.[71] He was fortunate to die when he did, spared a final disillusionment with the Communist Party, about whose crimes of commission and failures to establish a better society he had maintained a public silence, though he seemed to harbor many private doubts about the trend of events.

The foregoing Introduction addresses the matter of 'Kisch in English translation' and, in abbreviated fashion, several aspects of his life and work: his long career as a journalist; his travels and adventures, which resulted in thematic books; his ventures into fiction, including writing for the stage; his reputation during the interwar years as 'the master of reportage'; and the relationship between his writing and his political beliefs and commitments. With regard to the topic of Kisch in English, I note that my translation of the two cabaret plays is the first instance of any complete fictional work of Kisch—short stories, a novel, and plays — coming over into English; only a few small illustrative excerpts of these works have been translated to date.[72] It is my hope that this will contribute to a re-evaluation of Kisch as a more well-rounded and gifted writer, rather than as just a master of politically-framed journalism (a characterization that ignores his gifts as a feuilleton-writer and essayist).

The two plays selected were Kisch's most successful works for the stage. As to the Redl story, a combination of materials from his 1924 book and his Redl play was adapted into a 1931 film that gave Kisch writing credits. In the previous year the story of 'Toni Gallows' that Kisch had presented in feuilletons and three versions for the stage was also made into a successful film. These adaptations indicated that producers and directors believed that both stories had popular appeal. Other stage, film, and literary adaptations of the Redl srory appeared in the 1920s, 1950s, 1960s and 1980s. Along with the later television-plays of the Toni Gallows tale, these constitute the 'long afterlives' of the stories that are discussed in detail in Chapters 9 and 10.

To reiterate, the play about Colonel Redl is a historical melodrama with comedic interludes (Kisch called it a "Tragicomedy of the General Staff"). It derives its narrative materials from a successful book of investigative—and, at times speculative—reporting about the famous espionage affair. The shorter play about Toni Gallows, a pathetic yet defiant Prague prostitute who argues her way into heaven, is based on a feuilleton-style newspaper sketch that was framed as a posthumous fantasy. Though the character of Toni is a fictional embellishment of a woman allegedly known to Kisch from his days as a reporter in pre-1914 Prague, the social milieu she dwelled in was real enough. The plays bring to light fictional techniques that Kisch sometimes used in nonfictional reportages and essays and thus contribute to an understanding of his approach to writing in general. They also raise more general questions about how historical events are transformed into works of art, a topic that will be addressed in the final chapter.

Chapter 2.
Notes on the Plays: Sources and Translation

The texts of the two plays translated into English for the first time here were published in a wide-ranging 1926 collection of pieces Kisch had written during the early and mid-1920s, *Hetzjagd durch die Zeit* (Pursuit through Time, or, alternatively, Pursuit throughout the Ages).[1] Kisch (or his publisher) selected the book's title on the basis of the inclusion of his play about Colonel Alfred Redl, *Die Hetzjagd*. During the interwar era interest in the Redl case persisted in Germany, Austria, and Prague, where Kisch was a well-known reporter and Redl had been stationed at the time of his detection as a spy, though the day of his downfall occurred in Vienna. Kisch kept this interest alive and came back to the story several times between 1913, when he first reported on the case, and 1941–1942, when he devoted a chapter of his memoirs to the espionage affair and his role in bringing it to the public's attention.

The origins of the plays are quite different from each other. *Die Hetzjagd* relied for its basic material on Kisch's post-World War I research into the famous espionage scandal, resulting in his 1924 book of investigative journalism about the case. He didn't have to wait until his research was completed to work on the play —as discussed in Chapter 4 below, he could have easily used material from a more 'telegraphic' version of the Redl story written in 1921 but not published until 1936.[2] This version would have sufficed for the play's narrative outline. The story about the Prague prostitute nicknamed "Toni Gallows" first appeared as a newspaper feuilleton in *Prager Tagblatt* in early 1921.[3] Kisch had encountered Toni (or had heard of her story) during his pre-war years as a reporter covering his native city's demi-monde and criminal haunts. During the 1920s and 1930s Kisch returned to these two stories several times in prose articles of varying length, so the published and performed plays were bracketed in time by newspaper, magazine, and book-form treatments of their narratives. As with the Redl story, his last return to the tale of Toni the prostitute came in a chapter of his memoirs. The memoirs were among the first of the books he wrote after the Nazi ban of 1933 to be issued in Germany and Austria after World War II, thus bringing these two stories and the rest of the book's contents to the attention of younger German readers for the first time.

The word *Hetzjagd* carries the connotation of "harrying", as in the chase and hunting of game. If considered either in its widest extension of meaning or metaphorically, it supplies an interpretive framework for several other pieces in the collection. However, it is possible that with "pursuit(s) throughout the ages" Kisch was alluding to the fact that he himself was 'always on the hunt' for both gripping stories, and, in many cases, for 'the story behind the story'. The book came out at a time when he was writing prolifically and casting about for new publishing links and travel opportunities, having made up his mind that the kind of reportage that had succeeded so well in *Der rasende Reporter* (released in late 1924) laid out a promising path for future works. By the time *Hetzjagd durch die Zeit* appeared Kisch's historical melodrama about Redl and his sharp-edged comedy about Toni Gallows had been presented in variant versions in several venues in Germany, Austria, and Czechoslovakia.

These two cabaret plays (the Redl play was performed in small theaters as well) were Kisch's most popular works for the stage. They appeared under a variety of names in two languages during the 1920s and early 1930s. The play about Colonel Alfred Redl's last day on earth was performed as either *Die Hetzjagd* (The Pursuit) or *Der Fall des Generalstabschefs Redl* (The Case of General Staff Chief Redl, which was the title of Kisch's 1924 book about the affair). In Czech the play was called *Vyzvědacská aféra obstra Redla*. The play about Toni Gallows appeared as *Die Himmelfahrt der Tonka Šibenice* and *Die Himmelfahrt der Galgentoni* (The Ascension of Toni Gallows to Heaven), alternatively using Czech and German nicknames for the protagonist. In English "Toni the Gallows Girl" would also be an appropriate sobriquet, as will be seen when the origin of her nickname is revealed in the play. The Czech version of the play was titled *Tonka Šibenice na onom svété*. Variations in the plays' titles depended on their performance sites. Czech performances preceded German ones, for reasons discussed below in Chapter 7, which gives an overview of Kisch's playwriting career, the performance histories of his plays on Czech and German stages, and critical responses to them.

As to the published texts of the plays, variations depended on what Kisch thought would attract readers. For instance, in the 1926 German text for his play about Toni Gallows, the play is billed as "a real Prague legend". This entailed using the Czech names from the 1921 feuilleton for the play's characters and for the names of various dives, brothels, streets, and well-known neighborhood markers in Prague, familiar to readers there. Because his potential audience was larger in Germany, Kisch published two German-setting versions of the Toni Gallows play, in which local details of the story are altered accordingly. They are slightly less developed than the 1926 Prague version translated here. The earlier German version of the play was published in a 1922 issue of a Berlin weekly magazine, *Das Tage-Buch*, at a time when it was being performed in Berlin.[4] In this version Toni's life-story unfolds first in Hamburg and then in Berlin, and the language of the three deceased souls is in heavy regional dialect (a few Hamburg touches and a host of Berlin usages and pronunciations).

Here are the 1926-text Czech names used in the present translation and their German counterparts: Antonie Havlová (nicknamed Tonka Šibenice) is Toni Pelzer (nicknamed Galgentoni); Barbara Upejpavá is Frieda Kniefall ("on her knees Frieda"); Mungo Natscheradetz is Moritz Meseritzer; blondie Mirko is blondie Willy; and the repulsive murderer, Ferdinand Prokupek, is Hugo Klos. The third and last version of the play was published in Kisch's 1927 reportage collection, *Wagnisse in aller Welt* (Worldwide Exploits).[5] It is a slightly edited re-publication of the 1922 text,[6] taking us back to Hamburg and Berlin again.

In the 1922 and 1927 texts of the play, the slums and demi-monde of Prague have been transferred to Hamburg's Reeperbahn district, notorious throughout Europe for its brothels, streetwalkers, and dives that served the city's natives and foreign seamen who thronged the port. For the Berlin passages similar seedy neighborhoods and streets are named. Kisch had been in Hamburg several times, was fascinated by the city's hustle and bustle, thought of it as a potential 'red' city, given its large working-class population, and knew about its vice district, but he certainly did not have the long and close familiarity with its nooks and crannies that he had with Prague's neighborhoods, having resided there from his birth in 1885 until 1913. Presumably he became well-acquainted with Berlin's vice districts during his 1913–1914 and 1921–1933 years there. The Hamburg-Berlin version would have been more suitable for performance in German cities, while the 1926 Prague version would have played better in Vienna, where much of the population was more familiar with the Prague accent and everyday Czech expressions than they were with the dialects of Hamburg or Berlin (and, it was a tale of the late Habsburg realms and years, which resonated in Austria). Linguistic and narrative variations in versions of both plays will be discussed in more detail in Chapters 4 and 6 below.

In both fiction and nonfiction Kisch's language is usually colloquial and idiomatic, especially when it comes to direct and indirect speech; it has passages in local dialects. This stems as much from his intellectual commitment to socialism (implying that art about everyday people should be written in the language such people use) as it does from the kind of neighborhoods he covered as a Prague journalist. It has slang peculiar to various parts of the vanished Dual Monarchy and Germany. It is often 'breezy' and informal, never flowery or over-ripe. His dialogues in the Redl play go back and forth among the dreary clichés of love affairs going sour, comical banter among policemen, the imbecilic patter of a worthless Habsburg dynast, and the formalities observed by officials engaged in their duties. For the most part his language in the 1926 version of the play is the 'standard German' of his day, with a few Austrian touches. He had used more of the local dialect in his 1924 nonfiction book about the Redl case. For instance, in creating a conversation between detectives on the spy's trail and a porter at the hotel, he has the latter say:

> "Grad' jetzt saan zwaa Herren im Auto ankommen, Kaufleute saans aus Bulgarien" – "Under vorher eine Herr allein?" – "Im Auto? Dös waass i net. Vor einer Viertelstund' is der Herr Oberst Redl kommen. Im Zivil war er, dös waass i. Aber i waass net, ob er im Auto vorg'fahren is."[7]

To see how much this drifts from standard German: "Dös waass i net" is "Das weiss ich nicht" ("I don't know about that"). Kisch used this conversation in the Redl play, but dropped his phonetic representation of the broad Viennese accent, though this might have amused play-goers in Berlin, Prague, or Brno. Actors playing some of the roles may have used Viennese accents on the stage without the need for instructions in the working scripts of the play. As mentioned above, the 1922 and 1927 versions of the play about Toni Gallows employ a Berlin accent and local slang. A typical line, in Kisch's phonetic representation of this accent in Toni's mouth, is:

> Ick habe lange jenug jewartet. Zweeundfuffzig Jahre wart ick uff den Klimbim. Ich will direkt in den Himmel, sonst misch ick hier auf.[8]

In the play about Toni Gallows the language is inventively coarse and somewhat scatter-brained. The 1926 version includes Czech and German slang. Brief phatic phrases, adverbs, and interjections, often used as an ironic or questioning gloss on the ongoing conversation, can be translated in several ways. The Austrian "Na ja" is one such phrase — when in Prague, Tonka says, "No jo", using a local accent. I do my best in these instances to turn such short phrases and verbal tags into their era-appropriate (American) English counterparts. In the 1926 text of the play Tonka refers to locations in or near Prague in Czech and German. The editors of the Kisch *Gesammelte Werke* edition of the play published the 1926 text and footnoted its slang and Czech words and phrases (as well as a few in Latin and Yiddish) with German clarifications and translations.[9] Taking a position close to Kafka's, Kisch believed that Yiddish in particular did not debase German but, as a living spoken language, could be used to enliven and enrich German written in everyday language (rather than in the allegedly pure 'High German' of literary culture as defined by critics and by middle-class precepts). He felt the same way about 'Slavicized German' spoken in some quarters of Prague.[10]

Kisch's writing often contains foreign words and phrases and a wealth of allusions indicating his extensive background knowledge of history and culture from around the world, not just Germany, Austria, and the Czech lands, with which he was directly familiar at the time. He was widely read and usually well-prepared by specific research when it came to reporting and essay-writing, and he was a scrupulous self-editor and rewriter as well. He prepared himself for his extended trips, which began in late 1925, in the same way. In his cabaret plays this kind of learned material does not appear, but there are allusions to local matters in Vienna and Prague that require either free translation or footnoting. An example of free translation would be my referring to Ober-Pajdakov as "Upper Nowheresville", taking Toni's language to refer to a "dump in the middle of nowhere". Another example is turning a curt phrase and a sentence fragment into a sentence: "Meinetwegen in Prtschitz! Da hinein sind Ihnen Schwämme, Sie alter Vorreiter vom Ringelspiel" becomes "For all I care you can go pick mushrooms in the Jews' cemetery out in the sticks, you old wooden horse from a merry-go-round."[11] More literally it is something like: "For all I care [go to] Prtschitz! [Go on] out there, there are mushrooms for you, you old etc." Prtschitz is today's Sedlec-Prčice, forty miles south of Prague, known for an old synagogue and Jewish cemetery, and mushroom-picking in woods and cemeteries was a popular pastime of the era. The phrase has a broader connotation—even today Czechs say "jdi do Pričice" ("go to Pričice') to mean "get lost" or "beat it".

Some problems for the reader of the 1926 text stem from Toni's fractured grammar and run-on sentences, and some from practices such as Kisch substituting the letter "j" for the letter "i" in various words and slang terms. (Whereas, in the Berlin dialect, he substitutes "j" with a "yeh" sound for hard "g" at the beginning of syllables, turning "genug" into "jenug".) Thus in Prague the reader encounters "Hajl", in this case meant as a derogatory remark about another prostitute. You find "Hai" (shark) in a dictionary and then realize that Kisch is substituting a "j" and using a standard diminutive form (by adding "[e] l" at the end of a word), giving you "little shark". This is just one of numerous epithets that Toni uses to describe her fellow men and women. Men are bums, guys, drunks, mugs, gents, cabbage-heads, suitors (brothel clients), horse-radishes, and a variety of other things. Women are ladies (those she works with before they turn on her), sows, cows, floozies, broken-down things, and other objects of contempt. In a relaxed mood she compliments Heaven's High Judge as a friendly paprika (i.e., "peppery old gent"); in the Hamburg-Berlin version this becomes "congenial old rooster". Sometimes I translate these literally, at others with what I think makes more sense to readers of English. On account of the several different usages of "Herr" in German, I sometimes leave it untranslated in the Redl play. Through exposure to films and television American and English readers are used to the German word and would find phrases such as "Mr. Post Office official" or "Post Office official, Sir" awkward, though salutations such as "Mr. President" or "Mr. Chairman" are commonplace in English. In dialogues among military men and high-ranking civilians I often translate it as "Sir", just as it would be used in English. Also, where Kisch writes "Parlament", I use "Reichsrat".

Footnotes to the Redl melodrama, most of which are on the title-and-cast page, are long because they include necessary background information about specific historical characters and matters, who and which are probably little-known or unknown to most English-language readers, whether they hail from the USA, the UK, Australia, Canada or elsewhere (e.g., my long note on Conrad von Hötzendorf, who was one of the most important players in late Habsburg political and military affairs; or the note on how the army's 'marriage bond' worked). There are only a few footnotes to the Toni Gallows play, supplying supplementary information. In both plays I use asterisks to flag brief notes shown at the bottom of a page—these allow for continuous reading of the text while supplying information to make immediate sense of what is flagged (e.g., the name or reputation of a person or locale).

My formatting of the plays follows the appearance of the pages in the 1926 text of *Hetzjagd durch die Zeit*, which allows the reader to see the running headers that encapsulate material on the page, a common practice of the era—Kisch's headers use a telling phrase from the dialogue or summarize the page's contents; these are shown in italics, centered on the pages as they appeared in 1926. Kisch puts stage directions and background and mood descriptions in parentheses; I replicate these. The characters' names and their accompanying dialogue hew to the present-day formatting convention in English. My only apology to the reader is that I cannot supply the full context—sights, sounds and smells—of a Weimar-era cabaret theater, a place of sensory overload, where customers buzzed and hooted while partaking of alcohol, sausages, and a pile of cabbage and potatoes. Now, on to the plays.

Chapter 3. The Pursuit

THE PURSUIT
A TRAGICOMEDY OF THE IMPERIAL AND ROYAL[1]
GENERAL STAFF IN FIVE ACTS

Archduke Viktor Salvator, Inspector-General of the Troops[2]

Field Marshal Conrad von Hötzendorf, Chief of the General Staff of the Austro-Hungarian Army[3]

Major General Anton Höfer, Conrad's Deputy Chief[4]

Colonel Alfred Redl, General Staff Chief of the 8th Army Corps stationed in Prague[5]

Colonel Peter Umanitzky, Chief of the Intelligence Bureau of the General Staff[6]

Wenzel Worlitschek,[7] Major-Auditor*

Stefan Hromadka, Lieutenant in the 7th Ulan (Cavalry) Regiment[8]

Franzi Mittringer, Hromadka's fiancé[9]

Baroness Daubek[10]

Rigo, Leader of a gypsy band[11]

Strebinger and Steidl, Detectives of the Viennese Police Force[12]

The head porter of the Hotel Klomser

Franz, a bellhop at the Hotel Klomser

The events involving the above take place in Vienna on the evening of May 24, 1913.

* Rank and title of a lawyer serving as an officer in the army's Judge-Advocates Corps.

So then, who's going to provide for your wife

ACT I
IN COLONEL REDL'S HOTEL ROOM

Redl, Hromadka, Franzi enters later

REDL (he sits down on the sofa and throws his arm over Hromadka's shoulder): Tell me that you're not serious about this, I'm begging you, please tell me you're not serious. For God's sake, Stefan, you can't be serious, can you? Don't you realize everything that I've done for you ...

HROMADKA: Of course I realize it. And I'm certainly very grateful for everything ...

REDL: No, you really don't understand what I've done for you. How far out on a limb I've gone for you, Stefan, dangerously far out, and now you want to leave me. Tell me that you don't mean it, tell me that you don't really want to leave me.

HROMADKA: I don't want to leave you. I just want to get married.

REDL: Married? You call that not leaving me! With marriage it's all over between you and me. You're a young man, a good-looking lad too — everybody likes you, the whole world is there for you to grab. And now you want to give all that up, you want to put yourself in chains — and on top of it all, on account of a woman! On account of a woman! So then, who's going to provide for your wife? What, you'll hang around in bars, take business trips, stay in hotels, is that it? And all the time there are hundreds of wenches out there, far better than just one. And just what are you going to talk about with your wife? I'll lend you a book, it's called *On The Congenital Feeble-Mindedness of Women*.[13]

Something important has been pending for months

HROMADKA: But what if I really love her?

46

REDL: Hold on, you don't love her. You only let yourself get grabbed by her, you just let her nurse you along, and you let it happen because ... well, you were available because I haven't been around for you for so many months. It's been far too long since I've been in Vienna. I've been afraid to come here because— because I thought that you'd been unfaithful to me. I didn't come, even though there's something very important waiting for me here—something big has been pending for months—and yet I still didn't come ...

HROMADKA: Your appointment as Bureau Chief?

REDL: No, not that, not yet, anyway. Something else.

HROMADKA: What, something bad, some kind of unpleasantness?

REDL: Not unpleasant for you. But if you leave me, well then, there goes all my good luck, that's unpleasant. Look, Stefan, take a trip with me—we'll go to Switzerland, then Italy, and your thinking will change for the better. Blow off this whole idea of a woman!

HROMADKA: She loves me too.

REDL: And I don't love you? Aren't you the greatest good fortune in my life? Have I ever given you a reason to complain? It's not that I'm selfish, all I want is for you to love me. But this woman, what kind of person is she? Does she have enough money to cover the marriage-bond?[14] God only knows what kind of worthless slut she is anyway.

The faults of women

HROMADKA (resolutely): Excuse me, you can't insult her like that. If you had just asked me first, then I would have spared her these insults. My fiancé is the daughter of an official, and her mother is a teacher at a technical school here in Vienna. If she stays in school, then we don't need the money for the army's marriage-bond — that's an imperial ordinance. In any event I hope that she'll give up her place there ...

REDL: ... because you think that I'll come up with the money for the bond!

HROMADKA: Yes, I had hoped for that, though Franzi has forbidden me to accept such an arrangement. But now, since you've been running her down ...

REDL: Franzi knows about me?

HROMADKA: She knows about you, but only that we're friends.

REDL: Does she know that I'm in Vienna?

HROMADKA: I mentioned to her that I was going to see you.

REDL: And what else does she know?

HROMADKA: Nothing.

REDL. Oh yes, "nothing", as you put it! Just put something like that in a woman's head, you fool! She's definitely thinking about her part in all this — women have a nose for things that are none of their business. But in that they're mistaken. Look, Stefan, let women be women, but stay true to our friendship. Men don't ever

Promises

let other men down — stick with me, Stefan! Listen up, within a year I'll be a General — I'm already the most talked-about General Staff man in the whole monarchy. I'm bound to become Chief of the Intelligence Bureau, maybe even Chief of the General Staff or Minister of War, and you, (here Redl sits closer to Hromadka and hugs him around the shoulder) you'll move on up along with me, you'll make extraordinary advances, and, if you want to, you'll get into the War College.[15] I'll go to the Kladrub stable[16] and buy you a gray stallion with gold-braided riding blankets, I'll get you the best fur shako with beaver trim, the works, isn't that what you want? (there's a knock on the door, but they don't notice it) You do want all that, don't you? I'm not asking for anything in return, only that you love me ... (Franzi enters the room, unnoticed)

REDL (continues): ... that you truly love me, I don't want anything else from you, just that you remain my Stevie, while I'm still your Freddy ...

(Franzi steps forward)

HROMADKA (he jumps to his feet): Franzi! (he pauses) Franzi, let me explain this to you ...

FRANZI (her voice tinged with sadness): You don't have to explain anything at all to me, Stefan. I know you very well, and I know that you're a good person. And if you've been a little frivolous, maybe rash, still I know you're convinced that you love me and that we're good for each other. No, Stefan, *you're* not guilty of anything. (she gives Redl a measured gaze)

REDL (his tone is cold): You wish to say something else? That I'm "guilty of something," my dear young woman?

Conflict between Franzi and Redl

FRANZI (aggressively): Yes, I do want to say something, don't you worry about that, I'll say it alright. Shame on you, Herr Colonel, shame on you, you in your golden collar, that you ...

HROMADKA: Franzi, please, you don't understand what's going on.

FRANZI: No, I don't understand it, thank God for that, and I don't ever want to understand it. I'm not going to get mixed up in that business, what men do with each other. "Judge not, lest ye be judged," that much I've learned from my religion. And first of all I don't want to judge something that I don't understand... But what I do understand, Herr Colonel, is that you've led this young man astray, seduced him, and you want to lead him ever farther astray. You've pampered him and coddled him, and now you want to corrupt him, corrupt him for once and all. That's why I've come here, Herr Colonel, to tell you that you shouldn't ruin my Stefan. What do you want from him?

REDL: Don't get yourself involved in men's business, my dear young woman.

FRANZI: No, I don't want to get myself involved in your kind of men's business, Herr Colonel, you've got a heavy burden to bear when it comes to that. I can see from the way you look that you're an unfortunate man, but don't pull this young man into your own misfortune. Go on, carry on your men's business with other men just like you, but this young man isn't like that, a man like you, he loves me, do you understand, he loves a woman!

REDL: It's up to me to decide who my friends are.

FRANZI: Friends? We're not talking about friendship. Why are you lying to yourself about it? Is it friendship that he has with a man twice his age? What kind of a friendship is it for you to take an upright lad from the country and stick him in the middle of a

What the name "Redl" really means

bunch of cavalry officers, a bunch of titled idlers who would openly scorn him if you weren't protecting him, if you hadn't made him your so-called protégé, while in reality you don't want to do anything for him.

HROMADKA: But Franzi! Colonel Redl has already done more than enough for me!

FRANZI: That's what you think. Oh yes, he's bought you riding horses, had beautiful uniforms made for you, got you nice living-quarters, sent you bon-bons and champagne, but just why has he done all this? It's because he wants you to get used to his posh way of life, so you won't be able to break away from him. And hasn't he promised to get you into the War College? So why hasn't he told you that you should be studying, should be preparing for the examinations? Only because he's worried that if you show that you can accomplish it on your own, you won't need him anymore. It's the same reason why you haven't gotten into the military intelligence bureau even though he promised you that too. If he really wanted that, you would have been taken in by the bureau ten times over. Doesn't just one word from Colonel Redl suffice for that?

REDL: The dear young woman overestimates my powers.

FRANZI: Oh no, Herr Colonel, I've made all the right inquiries about the man who wishes to call himself the friend of my Stefan. And wherever I've asked, I've received the same information — in the army the name of Colonel Redl means almost as much as the Emperor's name. Colonel Redl is the ingenious organizer behind all of our intelligence services, Colonel Redl is the master recruiter of spies, Colonel Redl is flawless when it comes to unmasking foreign agents, he's the expert who can't be contradicted in espionage trials, he's the man who makes sure that the accused wind up in prison. That's who you are, Herr Colonel Redl. None of that makes

Recruiting spies, punishing spies

me very happy, because the one important thing I learned from my religion is, "Judge not, lest ye be judged." So, how can a man recruit spies and, at the very same time, punish spies — that I don't understand... But, first and foremost, what's been on my mind is this: if a man can so easily induce hundreds into criminality, then he should easily be able to lead one man who is his friend to honest work.

REDL: My dear young woman, I forbid you to get mixed up in my professional affairs.

HROMADKA: Franzi, your behavior is scandalous!

FRANZI: Certainly, Herr Colonel, here in this place you have the right to forbid what you want. I shouldn't get involved in your men's business, or in your professional affairs. Fine, Herr Colonel. But you shouldn't be getting my fine young Stefan involved in your dreary little men's business or your wretched professional affairs. That's what I'll forbid to you. Poor Stefan!

(she addresses Redl) : We'll see each other again.

(she exits)

REDL: Well now, you just got a preview of what kind of wifely lectures await you when you marry. Look how she's been snooping around after you! And how she's been collecting information about me. An international spy couldn't have discovered more! And how critical she is of my profession ...

HROMADKA: I really must beg your pardon for all this.

REDL: No, it's all right. But I do want to save you from the clutches of this woman, she's a real witch, I'm telling you. Come on, take a trip with me, we'll make a pleasant tour of the Alps ...

HROMADKA: I don't have any military leave time.

Arranging a trip to the mountains

REDL: I'll get your leave for you tomorrow, do you want that?

HROMADKA (hesitantly): But ...

REDL: No buts about it! Do you want to? (Hromadka is shaking his head) We'll travel by car. In a touring car, I'll buy you a touring car.

HROMADKA: An Austro-Daimler?*

REDL: Yes, an Austro-Daimler.

HROMADKA: When?

REDL: First thing tomorrow.

HROMADKA: Your word of honor on that?

REDL (smiling): My word of honor

* One of the most expensive cars of the pre-WWI era. Redl owned two and, in Kisch's 1924 report, he was having one ostentatiously refurbished while in Vienna to deal with Hromakda.

HROMADKA: You've got that kind of money?

REDL: Yes.

HROMADKA: Here in Vienna?

REDL (as he looks at the clock): Yes, but you should go now and pack your bags. And tomorrow morning you're coming, aren't you? Word of honor?

The Colonel rushes off

HROMADKA: Word of honor! Are you going out too?

REDL: No, not — that is, well, I do have to go out now.

HROMADKA: Good, then, we'll go together.

REDL: No, that's not on. I've got to change into civvies.

HROMADKA: Well, I don't mind waiting for you.

REDL: No, I have a private matter to attend to.

HROMADKA (as he drums his fingers playfully): Aha! An affair of the heart, is that what's up?

REDL: Not a bit of that! Something very different. Go on, get out of here.

HROMADKA: All right, all right, don't throw me out. Should I send for a car for you?

REDL: Yes, order me a car—No, forget that. I'll pick up a taxi while I'm on my way.

HROMADKA: As you wish. Well, with obedient respect, Colonel, Sir. (he exits)

REDL: Good-bye until tomorrow, my dear Stefan. (he hurriedly puts on an overcoat)

CURTAIN

The inebriated Inspector of Troops

ACT II
CRIMINAL INVESTIGATION FACILITIES IN THE OFFICE
OF THE COUNTER-INTELLIGENCE SERVICE

(The Chief of the Intelligence Bureau, Colonel Umanitzky; the Inspector General of the Troops, Archduke Viktor Salvator; and the Chief of the General Staff, Field Marshal Conrad von Hötzendorf)

UMANITZKY (sitting at his desk, on the telephone with the police chief): No, No, Herr Commissioner, release the man from custody at six o'clock this evening. I'll send someone to keep him under watch on the Elizabeth Street promenade. Something's bound to play out there.

(Salvator and Conrad enter)

UMANITZKY (jumping to his feet): With my obedient respect, your Imperial Highness! With obedient respect, Excellency!

CONRAD: Good afternoon, Herr Colonel.

SALVATOR (extending his hand toward Umanitzky): Greetings! So, how's everything with you? Still chasing the ladies? Yesterday I was over at Tabarin,* there's a little Hungarian girl there, Ilonka, she's flawless, her advance guard as well as her rear-guard. (he traces her figure in the air with his hands)

CONRAD: Herr Colonel, we've come to take a look at the facilities of the counter-intelligence service.

* An exclusive men's club in Vienna.

No cognac, No attractive young girls?

SALVATOR: Do you have any cognac, Umanitzky? Or a whiskey and soda? You know, just the other day I was at Sacher's* in the

* A popular hotel, with restaurant and café, home of the famous chocolate-cake confection, "Sacher-Torte".

afternoon, and I guzzled down a sherry-cobbler, enough to drown you, the whole thing through a straw ...

CONRAD: We're on duty here, Imperial Highness.

SALVATOR (with mock strictness): By all means, on duty, Colonel, Sir! I order you to show us the facilities of the counterintelligence bureau. I forbid you to speak of any private or personal matters here! (already he lapses from his role-playing) Don't you really have any cognac? (Conrad directs Umanitzky to get out a bottle of cognac for Salvator. Salvator sits down and takes a drink)

UMANITZKY (explaining things): Your Excellency, here's the photographic catalog of everyone suspected of espionage, foreigners and our own citizens, listed in alphabetical order, both male and female agents.

SALVATOR (jumping up): What the devil! You've got women in there too? Any good-looking ones in there, huh? I've got to see this for myself!

CONRAD: We're on duty here, Imperial Highness.

SALVATOR: Well, what nonsense! What do you really think about that, Herr Colonel? Over there we're on duty too, Herr Colonel. Do you think that in the military chancellery we spend all our time on our own pleasures? (here he falls out of his role) Come on, Umanitzky, show me a couple of lively young ladies, tell me their story ...

Secret Photographs

CONRAD: Herr Colonel, how do you come by the photographs?

UMANITZKY: The photographs you're looking at are of people who've been detained by the police, or even jailed, they're sent to us by various police agencies. There are some photos that we get from confidential sources who work for us, informants. And we take photographs of everyone who shows up here without them being aware of it ...

CONRAD: Without them being aware of it?

SALVATOR: Without them being aware of it? Now that's something really big, useful I mean. You ... well, you can certainly take nude photos, can't you? Of course, you must take nude photos. Umanitzky, come on, I beg you, please show me some photos of naked women, please, do me that favor ...

CONRAD: How do you actually photograph people without them being aware of it?

UMANITZKY: Anyone who sits in this chair, either to offer his services in our espionage work or to bring us some information, is photographed, both in full-face and profile. These two paintings on the walls have cut-outs with close-up lenses in them (he rotates the paintings out from the wall), and behind them is the photographic equipment.

CONRAD: Outstanding!

SALVATOR: Excellent! (he sits down in a club-chair). You really must take my picture now. Six photos, desk-top size, if you please. You know, a few days ago I was at Ronacher's,* and I arranged to meet the six Picadilly Girls in a private room – you know, they're from the English dance company, and each one of them asked for a photo of me.

* A Viennese musical theater.

The fingerprint trap

CONRAD (addressing Umanitzky): Please continue, Herr Colonel.

UMANITZKY: Moreover, each person has an impression of his fingerprints taken, though he has no idea that it's being done. The impressions are then printed out for entry into our fingerprint registry.

CONRAD: How do you get their fingerprints without them knowing it?

UMANITZKY: I arrange to have myself called, and when the phone rings and while I'm talking, I push over the cigarette case or ask my guest to take something from a box of chocolates. Or I offer my guest a cigarette, and then he pulls over the lighter and the ashtray. All the boxes and the lighter are coated with invisible red lead powder.

CONRAD: What happens when they take a cigarette or a chocolate?

UMANITZKY: Then I have myself called out of the room for a minute. If the person is some kind of agent, then he immediately reaches for the folder on my desk that's labeled "Top Secret". And the folder is also coated with a silky powder.

CONRAD: Extremely useful, that!

SALVATOR: It's not useful at all. When I think about it, you know, with me groping things all over the place with my fingertips — well, anybody can go around all over the place, find my fingerprints and reveal my incognito. For example, four days ago, just an example, I was with Madame Rosa in a private room ...

CONRAD: We're on duty here, Imperial Highness.

The cabinet that's not a cabinet

SALVATOR: Naturally, on duty. Let me ask you something, Colonel, related to duty of course, can you lift fingerprints from a woman's body?

UMANITZKY: Certainly, Imperial Highness.

SALVATOR: Well that's a filthy business, disgusting! Won't a man be able to enjoy himself anywhere in the world?

CONRAD: Please continue, Herr Colonel.

UMANITZKY: Here, for instance, this cabinet ...

CONRAD: This medicine cabinet?

UMANITZKY: ... is no medicine cabinet, Excellency, for inside it there is ...

SALVATOR: ... inside there's champagne. How about that, did I guess it right, Umanitzky? I'm pretty sly, huh? Ever since I was a kid I've been a clever one. We used to have a lady's maid, and she would always say that I was so clever they could use me to catch mice. I don't know how it's come about, but I can't catch mice any more. Just this afternoon, going home from the tavern, I saw so many white mice ...

CONRAD: So, what's in there, in the medicine cabinet?

SALVATOR: Champagne is what's in there, like I just said. I've already seen it for myself.

The technical preservation of conversations

UMANITZKY (as he opens the cabinet): Inside there's a gramophone's recording device, it's activated before any important conversation takes place. Here, look, you can see the speaker-horn.

SALVATOR (disappointed): I don't give a damn about that.

UMANITZKY: Everything that's said is inscribed by a needle onto a gramophone record, and then it's stored away and filed by protocol.

SALVATOR: That's splendid, magnificent! You, Umanitzky, you've got to play back everything I've just said here, right now. That will be fabulous!

UMANITZKY: I regret to say, Imperial Highness, that the device was not turned on.

SALVATOR: That's the usual nonsense from you scamps! Naturally — that's the way it goes, my best speeches and expressions are lost forever. What a pity, that every word a man says is lost. But I'm going to have one of these things made for me at home, then every evening I'll send off everything I've said that day to the Academy of Science, they can play it for their philosophy classes. You do know that I have the title of Protector of the Academy of Science, don't you, Conrad?

CONRAD: Certainly, your Imperial Highness. Just as your father before you was the Protector of the Academy of Science.

SALVATOR: Aha, I know what you mean to say — you think that I inherited the position, that everything's due to inheritance, the old protection racket. No, my dear man, it's not that simple. That having been born an Archduke has offered me some slight advantages, well, I'll grant you that, but a man must accomplish

All of our arrangements are due to Redl!

something else in this world before he becomes a Protector of the Academy of Sciences!

CONRAD: Certainly, your Imperial Highness! (addressing Umanitzky next): Your arrangements here are cunning, most interesting. Was all this put together according to your instructions?

UMANITZKY: No, your Excellency, the truth of the matter is that all of these arrangements come from Colonel Redl's work. As the leader of our counterintelligence program Redl organized everything, the criteria for recruiting agents, he wrote the book on methods of surveillance, he established the techniques for exposing foreign spies, all of it.

CONRAD: An ingenious fellow, that Redl. Someday he's going to be my successor.

SALVATOR: There's something disgusting about the man, I've never seen him with a woman.

UMANITZKY: Too bad he's not still with us here in intelligence.

CONRAD: Yes, well I definitely had to give him the job of General-Staff Chief in Prague. War could break out at any moment now, and Prague is dangerous terrain, what with all the Panslavism there, constitutionalism, anti-militarism, anti-dynastic sentiments, high treason just beneath the surface — there has to be a man there who knows secret police work thoroughly, someone like Redl.

UMANITZKY: By the way, if I may be permitted to say so, respectfully and without exaggeration, our facilities here are operating just as smoothly under my leadership as if Redl himself were still here.

Conditions along the borders are compromised

CONRAD: Colonel, it's just on that account that we came here. The intelligence services are not functioning to our satisfaction. What's the use of all of these criminal investigation facilities when our most secret preparations along the Russian, Serbian and Italian borders can be countered by the enemy within three days?

UMANITZKY: Excellency, we must have a very high-ranking source betraying us.

SALVATOR (making an aside): Oh my soul, maybe I'm about to come under suspicion. (Then speaking aloud): But, my dear gentlemen, I don't know a thing about our preparations along the borders, I give you my word of honor. The only secrets I could betray are the marching orders against the Ballet or the training regulations over at Frau Sachs's place.*

CONRAD: Most definitely, we're being betrayed by a highly placed source. And it's definitely the job of the intelligence bureau to discover just who this high-ranking source is. Herr Colonel, what steps have you undertaken about that?

SALVATOR: It's simple. I'd just arrest this highly placed source. And then string him up. It's all the same to me whether the spy is you or me — — I mean, not me, but you, Umanitzky, for example. Tell me, Conrad, why don't you just simply have this high-ranker arrested?

CONRAD: Pardon, your Imperial Highness, but we don't know who he is.

SALVATOR: Well, you've got to find that our right away!

CONRAD: Certainly, Imperial Highness. So then, Colonel, what steps have you taken?

* Presumably a "high-class" brothel.

Two packets of money at the post office

UMANITZKY: As your Excellency knows we've set up a so-called "black room" at the main post office, where we open suspicious-looking letters and packets — we do it in spite of the legal regulations guaranteeing the inviolability of the mails.

CONRAD: You know, Herr Colonel, you've got to take responsibility on my behalf for this, so that not a soul knows anything about it, otherwise we'll have a fine scandal in the Reichsrat.

UMANITZKY: The police officials who are carrying out the censorship open a thousand letters a day, on the average, and they themselves have not been told that they're working on behalf of the army. They all believe that the main objective is to uncover toll-tax swindlers and smugglers.

CONRAD: So, what's the result?

UMANITZKY: Besides the two letters that are being held at the main post office, nothing else special has popped up.

CONRAD: Those are the packets with cash sent from the Russian border, right?

UMANITZKY: Yes, Excellency, the ones from Eydtkühnen.*

CONRAD: And how long have they been lying around there?

UMANITZKY: The first one, containing a payment of eight thousand crowns, arrived back in February, the second one with a payment of six thousand crowns came in during early March.

CONRAD: So, already it's been almost half a year! Those are very big cash payments – and nobody has picked them up yet!

* A German town on the border with Russia, known as a smuggler's haven and an active center of Russian espionage activity.

The post office is under surveillance

UMANITZKY: Definitely not yet. Of course we have the postal pick-up counter under surveillance.

SALVATOR: Understood! Outstanding! A doubled guard with bayonets at the ready patrols the postal counter. And when the spy shows up, he'll be shot right away. An excellent plan, my dear Umanitzky, and I wish you all the luck with it.

CONRAD: How are you carrying out this surveillance, Herr Colonel?

UMANITZKY: I've got two plain-clothes detectives from the police housed in a room in the post office, and the room is connected to the pick-up counter by a wire that sends an alarm signal. Whenever somebody shows up to pick up the two letters with the code-name "Operaball 13" on them, the clerk will press a button, and the detectives will rush in.

SALVATOR: ... and seize him, right?

UMANITZKY: To be sure, your Imperial Highness, we'll seize him.

SALVATOR: Upon my word, that's just what I thought myself.

CONRAD: I only wish that it had already been done. Herr Colonel, I'm making you personally responsible for this — the whole matter of the two letters has to be cleared up.

UMANITZKY: Yes Sir, Excellency!

CONRAD: I have to go now. Does his Imperial Highness have any other orders for us?

SALVATOR: No, nothing urgent. You can go now, Conrad. (sotto voce): I'll snoop around here a little bit more. (aloud): Well, salutations, Conrad! We'll see each other this evening for a nice meal in the Grand Hotel. Best wishes! (Conrad exits). At last, Umanitzky we're finally all by ourselves. So now you can show me a couple of attractive lady spies. Don't you really have any photos of naked women?

UMANITZKY: Unfortunately not, Imperial Highness. But just yesterday there was a young Polish woman in here, dark looks, absolutely gorgeous.

Report over the telephone

SALVATOR: Can you send her my way? I'll fix up something for her, a fake report, something like that.

UMANITZKY: Imperial Highness, I don't know if she's coming back here again.

SALVATOR: Then at least show me her picture. You do have her photo here, don't you?

UMANITZKY: Certainly, Imperial Highness. (he goes for the photo catalog) Ah ...what was her name? Aha ... (the telephone rings, Umanitzky goes to pick it up)

SALVATOR: First the picture, Umanitzky, if you please.

UMANITZKY: Just a moment, Imperial Highness

SALVATOR: The telephone's not going anywhere!

UMANITZKY: I'll take care of it quickly. (He picks up the receiver): Colonel Umanitzky here, who's on the line? Uh-huh, the main post office, good. What's up? Taken care of?

SALVATOR: The Operaball stuff? (Umanitzky nods yes). Give me the phone!

UMANITZKY (he fends him off gently): Picked up by an elegant, fit-looking man. Got it. Didn't you apprehend him? What? No? Why's that? What's this you're telling me? The two detectives were pressing their pants because it's Saturday evening? What a disgusting mess! They've been hanging around half-a-year, waiting just for this moment. And they weren't able to run him down? How's that? He jumped into a car right away, and they didn't have a car? Why didn't they have a car?

Escaped!

SALVATOR: Why don't they have a car? Every detective ought to have a car — better yet, he should have two cars, one on each sidewalk

UMANITZKY: Where are these fellows? They're trying to find the car? What kind of a car was it? What, a taxi?

SALVATOR: Thurn and Taxis? Aha, the famous postal service of Thurn and Taxis!

UMANITZKY: A taxi, the devil take it, searching for that won't help us much, the scoundrel's probably been driven directly home, he's given us the slip! Horrible! Yes, send the postal clerk over here right away, maybe he'll be able to recognize the fellow from our collection of espionage agent photos. (he hangs up the receiver)

SALVATOR: Yes indeed, send the spy over here right away, maybe he'll recognize the postal clerk from the photos.

UMANITZKY: It's dreadful! (yelling into the adjacent room): All of you are staying put right here. We're on emergency duty.

SALVATOR: Good, good, emergency duty! (to the adjacent room): On my command. Emergency duty! (into the telephone receiver): Get the whole garrison at the ready. Cavalry, saddle-up! Attack!

UMANITZKY: (he paces around frantically): What an unholy mess! They let the man slip away. They just had to be pressing their pants!

SALVATOR: Oh well, their pants were probably all wrinkled.

UMANITZKY: But why did they have to be doing that just when the letters were being picked up!

Escaped!

SALVATOR (secretively): You know, maybe they didn't know the letter was going to be fetched just then. You, come on, show me the photos of the Polish spy-lady, right now, Umanitzky!

UMANITZKY: I can't do that just now, Imperial Highness, now's the time for work.

SALVATOR: Of course, now's the time for work. (he runs all over the office, from one device to the next, trying to get something going; then, into the telephone): Aim the cannons! Post office at the ready! All mailmen to their horses! Yes! And now the spy will be flushed out right away!

UMANITZKY: Your Imperial Highness, you ought to notify Conrad that the letters have been picked up.

SALVATOR: Of course! Pick up Conrad — Notify the letters — it will be done!

UMANITZKY: It's rather urgent, Imperial Highness.

SALVATOR: Of course! (he uses the cognac bottle as a telephone): Get the war-fleet out on the Danube! All spies on emergency duty! Salutations, Umanitzky, I've got to get a move on, (clarifying the point): ... there's a bit of a rush on.

UMANITZKY: With the most obedient respect, Imperial Highness.

CURTAIN

Two men on the trail

ACT III
THE DETECTIVES IN THE HOTEL LOBBY

HEAD PORTER (clapping his hands): Franz! Baggage from room number 64. (as he runs to the office): Bills for room numbers fifteen and sixteen! (he runs back): Klara, change out room 64! Franz! Where is that little rogue? (Franz comes in). Get the bags from room 64, and make it quick!

(Strebinger storms in, wearing a raglan coat with a plaid cap; he's smooth-shaven and is nervously swinging an English pipe back and forth. Steidl enters behind him, wearing a yellow mackintosh and an old gray hat with a stiff brim)

PORTER: The bills for rooms fifteen and sixteen. (to the two men): A room with a bath?

STREBINGER: With a bath?

STEIDL: No, we only want to ask you ...

PORTER (rushing around): Hang on a minute, please.

STREBINGER (trying to block the porter): Hey there ...

STEIDL: Leave him alone. There's really no need for us to be in a hurry now.

Damned trouser creases

STREBINGER: With you there's never a hurry! Just like with your pants-pressing, you messed around with that for half an hour.

STEIDL: But they do look like they came straight from the tailor's shop, right?

STREBINGER: I don't give a damn about the crease in your trousers! We hang around this stupid post-office for half a year, and when the buzzer sounds we're both caught with our pants down.

STEIDL: Well, yeah, so what? How did that hurt us?

STREBINGER: Please don't make me crazy, you're talking nonsense. How did it hurt us? Our man gave us the slip, that's how.

STEIDL: And if we'd had our pants pulled up?

STREBINGER: We could have grabbed him before he got into the car.

STEIDL: Oh yeah, sure. Then he would have shot us.

STREBINGER: But in that case we would have fulfilled our duty.

STEIDL: What kind of a duty is that, to get yourself shot? That's not in the service regulations.

STREBINGER: So we've been letting him lead us around by the nose!

STEIDL: And now we know that he's right here.

They encounter the taxi − − −

STREBINGER: On account of a lucky break.

STEIDL: Well then, don't you see it, if we hadn't been pressing our pants, then we would have been shot and we wouldn't have had that lucky break.

STREBINGER: Naturally, you have all kinds of excuses for your foolishness.

STEIDL: And you, you're always in a rush. You wanted to call the police chief right then and there in the post office and tell him the spy got away from us. Then both of us would have been fired.

STREBINGER: How was I to know that we were going to run into the same taxi? And I'm the one who yelled out at it to stop, even though it was empty.

STEIDL: Oh yeah, sure.

STREBINGER: I did yell out, I'm the one who yelled.

STEIDL: Big deal.

STREBINGER: Why didn't you yell anything?

STEIDL: Because you were yelling! What do you think it looks like when two people are standing together on the Ringstrasse* and they're both yelling at a taxi-driver?

STREBINGER: And just who asked the driver where he went with the man from the post office? And just who said that we should trail him to the Kaiserhof Café?

* The showpiece boulevard surrounding Vienna's Old City. It was built atop the polygonal lines of the city's fortified wall demolished during the early years of Franz Joseph's reign.

– – – and find a penknife sheath in it

STEIDL: Well, what do you think, that I would have gone to the Prater?* And the penknife sheath? I'm the one who found it in the car!

* A strip of wooded parkland located along the Danube. It had inns, housed seasonal fairs, and was one of Vienna's most popular areas for strolling, carriage-driving, and recreation.

STREBINGER: That's no great work of art, when I'm the one who yelled at the cab and ordered the driver to take us to the Kaiserhof Café.

STEIDL: Well, he wasn't at the Café.

STREBINGER: But I'm the one who found out at the next taxi stand that he'd moved on to somewhere else.

STEIDL: Yeah, but not where he went! I'm the one the guy talked to, the guy who waters the horses, the guy who washes the carriages, the guy who juggles the jobs for the cabbies; he heard what the man said, "Take me to the Hotel Klomser."

STREBINGER: Oh yeah, sure, so we both get the same amount of credit for finding out who the man is?

STEIDL: Yep, neither one of us knows who he is.

PORTER (passing by): What's going on with the bill for numbers fifteen and sixteen?

STREBINGER: Excuse me, Herr Porter, who's recently arrived by car?

PORTER: Hey, listen up here, do you think that I've got the time to talk with people about whether a guest came in by car or trotted in by foot?

The recent guests

STREBINGER: We're detectives, operating under the authority of the police.

PORTER: Ah, that's altogether different.

FRANZ (loaded down with bags): Baggage from room 64.

PORTER: I don't have time for that now. (Franz exits). So, you want to know who recently came in by car?

STREBINGER: Yes, during the last half-hour.

PORTER: All right, first there was Miss Schönemann from Berlin, she's got room number eighteen, with a bath. Then around six o'clock ...

FRANZ: The bill for rooms fifteen and sixteen!

PORTER: Don't bother me with that now, you stupid little scamp! So then, after that Mr. Nicolic came in, he's from Sarajevo.

STREBINGER: Oh yes, he's our man ...

PORTER: How's that? He was taken up to his room in a wheel-chair, the poor guy is missing his legs ... and he's your criminal, who'd ever believe that?

STREBINGER: No legs? Then he couldn't have jumped into a car.

STEIDL: Who else came in?

The spy has a room next to Colonel Redl!

PORTER: Then another one came in, he's in room number 25, he's a Russian ...

STREBINGER: Aha ...

PORTER: Oh, what's his name? (he looks it up): Nijinsky, he's a member of the Petersburg Imperial Court Opera-Ballet company...

STREBINGER (to Steidl): "Operaball 13", get it?

PORTER: Yeah, he just arrived, directly from the West Side rail-way station, he had fifteen trunks full of costumes, the real thing, and there were three cars full of ...

STEIDL: Nobody else, then?

PORTER. Yes, just before that Colonel Redl came in.

STEIDL and STREBINGER: Who? Colonel Redl? *Our* Colonel Redl?

PORTER: The one from the General Staff.

STREBINGER (to Steidl): Well now, that's downright precious! Now the spy is staying under the same roof as our Colonel Redl.

(he laughs): Maybe even in the room next to him, wall to wall. What would a writer call it in a spy novel? "Traipsing into the trap" or maybe "Into the lion's den"? No, not even a fanciful writer would come up with this one, nobody would ever believe him. That a spy would actually take lodgings in a place where the great spy-catcher lives! Hahaha! Colonel Redl's eyes will pop wide open when I report this to him — I'm going to notify him right now.

Telephone conversation with the police chief

STEIDL: There's no need to rush into this. First you ought to call the police chief, we've got to tell Privy Councilor Geyer that the trapped man is here in the Hotel Klomser.

STREBINGER: You're right, the rest can wait. (he goes to the phone booth)

STEIDL (to the Porter): Did Colonel Redl also come in by car?

STREBINGER (speaking into the phone): Please Miss, give me number 12–3–48 ...

PORTER: I can't tell you that, I wasn't looking out the door at the time.

STREBINGER (on the phone): Herr Privy Councilor, your humble servant here, Sergeant Strebinger from the surveillance detail at the main post office.

PORTER: He came back about twenty minutes ago, he's in room number one.

STREBINGER: Yes, right, I identified the taxi, and Steidl and I took it directly back to the Kaiserhof Café.

PORTER: He always wants a room that overlooks the courtyard.

STREBINGER: The porter at the taxi-stand told us that our man was driven to the Hotel Klomser.

PORTER: The Colonel got here earlier this afternoon, he came in from Prague.

Redl gives himself away

STREBINGER: We found a sheath for a pen-knife in the taxi. The man probably mislaid it when he opened the letters.

STEIDL: Herr Porter, when the guests who came in this afternoon come by, ask each one of them if he mislaid his penknife sheath.

STREBINGER: Yes, certainly, Privy Councilor, Sir, we'll run a police operation, a raid, check every last penknife to see if it fits into the sheath. Yes, of course, you're right, Herr Councilor, that's not real proof that the sheath belongs to the man.

(Colonel Redl appears on the stairway, pulling on his gloves. He's wearing a military overcoat, sword, and gray General Staff cap.)

STREBINGER: And I and have to respectfully report one more very interesting thing to you, Herr Councillor. By coincidence Colonel Redl is also staying at the Hotel.

REDL (to the Porter): Has Lieutenant Hromadka asked after me?

PORTER: No one has, Herr Colonel. Is there a chance that the Colonel lost this penknife sheath?

REDL: Yes. (He takes out his penknife and examines the sheath.)

STREBINGER: Yes, if we only knew whose sheath it is, then we'd know who the spy is.

The pen-knife sheath is Redl's

REDL (he sticks the knife into the sheath): Now where did I leave this thing lying around ... (He freezes suddenly, in a state of inner terror. He turns around and notices Steidl leafing through the hotel's guest book.)

STREBINGER: Certainly, Herr Privy Councilor, I'll request Colonel Redl to head up our investigation until the police commissioner and the other officials arrive.

REDL (leaves the hotel)

STREBINGER: Your obedient servant, Herr Privy Councilor. (He hangs up the phone, steps out of the phone booth, and says to Steidl): I've reported everything.

STEIDL: About the sheath, too?

STREBINGER: Sure, why?

STEIDL (to the Porter): Ring up 12-3-48 immediately and tell them that everything's in order now, the pen-knife sheath belongs to Colonel Redl.

STREBINGER: What?!

STEIDL: Let's go! (they both exit)

PORTER: Franz! The bills for numbers fifteen and sixteen!

CURTAIN

Operetta Music

ACT IV
"YOU'RE MY GOOD LUCK SMILING AT ME..."

(A semi-private dining alcove in Vienna's Grand Hotel, the evening's table is fully laid out. Conrad von Hötzendorf, Baroness Daubek, and another woman sit there, chatting; the place at the head of the table is open. Music is playing. Salvator enters. The other three jump to their feet. The ladies give him a humorous greeting: "Hofnix"[17])

SALVATOR: So then, what's up? It's a real pig's mess, I can't be in two places at one time, and besides it's all a waste of time. I'll put it to you, Conrad, something you'll find colossally interesting, the man's coming out, the man from the opera ball ...

(The band's leader and first violinist approaches them, bowing deeply)

SALVATOR: Jó estét kivánok, Rigo-báczi! Hogy van?* How does
* Hungarian for "Good evening, Uncle Rigo, how are you?"

that big hit from the latest operetta go? What's it called?

BARONESS DAUBEK: The "Dream Waltz"?

SALVATOR: No, no, there's a man's name in the song's title ...

BARONESS DAUBEK: "Orpheus in the Underworld"?

SALVATOR: No, it's a nobleman's title ...

BARONESS DAUBEK: "The Gypsy Baron"?

SALVATOR: No, no, it's a higher title than that. A Count, I think.

Melodrama

ALL TOGETHER: "The Count of Luxembourg!"

SALVATOR: Right! You've all got the right picture now! (The violinist plays, and Salvator sings along): "You're my good luck smiling at me, I've been floating in the air since time gone by ..." À propos floating in the air, your man's been floating in the air right in front of you, jumping into a taxi, and two people are pressing their pants, and of course they couldn't chase after him without their pants -- how would that look, them in their underpants — I beg your pardon, dear ladies — running around in the streets in their underpants? That looks like, well, it's hideous.

BARONESS DAUBEK: What two people?

SALVATOR: Huh? The two detectives, you understand me, right, Conrad? The two detectives — à propos detectives, tell me, Conrad, and be straight with me about this, hands across your heart, in your opinion how many cars does a detective need?

CONRAD: That depends on circumstances, Imperial Highness.

SALVATOR: It doesn't depend on any such thing, every detective should have a car, better yet two or more. That has to be enacted in the regulations at once, the Reichsrat can bite its tongue about it. I think that Sherlock Holmes had fifty or sixty cars at his disposal. You know, Sherlock Holmes must have been a very clever fellow, I think, (speaking softly now) — upon my soul, I believe that Sherlock Holmes is even more clever than Nick Carter — keep that between us. (speaking aloud again) Sherlock Holmes wouldn't have let that fellow escape, that much I know for sure!

BARONESS DAUBEK: What fellow is that, Imperial Highness?

"What nice little thing are you bringing me"

SALVATOR: Well now, the fellow who betrayed our deployment plans for operation Operaball, who in 1913 betrayed the whole Operaball thing, and sold it to Russia ...

CONRAD (pricking up his ears for a second): What?

SALVATOR: Yes, my dear Conrad, like the first time I attended an opera ball, I was only a youngster at the time, a major in the Savoy Dragoons Regiment—do you know what ever became of the regimental doctor, Popper — he's the one who treated my first case of — pardon me speaking about this, ladies — —

BARONESS DAUBEK: Please, please, Imperial Highness.

SALVATOR: All right, all right, those really were golden days! (He dances and sings a little song.) "You're my good luck smiling at me..."

(Umantizky enters, seemingly astonished by the dancing Salvator)

CONRAD (to Umanitzky): Greetings, Umanitzky, what nice little thing are you bringing me?

SALVATOR: Greetings, Umanitzky, are you bringing me something nice too? Come on, sit down with us, grab a glass of wine and get something to eat.

UMANITZKY: May I respectfully request a moment with you, Excellency?

CONRAD: Do you have to, right now?

SALVATOR: Now, in the middle of the night, when everybody's asleep?

Umanitzky delivers his report

CONRAD: Is it really that important?

UMANITZKY: Indeed it is, Excellency.

CONRAD: Well then, there's nothing but to do it. (He gets up.) So where do we go now?

UMANITZKY: We can retire over here for just a moment. (The ladies leave. The door is closed. The music goes on, muted.)

CONRAD: So now, what's the matter?

UMANITZKY: His Imperial Highness will have already told your Excellency that the letters have been picked up.

CONRAD: What letters?

UMANITZKY: The two spy's letters with money in them, the ones with the code-name "Operaball 13" on them that have been lying around at the post office.

CONRAD: What? I don't know anything about it.

SALVATOR: Of course you do. Well, if only you listened to me when I'm speaking! I already asked you about the cars—on account of Sherlock Holmes!

CONRAD (to Umanitzky): What's this thing really about? Quickly!

UMANITZKY: At five-thirty today the letters were picked up by a man. Before the detectives could grab him, he'd jumped into a car and was driven off. He was followed to the Hotel Klomser, and after he left the hotel, he was tailed on the street. He saw he was under surveillance, so he tore up some papers while he was in a

Who? What? Have you lost your mind?

passageway—he was hoping to slow down the agents following him while they picked up the pieces, while that was going on he could get into a car and make his escape. In spite of all that they still followed him, they picked up the paper scraps, then had them reassembled later.

CONRAD: What was in them?

UMANITZKY: Confirmations of receipts from known espionage cover-addresses in the Hague and Lausanne.

CONRAD: From which countries?

UNMANITZKY: Russia, France, Serbia, and Italy.

CONRAD: Italy too?* Who's the man?

UMANITZKY (haltingly): He is — — is — —

CONRAD: The devil take you! I want to know who the man is!

UMANITZKY: Colonel Redl.

CONRAD (screaming): Who? What? Have you lost your mind! Do you realize whom you're accusing here? Stand at attention!

UMANITZKY: Your Excellency!

CONRAD: Forgive me — — Colonel Redl? Are you certain?

UMANITZKY: Definitely, completely certain.

* Although a member of the Triple Alliance with Germany and Austria-Hungary, Italy's reliability in the case of war was doubted, especially by Conrad, who constantly urged a pre-emptive strike against Italy.

Suicide is commanded

CONRAD: For God's sake, for God's sake! What's the old Emperor going to say? He put so much stock in Redl.

SALVATOR (secretively): Aha, perhaps the Emperor is also involved in this.

CONRAD: If the world gets wind of this — our allies — the Reichsrat — horrible! — Not a single soul is to know of this —

UMANITZKY: But, Excellency, it can't remain a secret, not if Redl is taken into custody.

CONRAD (with decisiveness): We can't allow him to be taken into custody. He has to die tonight.

SALVATOR: Of course, a fellow like this one has to hanged!

CONRAD: Thinking it over, of course, he himself should ... have I made myself understood?

UMANITZKY: At your command, Excellency, suicide.

SALVATOR: For God's sake, you can't just go grasping after suicide! Suicide is strictly forbidden by our religion. At least you have to send the rotten swine a priest for his soul, then you can string him up.

CONRAD: Have I made myself understood?

UMANITZKY: At your command, Excellency.

CURTAIN

Collapse

ACT V
HARAKIRI

(Redl's darkened hotel room)

REDL (he enters, turns on the light, collapses into a chair): It's all blown away! (He slowly sits up straight and lays his military cap aside.) Adieu, you cap with your cockade! (He unfastens his sword.) They're going to break you in half. (He looks at his decorations, touches the military stars on his collar, and then tears off his overcoat.) Away with it! (There's a soft knock on the door, he pulls himself together.) You're already here? (There's another knock. He tries to call out "Enter", but only makes an inarticulate sound.)

FRANZI (she opens the door): Please forgive me, Herr Colonel ...

REDL: Who's there?

77

FRANZI: It's me, Herr Colonel.

REDL: Oh yes, excuse me, young woman. (He quickly pulls his coat back on. Franzi remains standing at the door.) Please, come right in.

FRANZI: Herr Colonel, I've come to request something from you.

REDL: "To request something from you"! Somebody comes to request something from me! (He laughs hysterically.)

Two hours are a long time

FRANZI (startled): Are you sick, Herr Colonel?

REDL: Yes, sick. Just a little bit sick, it's only a lethal illness. But, what ... (he pulls himself together) How may I be of service to you, my dear young woman?

FRANZI: I've come here from Stefan. He's made all his preparations for the trip.

REDL: For the trip?

FRANZI: Yes, he told me that he's taking a trip with you ...

REDL: Taking a trip with me?

FRANZI: He told me all about it, he didn't hide anything − − he said he'd given you his word of honor.

REDL: Yes, he did give his word of honor. But that was a long time ago, a frightfully long time ago.

FRANZI: No, it was just two hours ago, right after I left here.

REDL: Two hours ago! ... Two hours is a long, long time, my dear young woman. You don't realize what can happen in two hours, two hours is the difference between supreme good luck and the worst misfortune, two hours suffice to split up a beautiful blooming tree into firewood − − is it really only two hours since you were last here?

Tell Stefan I send him my greetings

FRANZI: Yes. And I learned something too during those two hours. I've behaved badly, I demanded things when I should have been begging a favor from you. I should have presented myself to you for what I am, a weak young woman, a woman who doesn't have anything else in the world besides him, besides my fine, dear Stefan, and I can't live without him. I should have thrown myself down at your feet (here she kneels down) and begged of you: Let me have my Stefan. You're a very big man, Herr Colonel, you enjoy the respect and trust of others, you've got the brightest of futures, thousands envy you your good fortune, yes thousands ...

(With a quick glance Redl sees that Franzi is kneeling down. He reacts to her words with a perplexed laugh, which, when he hears "good fortune", turns into a burst of sobbing. He staggers.)

FRANZI (she jumps up, startled; she props him up): For heaven's sake, what's going on with you?

REDL (after pausing): It's nothing. Don't worry about it − − I'm not going to stand in your way. Stefan won't ever see me again. Tell him I send him my greetings, that I wish him better luck than I've had, tell him ...

FRANZI: What's the matter, Herr Colonel? What's happened to you?

REDL: ... tell him that I was thinking of him right up until the very last minute ...

FRANZI: What do you mean to do? − − Look, Herr Colonel, I'm only a woman, and I know that you despise women, though I don't know what's behind your desperation right now − − but I want to say something to you: an hour ago I realized that my Stefan had made a decision for you and that he wanted to get away from me − then, just for a second, the thought came to me that maybe it would be better if I did away with myself. But in that same instant I also knew that's not the right way for a decent human being to go. As long as you can work and love there's no

It's too late

need for you to die. And that goes for you too, Herr Colonel. (She takes his sword.) What kind of a thing is this for men to make, a thing made to wound others? (She picks up his cap.) Why do you wear the monogram of other men on your head? (She points to his military overcoat.) Why do you wear somebody's livery, like a lackey. (She fingers the decorations on his coat.) Why do you wear these tinplate awards, like some kind of prize-winning animal? If it's life you want to pursue rather than death, and if all these things oppress you, then throw them all away! Whether you sweep streets or clean up canals, that's far more honorable work than recruiting spies and unmasking spies!

REDL: I thank you for that, my dear young woman. Unfortunately, it's too late for that now.

FRANZI: It's never too late.

REDL: Perhaps you're right. But summoning up courage won't help me now. I must ask you to please leave now, my dear young woman.

FRANZI: I thank you, Herr Colonel.

REDL: It's you I have to thank, gracious lady.

FRANZI: Good-bye.

REDL: Good-, Good- ...Live well!

(Franzi exits)

A Homosexual? Horrible!

REDL (he goes to his desk and takes out writing paper): Whom should I write to first? The Corps Commander. (He starts to write, tears it up, then starts again. There's a knock on the door.) Already? Come in!

(Umanitzky, General Höfer, and Major-Auditor Worlitschek enter, wearing their military caps.)

REDL: I know why you've come. I won't waste time denying anything.

UMANITZKY: I have to ask you if you have any accomplices, Mister Redl?

REDL (he startles when he hears the words "Mister Redl"): No, no one.

UMANITZKY: Who recruited you as a spy?

REDL: The Russian military attaché, he had me under surveillance when I was acting as an expert witness at an espionage trial, and he found out then that I ... (he pauses) ... that I'm a homosexual.

I'm a victim of blackmail.

UMANITZKY: A Homosexual?

HÖFER: Horrible!

WORLITSCHEK: Achh ... the devil take you!

UMANITZKY: Mister Redl, under the highest orders you have to bring this affair to its end within the hour in the only way possible. Have I made myself clear?

You are allowed to ask for a pistol

REDL (after a moment): Yes.

UMANITZKY: You are allowed to ask for a pistol.

REDL: Please — I respectfully — request — a pistol.

(Umanitzky gives the Major-Auditor a signal, whereupon he hands over a revolver: Umanitzky then confirms to General Höfer that he has given it to Redl.)

UMANITZKY (he salutes): Herr General, I respectfully report the completion of our official mission.

(Höfer salutes back to Umanitzky. The three men leave the room. Redl takes the revolver, lifts it toward his open mouth, and the curtain falls, after which a shot is heard.)

THE END

Chapter 4. Kisch and the Redl Case: Reportage into Melodrama

Viewers and readers of *Die Hetzjagd* were exposed to a constricted presentation of the complicated Redl affair, the culmination of a series of events that occurred over a decade before reaching its unsavory end in 1913. Therefore in the present chapter I supply information on the historical events on which the play was based. Even within the confined temporal frame of one day on which the strands of several narratives concluded in Redl's death, there was more to the story than Kisch could show on stage. My historical exposition is followed by analytical remarks about the structure and themes of the play, and then returns again to historical issues: first, the accuracy of Kisch's reporting on the case; and, second, how historians assess the significance of Redl's espionage. A more detailed look at other aspects of the play — its performance history, contemporaneous critical responses, and its placement in a series of plays written by Kisch during the 1920s — is undertaken in Chapter 7.

During the 1920s the names of Kisch and Redl became intertwined to the extent that readers and critics considered it 'his' story in an almost proprietary way. This was due to the success of Kisch's 1924 book about the case, *Der Fall des Generalstabschefs Redl*. In the chapter of his memoirs re-telling the Redl story Kisch reminisced about his lead role in breaking the case during the two weeks in May and June of 1913 when he had written numerous unsigned articles about the affair for *Bohemia*.[1] The General Staff immediately issued a 'cover story' that Redl's suicide resulted from overwork, insomnia, and anxiety; in the terminology of the era, he had a "nervous breakdown". To keep up the pretense, in recognition of his years of diligent service he was to be given a full-ceremonial military burial later in the week. This deliberately misleading version of what had happened came out in Vienna's *Neue Freie Presse* on Monday, May 26, a day after Redl had taken his own life.[2] By the next day this version was undermined by

Kisch, who had an 'inside source' who gave him enough information to indicate the falsity of the official Viennese press release. As he explains in *Sensation Fair,* he and his editor averted foreseeable censorship by using the ruse of printing a brief notice that the authorities in Vienna denied the truth of rumors of espionage as the real reason for Redl's suicide.[3] Kisch noted that this would lead the average reader, skeptical about government press releases, to the conclusion that an official denial meant that what was being denied might well be true. The local censors in Prague did not check with Vienna, so the notice was not blocked and the first challenges to the army's version of what had happened soon followed.

Kisch's claims about his priority and singular importance in reporting the story in 1913 were exaggerated, as shown by excerpts of articles published in other newspapers that are noted by Patka[4] and quoted in John Sadler and Sylvie Fisch's 2016 re-examination of the Redl case.[5] Between May 26th and June 6th, 1913, *Bohemia* published 17 unsigned articles about the Redl case that have been attributed to Kisch.[6] They vary greatly in length. Their sourcing is often anonymous, though Kisch also wrote longer pieces that paraphrased reports in other newspapers (mostly Viennese). They were speculative at times, repeating various rumors about aspects of the case that made for an exciting story. The speculation took place in a context of meager and deliberately misleading or outright false information released by official sources (whom Kisch also quoted).

Kisch's 1913 pieces about the case were an integral part of a swelling 'call and response' effect in the local newspapers, with each day's succession of competing speculations about the case driving further criticism of the General Staff by parliamentarians, factional politicians, and the designated Successor, Archduke Franz Ferdinand. By May 29th the General Staff had to reverse itself, cancelling Redl's military funeral and admitting through a terse published notice that Redl had committed suicide in order to avoid prosecution for espionage on behalf of a "foreign power" and for engaging in homosexual activity, an offense under both civil and military law.[7] As stated, the two clauses of the indictment implied that Redl had been blackmailed into espionage by foreign agents aware of his homosexuality. The link between Redl's homosexuality and his spying had not, in fact, been established through forensic investigation in 1913 and is still an open question (that is, Redl might have been blackmailed into espionage, or he might have volunteered his services in order to fund his increasingly lavish manner of living—the point is still moot and, historically, inconsequential).

By the time he wrote his last article on the Redl case for *Bohemia*, Kisch had established the following (with the assistance of reports from other papers), more or less correctly: Redl's espionage on behalf of Russia; his homosexuality, including an affair with his protégé, the cavalry lieutenant, Stefan Horinka; the fact that, in spite of an official counter-version, Redl had not been under suspicion before May 24th; police (Secret Service) involvement in the case as well as active investigation by members of military intelligence; the existence of the letters carrying cash, which had been under watch at the Central Post Office for about seven weeks; the police surveillance trap; the detectives' pursuit of an unknown suspect and their discovery of a pen-knife sheath in a taxicab used by Redl; the detectives' recovery of incriminating scraps of paper disposed of by Redl while under surveillance; the successful ruse that ensnared Redl at the Hotel Klomser; Redl's dinner with his old friend, the jurist Viktor Pollak; the commission of officers that visited Redl on the night of the 24th; his suicide by pistol; and, based on the first (false) news releases, the General Staff's attempt to cover up the real reasons behind Redl's suicide. Kisch had also passed along incorrect speculations and, like other reporters, remained ignorant of various details of the case. He learned some of these through research and interviews in the early 1920s. His 1913 coverage of the case was aggressive journalism, skeptical of the authorities, but in no sense reportage. But his 1924 book on the case, discussed below, was hailed as one of his first "great" reportages, though this term might also be applied to his war diary published in 1922. Note that the 1924 book dealt with recent history, not ongoing events, indicating the suitability of reportage techniques for dealing with the past as well as the present.

Hostile public and parliamentary reactions to the Redl scandal continued to flare up during the latter half of 1913, by which time Kisch had departed for Berlin. Because important members of the Austro-Hungarian leadership class and a sizeable proportion of the general public believed that Redl's espionage had disastrous consequences in 1914–1915, dissatisfaction with the official 'resolution' of the case in 1913 lingered on at the end of World War I. In this climate of suspicion Kisch became the journalist who pursued the case in the face of resistance thrown up by conservative elements in Austrian political life, who, even under the new post-1918 regime, wished to divert responsibility from the General Staff and the higher reaches of Austrian officialdom. He interviewed military and civilian officials who had been involved in the events of May 24–25, 1913 and in the subsequent official investigation. He also examined any documents he could find that might shed light on what had really happened. However, official files on Redl's career and on the case and its investigation by the General Staff and various ministries remained sealed and off-limits, to both journalists and historians. The first 'outsider' to gain access to many of these files, dispersed among half a dozen archives, was Robert Asprey, an American who wrote an "interpretive biography" of Redl during the late 1950s.[8] Georg Markus, an Austrian journalist and television personality, duplicated some of Asprey's research for his 1985 book on the Redl case and also claimed to have made new discoveries based on Russian sources; the probative value of this Russian material was far from definitive in resolving contested aspects of the case, discussed below. And historians came back to the case in the 2010's, often in conjunction with revisionist histories of World War I and its causes. Some of the relevant files about the Redl case may have been deliberately destroyed, and there were claims that Russian files bearing on Redl had been confiscated by the Germans in Warsaw in 1915 and thereafter "gone missing".[9]

The 1924 book can be broken down into five separate stories that Kisch wove together, combining investigative journalism with speculation and an historical appraisal: the events of May 24–25, when Redl was detected as a foreign agent and persuaded to commit 'compulsory suicide'; a survey of Redl's long career in military intelligence; the serendipitous tale of how Kisch acquired his first clue that the official press release about Redl's death was false; an assessment of how much damage Redl's espionage had done to Austrian military plans and foreign policy during a period of increasing international tension over the Balkan Wars and during the opening months of the world war; and a depiction of the behavior of the General Staff officers in their failed attempt at a cover-up. Viewers and readers of *Die Hetzjagd* are exposed to only the first story that describes the detection and apprehension of Redl on his last day on earth, a tale of crime and dereliction of duty at the highest levels of Austria's military-political leadership.

What exactly, according to Kisch, happened on that day? Although many particulars of his 1924 version of the story have been challenged by historians and by Redl's and Kisch's biographers, his account supplies the basic timeline and record of events that have been written about time and again. It is given immediately below, with some supplementary information from Robert Asprey's 1959 biography of Redl, *The Panther's Feast*.[10] Its errors and misleading parts (whether inadvertent or deliberate) will be discussed farther below, though they have no actual bearing on the construction and narrative of the play derived from Kisch's reporting about the events of Redl's final day.

On the morning of Saturday, May 24, 1913, Colonel Alfred Redl left Prague for a short trip to Vienna, where he planned to deal with problems he was having with his protégé and paramour, Lieutenant Stefan Horinka (named Hromodka in *Die Hetzjagd*), whom he had led his friends and colleagues to believe was his nephew. He told his commanding General, Arthur Giesl von Gieslingen, that his 'nephew' wished to leave the army in order to marry a woman of modest means and that he was going to attempt to talk him out of this rash decision that would terminate a promising career as a professional cavalry officer. Redl had been stationed in Prague since early 1912 as the General Staff Chief of the VIIIth Army Corps, an important liaison position that included training officers and evaluating the readiness of the Corps in the case of war. In keeping with his special skills, he also had an intelligence remit to report on nationalist unrest in Prague.

Redl's chauffer drove him to Vienna in his expensive Daimler-Benz convertible, an extravagance he explained by false stories about having inherited a considerable sum of money from an uncle (he could have hardly afforded the automobile, much less all the other tokens of his luxurious life-style, on a Colonel's pay). He was dropped off at the Klomser Hotel, close to military intelligence headquarters, his old workplace for eleven years between 1900 and 1912. During those years he had risen in rank and responsibility, becoming deputy director of the *Evidenzbüro*, where he was considered to be most adept professional in military intelligence and counterintelligence, a reputation bolstered by his appearance as the prosecution's formidable expert witness in a series of espionage-treason trials held in Vienna in the middle of the previous decade.[11] He had his chauffeur take the car to a workshop, where its interior was to be refurbished with red silk lining.

Sometime during the afternoon of the 24th Horinka arrived at Redl's suite of rooms in the Klomser. Redl tried to persuade him to drop the idea of marriage—or to at least postpone it—by promising to buy him a touring car, after which they would go off on holiday together. Whether the meeting was stormy or calm and business-like is unknown. Soon after Horinka left the hotel, Redl, dressed in civilian clothes, went to Vienna's main post office in order to pick up two letters at the general delivery window. They contained 14,000 crowns in large-denomination bills and were addressed to one Nikon Nizetas. According to Kisch the envelopes also bore the code-phrase "Opernball 13". This cipher has a role in the play, but later researchers discovered that no such coded phrase existed (this will be discussed below). Redl arrived at the post office shortly before its 6:00 p.m. closing time. Unwittingly, he had walked into a trap organized by the *Evidenzbüro*, with assistance from Vienna's police.

In March, 1913, German military intelligence officials contacted their Austrian counterparts, alerting them to a letter they had inspected before sending it along to its general-delivery address in Vienna. German officials opened it because it came from

Eydtkuhnen, a town on the German-Russian border well known for smuggling and espionage activity. They found a large amount of cash. An accompanying letter indicated that the addressee ("Nikon Nizetas") was ostensibly being paid for unspecified services. After the letter was forwarded to Vienna, Redl's old colleagues at the *Evidenzbüro* set up the trap. Stationed in Prague, Redl was unaware of the operation. They installed an electric wire that ran from the general-delivery window to a buzzer at a nearby surveillance post, where plain-clothes detectives would be alerted when the suspicious letters were picked up (by May there were two). When Redl arrived, posing as Nizetas, the desk clerk activated the alarm, but the detectives were slow in responding. They saw their quarry get into a taxicab and managed to jot down its license number as they bemoaned their fate after their egregious fumbling of the surveillance. And then they had what is called 'hunter's luck', seeing the cab return along the same street by the post office. They hailed it, climbed in, and asked the driver to take them to where he had driven his last fare. They found a distinctive penknife sheath in the back of the cab, presumably lost by its previous occupant. They went to a cab-stand at Kaiserhof Square, where they found a porter who told them that their suspect's next destination was the Hotel Klomser.

Detectives Strebinger and Steidl (as Kisch named them in his play, though his memoirs recall the first as Ebinger) repaired to the hotel, where they conversed with the head porter, questioning him about who had come into the hotel from a taxi during the preceding hours. They found the fact that Redl was staying in the hotel deliciously ironical—the master spy-catcher might now be enlisted to help them find their quarry. They telephoned in the status of their surveillance (still not knowing the identity of the suspect) and were told to remain on the alert at the hotel. Rather than contacting Redl for assistance they settled on a plan of leaving the penknife sheath with the porter, who was to ask each departing guest if he had misplaced it. As the detectives loitered in the lobby Redl came downstairs in civilian dress. He was going to have dinner with an old friend, a jurist named Viktor Pollak, at the nearby Riedhof Hotel's restaurant. When asked, Redl identified the pen-knife sheath as his and immediately suspected that he had been detected (he noticed one of the detectives feigning interest in the guest registration book). The detectives instructed the porter to phone the police and inform them that everything was under control and that Redl was the wanted man.

Redl then went on a counter-surveillance route, walking through passageways with multiple exits and deliberating with himself how to handle the situation. At some point he removed papers from his pocket, tore them up, and scattered the shreds in the street. One of the detectives picked up the scraps while the other remained on his trail. He kept his dinner appointment. At the Riedhof's restaurant Redl made a veiled confession to his old friend that he was guilty of "sins and moral failings", requesting Pollak to contact the police in order to see if they would supply him with transportation back to Prague, or possibly to a sanatorium. Pollak reached Police Chief Gayer, who advised him to tell Redl to return to his hotel and not do anything rash. The detective was on the scene and followed Redl back to his hotel.

As this queasy meal took place the police and the *Evidenzbüro* took a number of steps to confirm the identity of the suspect. Major Max Ronge, who had been trained in counterintelligence by Redl, recognized his old boss's handwriting on the post office receipt for the letters to Nizetas and the pieced-together shredded papers. These included receipts for a letter mailed to Horinka, and, more incriminating, for letters mailed to 'cover addresses' abroad known to be used by Russian and French military intelligence; one cover address was possibly a French relay point for conveying information to their Russian ally. Now Colonel August Urbanski, the Chief of the *Evidenzbüro*, had to report the shocking news to Conrad, Chief of the General Staff. Conrad's dinner engagement at the Grand Hotel was interrupted by Urbanski and Ronge. He immediately decided upon a confrontation at the Hotel Klomser, during which a commission of four officers would interrogate Redl and then encourage him to commit 'compulsory suicide' (a common escape route from prosecution for violations of the officer corps honor code). He appointed Urbanksi and Ronge to the commission and told them to pick up his executive officer,

General Franz Höfer, and a high-ranking member of the army's Judge Advocates Corps, Auditor Kunz. Kunz was not in Vienna, so Wenzel Vorliček, an Auditor who held the rank of Major, was substituted. Conrad instructed Urbanski that everyone involved in the case up to this point had to be sworn to secrecy and that all communications to the government and the dynasty regarding the case were to be handled by the leadership of the General Staff (i.e., Conrad himself would filter and sanitize any investigation results before forwarding them).

The commission arrived at Redl's suite sometime near midnight, noticing evidence that Redl had tried to hang himself but had failed. Their interrogation focused on two points: Did he have any military or civilian confederates? And, how long had he spied on behalf of Russia? To the former question Redl replied, "None." To the latter he stated that he had begun working for Russia in 1912, when he had sold the enemy some training manuals and a classified report evaluating that year's annual field maneuvers. He told them that they would find evidence of this in his quarters in Prague. Establishing that he had no personal weapon with him, the commission advised him to request a pistol, which he did. Unfortunately they had forgotten to bring one along, so Ronge was posted to retrieve a pistol and return to the room. After this had been done the commission left, lingering outside the hotel in the square that had the popular Café Central on its opposite side. They decided to change into civilian clothing so as not be so conspicuous; in alternation two remained while two went home to change. They heard no gunshot (Redl's rooms faced an interior courtyard), so after several hours had gone by they phoned the police to send one of the detectives involved in the surveillance. Upon arrival he told the desk-clerk that Redl had summoned him to come to his room as soon as possible. When he entered the unlocked room he found Redl dead on the floor, a victim of a pistol-shot through the mouth that exited the back of his skull. There were two suicide notes, one to General Giesl, the other to one of his brothers. The detective reported this to the commission, who then arranged to have someone (either the police or military intelligence) call the hotel and request the desk-clerk to go to Redl's room and bring him to the phone for an urgent message. The clerk reported back on Redl's corpse. Officially, it was the clerk who had 'discovered' the evidence of suicide. Soon thereafter a coroner and military officers arrived and had Redl's body removed for an autopsy.

The foregoing events of the day are, in part, the story told in *Die Hetzjagd*. For the sake of completion, however, the rest of Kisch's narrative will be given here. Colonel Urbanski and Auditor Vorliček rushed to Prague on the morning's first train and informed General Giesl about the distressing news. The trio secured the services of a local locksmith to break into Redl's quarters, desk, and cabinets. They noted the effeminate character of his apartment—red and pink silk everywhere, kitschy erotic knick-knacks, a strong smell of perfume. More important, they found sophisticated equipment used to photograph documents and logbooks with notations of classified documents sold and payments received (much more than Redl had hinted at). They also found a closet full of women's clothing, a cache of scented love-letters, and lurid photographs that incriminated a large number of men, including army men, who had engaged in homosexual activities. The commission members were in a state of shock, lest any of their discoveries be revealed to the public; such leaks would supply anti-militarists and the numerous critics of the General Staff with information that could be used to undermine its 'executive control' of military affairs and the political-diplomatic influence that Conrad exercised.

In dealing with Redl the man, Kisch provided a dismissive character sketch. He mistakenly reported that Redl's father was a "Garrison court official" in Lemberg. In fact he was a railroad freight dispatcher supporting a wife and fourteen children on a modest salary. He gave an accurate account (as far as it went) of various infantry and other assignments Redl had held and commendations he had received over the course of his career. Noting that Redl had attended the War College in Vienna (a definite 'gate' for entry into the General Staff), Kisch disparaged that institution for producing martinets and "pathologically ambitious" officers. He suggested that Redl may have been recruited by Russian intelligence when he was posted as a Russian-language student and "observer" to Kazan in 1899; there is no proof of this. He covered Redl's much-praised role as an expert witness in a series of espionage trials in Vienna, opining (as many others did, long after the event) that Redl's tergiversations in one of these, the complicated "Hekailo-Wieckowski-Acht" espionage affair of 1903-04, indicated that he was definitely working for the Russians at that time. And he wrote of Redl that his taste was mediocre and his mind incurious, even pedestrian (a judgment contradicted by his colleagues and superiors whenever they went on record about his character and deportment[12]).

One other aspect of Redl's career was treated by Kisch, his professional diligence and mastery of espionage and counterespionage 'tradecraft'. In addition to writing guidance manuals on the technical side of intelligence operations Redl had introduced the new criminological techniques of dusting objects with invisible powder used to collect fingerprints, positioning hidden cameras and recording devices in interview rooms, tempting interviewees with official-looking files that they might be recorded viewing when agency officers left the room, etc. These 'tricks of the trade' were introduced into the Redl play in Act II, educating the audience while providing props for Archduke Salvator's nonsensical comments.

As to long-term considerations, Kisch's 1924 book provided information that would allow the reader to infer that Redl had been spying for perhaps a decade before 1913 and that he had earned immense amounts of money over the years, with the implication that the information he had sold to the Russians (and, as it proved, to Italian military intelligence) was highly valued by his paymasters. Two probabilities were especially worrying: the sale of current mobilization plans; and the likelihood that Redl had betrayed almost all of Austria's agents spying in Russia, thus leaving Austrian military intelligence in the dark about Russia's military establishment and its strategic plans. This was the 'maximalist' position that many in Austria believed to be true (as did some later historians), and it would come to haunt everyone after the disasters on the Serbian and Russian fronts between August 1914 and the failed winter operations in Galicia in early 1915. Kisch agreed with this devastating assessment, though it has often been challenged. In the end it may have been nothing more than scapegoating.

Kisch continued his 1924 report with an account of the adverse parliamentary and dynastic reactions to the laxness of the General Staff with respect to Redl's extravagant expenditures and to their attempted cover-up in the Redl affair. He painted a portrait of a furious Archduke Franz Ferdinand, who wanted as many General Staff heads to roll as possible and who kept up pressure throughout 1913, though he was kept in check and only managed to force Urbanski's early retirement for "medical reasons" (after the Archduke's assassination Urbanski was recalled to the colors, achieving the rank of General during World War I). Kisch concluded his 1924 book with a section on the "story of how he got his story from a locksmith in 1913." He listed six officials involved in the Redl investigation as sources whom he interviewed during the early 1920s. Among them was the retired General Urbanski, whom he visited and from whom he received a "memoir" on the Redl case and its political aftermath, including remarks that reflected the view of Conrad and Urbanski that the Successor was "pathological". Kisch wrote that he slipped into their conversation innocent-sounding questions regarding the locksmith who had been conscripted on that Sunday morning. Urbanksi dismissed his hints about this as irrelevant.

But this was a portion of his book that Kisch was extremely fond of. In his telling the locksmith was named Wagner, the right end on a football team managed by Kisch. On Sunday, May 25th, Kisch's club, "Sturm", had a match with a Czech club, "SK Union Holeschovice". Wagner missed the match, and Kisch blamed his team's loss on his absence. Wagner came to Kisch's office at *Bohemia* the next day and apologized, claiming that he had been conscripted by high-ranking military men from Vienna to break into an officer's apartment. At first Kisch scoffed at his excuse, then he remembered seeing a telegraphed news summary from Vienna about the suicide of a Colonel. Putting two and two together, he realized that Redl was involved. Inquiring further, he learned from Wagner what evidence the commission had found and how agitated they were by their discoveries. From this Kisch jumped to the conclusion that Redl had been forced to commit suicide because he was guilty of espionage and that it was possible he had been blackmailed into treason because foreign agents had discovered his homosexuality and used it as leverage against him. Within a day he and his editor had concocted their 'official rumor-denial' approach to getting this information out to the public.

In addition to hewing to the trope that 'a lowly working man had contributed to the undermining of a powerful institution', which Kisch found satisfying, he thoroughly discredited Urbanski's memoir by presenting it as just one more attempt of the General Staff to deflect criticism and deny their responsibility for the Redl scandal and its dire implications in case of war. (Even after admitting a selectively qualified version of what had happened, Conrad publicly minimized the consequences of Redl's espionage—his private opinion was quite different.) And he ended his 1924 book with a stirring declamation about the socially damaging effects of the then-prevalent combination of militarism and chauvinism. Strongly committed to the socio-political theories of international communism after 1918, Kisch viewed nation-states and empires as fundamentally flawed and outmoded, as seen in his final remarks on the Redl scandal, with its allusion to the Dreyfus affair:

> The criminal case of Redl may appear to be unique, but it will always be repeated in one form or another, for nations themselves are the instigators of this crime, which nations themselves punish with death by means of the noose, exile to Devil's Island, or the order to commit suicide.[13]

Readers of the 1924 book can see just how much of its narrative and broader set of considerations were omitted from the play. With respect to Redl's final day itself, Kisch had chosen to excise elements that would have extended the time-line of the story or complicated the tale of Redl's pursuit: the day's start in Prague; the on-foot surveillance of Redl after he had claimed his penknife sheath and left the Hotel Klomser; his meal with his old friend, Pollak; and most of the activities of the police and the *Evidenzbüro* on that day. Still, the play captured the basic outline of the story of Redl's detection and apprehension. His 1924 version, whatever its flaws, was more truthful than any admissions by the General Staff, who also prevaricated about the length of time Redl had spied against Austria and the damaging effects of his treason. All of the other wider-ranging themes of his 1924 book were ignored in order to construct a tight play focused on criminality detected and punishment decreed on 'Redl's fatal day', a convergence of events that was almost ready-made for theatrical and film treatment.

Those were the omissions. What were Kisch's inventions, i.e., elements of the play not reported in 1924 or in his memoirs as actual events occurring on May 24-25, 1913? First, the presence of Horinka's fiancé at their afternoon meeting; this is "Franzi" (based on a woman named Marie Dobias).[14] Second, the comical fumbling of the detectives at the post-office, a deviation from the record which requires a more elaborate explanation, given further below. Third, the meeting of Conrad, Urbanski, and Viktor Salvator (an invented character) at *Evidenzbüro* headquarters. Fourth, the second meeting between Redl and Franzi later in the day. And, fifth and finally, the reconstructed conversations among all of the play's characters, a practice that has to be treated more cautiously in journalistic accounts than it does when it emerges in an artistic representation of historical events. On this last point it can be said that some of the conversations were invented strictly for comic and melodramatic effects in the play. This would apply to all scenes involving Viktor Salvator and the whole of Act III, where the detectives go at each other, as well as anything said by Franzi. Other conversations are (probably) paraphrases of information that Kisch obtained from the men he interviewed for his 1924 book.

Taking all of these departures from the factual record into account, one can now concentrate on the internal construction and effectiveness of the play itself. Most simply put, we have, in dramatic terms, two independent story lines, each of which embodies a conflict. The lines suddenly converge at the end of Act III, when Redl is discovered to be a sought-after spy and his fate is decreed by the powers on high. The play's opening conflict is straightforward, built around each member of a love-triangle feeling that he or she is the most aggrieved. Redl resents the rebellion of his protégé and former lover. Stefan resents Redl's interference in his plan to leave the army, marry, and begin a new life. And Franzi feels betrayed by Stefan, who might be bribed into maintaining his relationship with his 'Uncle Redl', though she takes the noble position of granting him his freedom of choice. Her attitude toward Redl mixes severe criticism of his personal values with sympathy for the man based on his choices in life, which have led him down a path of tawdriness and self-destruction. Other conventional theatrical stratagems in the opening act foreshadow Redl's fate later in the play. For example, Redl's remarks to Horinka that "he is his good fortune" anticipate the popular operetta song on the same topic, as sung by the Archduke to the amazement of his dinner companions in Act IV. Here "good fortune" implies Redl's complete misfortune. Franzi's remarks on Redl's golden collar also come to haunt him in the end, as he takes leave of the tokens of his military life.

The other conflict, somewhat obliquely presented, is within the leadership of the General Staff. Conrad and Urbanksi are aware of the existence of a high-ranking traitor within their ranks, and yet, as becomes apparent once the traitor's identity is discovered, they must do everything possible to suppress any and all information about the matter, lest they expose themselves to an onslaught of criticism that will undermine their power and influence. They can claim no public credit for concluding an investigation successfully, because that in itself would lead to discomfiting questions about why they had been unaware of Redl's true nature and activities for over a decade, while praising the man and expediting his rise through the ranks. As a socially-minded journalist the second conflict was weightier in Kisch's mind than anything having to do with Alfred Redl's character and personal life, including his relationship with his protégé.

Kisch called the play a "Tragicomedy of the General Staff", itself an interesting choice of words. Considering its comic elements first, there are two obvious yet different approaches taken by Kisch. They are equally overt, but differ in their social content. The banter between the two detectives is all on the surface and farcical, pitting Strebinger, an officious policeman who gets things wrong, against Steidl, who seems feckless, but is sly. They have different opinions of fulfilling one's duty as a policeman, as indicated by Steidl's remark that if they had been more alert they might have apprehended the suspect right off the bat at the post office, but might also have put themselves at risk of getting shot—as he says, "that's not part of the service regulations." Like a shrewd infantry sergeant disregarding the enthusiasm of an inexperienced lieutenant in search of glory, he is not game to impale himself on an enemy bayonet in a 'do or die' assault; rather, he prefers a less self-sacrificing approach to the problem at hand. Archduke Viktor Salvator's continuous spate of nonsense is equally farcical and readily apparent, consisting of always bringing the conversation back to the events of his own dissolute life as a career womanizer and alcoholic who believes in the reality of fiction's great detectives (Sherlock Holmes and Nick Carter). His sotto voce remarks addressed to the audience of the play are equally delusional and absurdly comical.

In contrast, the conversations between the two military men and Archduke Viktor Salvator are built around the social convention that even high-ranking officers have to defer to the continuous stream of nonsense issuing from a member of the ruling dynasty. They can gently brake or deflect his risible suggestions and enthusiasms, but they may never contradict him to his face. They should apologize even when they are obviously correct and sensible on a point of conversation while the Archduke is the opposite, but should never expect an apology from him. This is an implicit comedy of manners that might emerge in any society in which a rigid hierarchy of ranks determines what is allowable or not in public, and exactly who may say what to whom. Merit (the professional achievements of General Staff officers) must bow to status, which is all the Archduke possesses, though he imagines himself a paragon of achievement in the arts and sciences, a man who deems his every stray thought worthy of being recorded for posterity.

What about tragedy? While Redl's fate encompassed hubris followed by nemesis, he does not fit the old classical definition of a tragic hero in any other respect. Rather than a man caught in a conflict between the necessity of a deed and its incompatibility with the strictures of divine law, he is a mere malefactor who receives his just desserts. He has not sacrificed himself in order to achieve some goal on behalf of a broader community, often the tragic hero's role. Neither Stefan Hromodka's nor his fiancé's fate fills this strict definition either—they become 'collateral damage' in the legal follow-up to the scandal, but are in no sense heroic (though Franzi is thoroughly blameless). In point of fact the real cavalry lieutenant, Horinka, the only man punished in the Redl affair, was stripped of his rank and given three months of hard labor as punishment for having engaged in homosexual activity. But, as Markus discovered, he was back in the saddle as a cavalry sergeant as World War I progressed; he survived the war and later married and had several children.[15] During the late 1950s Asprey learned about Horinka's subsequent life when he interviewed the old man, now a butcher using a different name.[16]

Kisch's intention was clearly to attach the "tragic" label of his play to the General Staff, but in a manner implying that they were the authors of a tragedy, not its victims. Because he believed that the General Staff's fall into disrepute on account their role in the Redl scandal was another instance of just desserts, the clear intention of his play's sub-title was to hold the General Staff responsible for the thoroughly negative consequences of World War I. A year after the scandal, through a combination of fatalistic decision-making, self-dealing, and incompetence, Conrad and his abettors mismanaged the situation resulting from Franz Ferdinand's assassination by encouraging Austria's political leaders to seek war instead of a diplomatic solution (in some respects they were only reinforcing the political establishment's desire to have a final reckoning with Serbia, sooner rather later). In spite of their rhetoric on the point, both Conrad and his civilian counterparts knew that Austria-Hungary would not be able to isolate the war against Serbia and therefore a general European conflict among the Great Powers would ensue—about this they became fatalistic, almost suicidal. Having played their part in recommending war, the General Staff thoroughly botched its own mobilization plan and the opening campaigns in Serbia (where General Oskar Potiorek, a lax and ill-informed 'headquarters general' and court favorite, was at fault) and Galicia. They had done the same in the Redl case. Kisch firmly believed that they were an "elite within a caste" who had no regard for the welfare of the average citizen or the common soldiers under their command. The tragic consequences facilitated by the General Staff were the unnecessary deaths and damaged lives of millions of Austrians, Hungarians, and other Europeans. This is the brunt of Kisch's indictment, obvious in his 1924 book, less so in his play about Redl's downfall. Perhaps Dieter Schlenstedt, one of Kisch's biographers, was right about the play's effective comedy undercutting its more serious message.

The officers in *Die Hetzjagd* are modeled (somewhat realistically) on the actual participants in the Redl affair, while whatever Kisch learned about the police detectives is heavily embellished to establish their comical role. Viktor Salvator, however, is a confabulation who is meant to embody the combination of tawdry behavior and privileged immunity seen in the lives of members of Austria's hereditary nobility, and most especially its royal dynasty. In his book about the eccentric Wilhelm Habsburg, cosmopolitan and transvestite but effective as a military man and self-appointed temporary ruler of Ukraine at the end of the war, Timothy Snyder described several members of the royal family known for their conspicuous sexual eccentricities and distasteful public behavior.[17] Foremost among these was the old Emperor's brother Ludwig, a flamboyant homosexual and transvestite known as "Lutzi-Wutzi". Viktor Salvator is a composite of several such men. He is not meant to stand in for Franz Ferdinand, whose own character defects were of a different variety: raw racial and ethnic prejudice, a particular contempt for Hungarians, and abrasiveness in his dealings with other members of the royal court, a byproduct of the Emperor having forced a morganatic marriage on him. He was certain that only he could save the Empire from disintegration. A strong family man, he was neither womanizer nor heavy drinker. He practiced a rigid, doctrinaire Roman Catholicism. The only real aspect of the Successor's character assigned to Viktor Salvator relates to his religious beliefs—he was shocked by Conrad's willingness to encourage and abet suicide, stating that every scoundrel deserved to be allowed to confess and receive the last rites before being justifiably hanged. Conrad's obvious indifference to religion and his desire to marry a divorced woman also irritated the Successor, who had originally been a strong advocate of the General's appointment to the position of Chief of Staff. The equation "Salvator equals Franz Ferdinand" is a false one. An even more questionable portrait of the Successor's role in the Redl case was to come in a 1980s film that is discussed in Chapter 9.

As noted, Kisch omitted the longer-term considerations brought to the fore by the Redl scandal. They could hardly have been treated effectively in a cabaret play, but his thinking about them was clear in his 1924 book. This aspect of Redl's actions was part of the 'mental furniture' that German and Austrian playgoers would have brought into the theater with them, i.e., that the traitorous Colonel had contributed significantly to the Austro-Hungarian army's failed offensives in 1914-1915. Though the exact nature and extent of how Redl's treachery had damaged the war effort were debatable, it was certainly a popular belief in Germany and Austria that his betrayals made him 'the spy of the century'. While not using that phrase, Kisch opened his 1924 book in a way that put the espionage case in the broader purview of its assumed effect on the opening of the war:

> In the year before the outbreak of the World War the compulsory suicide of Colonel Alfred Redl, the chief of the General Staff of the Prague Corps, and the leaking soon after of his espionage activity caused an unprecedented stir, which was well founded politically in view of the tense European situation and criminally in view of the perpetrator's rank and sphere of influence. Rumors, protests, accusations suspicions, and conjectures followed in rapid succession down to the winter of 1914, when the deployment of the Austro-Hungarian army was judged a failure.[18]

It must be said the Kisch's biographical sketch of Redl is lacking in the kind of detail that would offer a sound explanation for his treachery, but this was not Kisch's objective. However, Redl's several biographers have remedied this lack of detail. Robert

Asprey's 1959 *The Panther's Feast* has been both praised and denigrated. The foremost American historian of the Habsburg army, Gunther Rothenberg, found its research and biographical portrait excellent, though he thought Asprey had overestimated the effects of Redl's treachery.[19] Some critics of Asprey's book were put off by its 'purple prose' whenever the author speculated about Redl's innermost character and the psychological basis of his homosexuality. In a comparison between Asprey and Georg Markus's 1985 book on the case (which dismissed Asprey's book as "novelistic") the historian Ian Armour came down on Asprey's side as having produced a more thorough and better-sourced work than Markus had done.[20] If the novelistic portions of Asprey's book are treated with caution, his narrative meets historiographical standards in its presentation of Redl's military and espionage careers and gives a solid account of the background conditions of service and typical career paths of professional officers in the late Habsburg army. A more rigorous and detailed examination of Austro-Hungarian army life can be found in Istvan Deak's *Beyond Nationalism: A Social and Political History of the Habsburg Officer Corps, 1848-1918*, which also attends briefly to the Redl case, explaining how the manners and mores of the officer corps provided the perfect camouflage for the Colonel.[21] The most recent biography of Redl is John Sadler and Sylvie Fisch's *Spy of the Century: Alfred Redl and the Betrayal of Austria-Hungary*, published in 2016. One of its merits is that it brings over into English the well-researched findings of Verena Moritz and Hannes Leidinger, whose *Oberst Redl: Der Spionagefall, der Skandal, die Fakten* (Colonel Redl: The Espionage Case, the Scandal, the Facts) came out in 2012. As to motives, Sadler and Fisch find no mysteries: greed and ambition motivated the traitor.

In contrast to biographers, who often aim to limn 'the inner man', historians approach the Redl affair with the goal of clarifying two very different issues: first, the accuracy of Kisch's account; and second, the actual consequences of Redl's espionage on Austro-Hungarian political-military affairs in 1913-1914 and on military operations at the war's outset in August–September, 1914. The present chapter is no place to give an expansive treatment of these interesting topics, so they will be summarized briefly in the hope that readers will go to some of the sources cited for more information.

The first parts of Kisch's 1924 account to be assailed had to do with the actual surveillance and apprehension of Redl and the story about the locksmith Wagner who missed a football match. In brief, there was no such locksmith and no such match, as discovered by Poláček, and restated by Patka,[22] Horowitz,[23] and Sadler and Fisch.[24] The existence of the code-term "Opernball 13" on the envelopes full of cash mailed to Nikon Nizetas was either a colorful Kisch invention or incorrect information received from someone he interviewed.[25] As Georg Markus discovered, Kisch's description of the surveillance differed greatly from a reminiscence of the lead detective in the case, published in the *Neues Wiener Tagblatt* in 1930. In fact there had been three detectives assigned to the surveillance at the post office, named Michael Macha, Ferdinand Watzek, and Vinzenz Volny.[26] That the post-office trap had not gone awry in the manner described by Kisch was confirmed by a 1953 newspaper reminiscence of the desk clerk, Betty Österreicher, who had passed the letters under surveillance to "Nikon Nizetas" (Redl).[27]

The detectives had not missed their man at the post office, but had trailed him from there in another taxicab, following an operational plan designed to see if the suspect might lead them to any confederates. They noted several stops where Redl got out and walked around, apparently to check if he was being followed. They lost him when their own cab stalled out temporarily, but easily managed to locate his cab, where they found the penknife sheath and learned that his destination had been the Hotel Klomser. They left the sheath with the porter, requesting him to give it to anyone who might claim it and to tell the suspect that it had been brought to the hotel by a cab-driver who realized his fare had misplaced it. They set up surveillance at two positions from which they could see the entrance to the hotel. When their suspect, wearing civilian clothes, passed them he shredded some papers and disposed of them on the street as he approached the Klomser. They picked up the pieces, detailed one man to take the scraps to military intelligence headquarters, and, when returning to the hotel, discovered that it was Redl who had claimed the pen-knife sheath. They telephoned in their results. In Macha's telling the military and police responses that followed, for the most part, adhered to the evening's events as described by Kisch in his 1924 report. In his 1933 book on his career in Austria's pre- and post-war military intelligence services, Max Ronge gave a slightly different version of the suicide commission's confrontation with Redl, noting that Redl had requested a pistol as soon as the commission arrived; Ronge also emphasized his painful private conversation with Redl.[28]

One more aspect of the Redl case that Kisch reported on became debatable when historians re-examined it in detail. That is, who were Redl's espionage managers (also called "case officers" or "agent handlers" in current intelligence terminology) and how did they go about maintaining contact with him? Asprey had written a great deal about Colonel Nikolai Batjuschin, working out of Warsaw, as Redl's blackmailer, recruiter, and main handler. He seems to have received this information from 'Tristan Busch", whose book on Austrian military intelligence matters contained a chapter on the Redl case and came out in German in 1946, with an English translation to follow in 1950.[29] On the other hand, in 1924, 1926, and 1941–1942 Kisch had written that on the day of his detection Redl stated that he had been blackmailed into espionage by the Russian military attaché in Vienna, Colonel Mitrofan Marchenko. Markus assigned agent-management roles to both men (as well as others who allegedly were in contact with Redl in Karlsbad). In his 2005 review of the case in a specialized military intelligence journal John Schindler, a military historian, dismissed Kisch's 1924 book in general and "Busch" as a source in particular. He cited diverse documentary evidence that led him to the following conclusions: Batjuschin had nothing to do with Redl; the links with so-called 'illegals' in Karlsbad were entirely unlikely; in the main Redl had been managed by a series of Russian military attachés stationed in Vienna; the Russians had not been aware of his homosexuality and had not blackmailed him (implying he had offered his services to them); when contacts with the attachés were too risky or inoperable, Redl had been handled through the mails (or by 'cut-outs'); Redl had definitely volunteered his espionage service to Italian intelligence; and, it appears, he was the best-paid spy of his era (though he still died in debt).[30]

Concerning the military attachés, Colonel Vladimir Roop held the position between 1900 and 1905 and had told colleagues in Kiev of a "highly-placed" Austrian army source ("R") who most likely was Redl. Roop was expelled by the Austrians under suspicion of espionage. His replacement, Marchenko, was the attaché from 1905 through 1910, when he was expelled for the same reason. Marchenko's successor was Colonel Mikhail Zankevich, who hurriedly left Vienna in April, 1913, presumably because of his soon-to-be-discovered role in the Lieutenant Cedomil Jandrić espionage affair (which had explosive implications on account of Jandrić's friendship with Conrad's son, Kurt). If Schindler is correct in his conclusions, then Redl could have been on the Russian payroll as early as 1900. Schindler cites a 1907 cable between Marchenko and Moscow as 'smoking gun' evidence that the Russians were unaware of Redl's sexual proclivities.[31] The key passage is translated from the Russian, describing Redl as, "A cynic. A lover of women who loves diversion." However, citing the same cable in his 1985 book about Redl, Markus has the passage translated into German as "*Ein Zyniker, der die Zerstreuung liebt.*"[32] This is plainly, "A cynic who loves diversion." The "lover of women" has gone missing. Readers proficient in Russian must decide for themselves which translation is more compelling. The point remains moot. In any event, whatever motivated Redl's entry into espionage against his own country—blackmail or simple greed based on his need for funds to maintain his increasingly lavish manner of living—he took to the task with zeal and professionalism and was extremely well-paid by both the Russians and the Italians.

Concerning the weightier question of how badly Redl's espionage had damaged the army's operations at the outset of World War I, historical opinion remains divided, though the current consensus of those who have looked at the Redl affair carefully has settled on three points of agreement. First, the general demoralization of both military and political leaders that occurred in response to the Redl scandal contributed to a period of diplomatic confusion and hesitancy during the crises sparked by the end of the First Balkan War and the quick outbreak of the Second Balkan War (Conrad viewed 1908–09 and the Balkan wars as Austria's "last best chance" to attack Serbia with a low risk of Russian involvement). There was a 'rebound effect' from this diplomatic hesitancy in late 1913–1914 that made policy toward Serbia from this moment on extremely bellicose and fatalistic, contributing to a lack of caution during the weeks following the Sarajevo assassination.[33] Second, detailed military information that Redl sold to the Russians *may* have assisted the Serbians enough in their planning and troop dispositions to have a serious negative effect on operations directed against Serbia in the late summer and fall of 1914. Third, even if Redl had sold the Russians the Austro-Hungarian mobilization plans (which applied to both the Serbian and Galician fronts), this information had no significant effect on how military campaigns against the Russians unfolded after the war broke out.

The agnosticism of historians about the impact of Redl's espionage on the Serbian campaign and their clear-cut rejection of the idea that Redl's treachery influenced the outcome of battles in Galicia are based on a current assessment that the Dual Monarchy was ill-prepared to engage in any serious war in 1914. Its army was underfunded, its first-line troops were undersized, it lacked sufficient modern artillery and ammunition stocks, the training of its reserve troops was thoroughly inadequate, it had no idea how to transition to a major-war economy, and its military and civilian leadership performed poorly, lurching from one disaster to the next without learning how to conduct warfare in the face of overwhelming modern firepower (i.e., how to adopt cautious but well-prepared 'offensive-defensive' positions in order to limit casualties and losses of equipment). Kisch himself (citing the parliamentarian Count Adalbert Sternberg's remarks) inclined toward the maximalist position that Redl's espionage was directly responsible for disasters on both fronts in 1914 through the winter of 1915.[34] Two of Redl's biographers, Asprey and Markus, agreed with this in the main. However, the consensus of modern historians tends in the opposite direction, for the reasons given summarily above. In particular they are dismissive of the older Austrian and German evaluation of Conrad as an unsung military genius who had bad luck or whose plans were inadequately carried out due to the flaws of other officers and civilian leaders. Conrad's mobilization plan was a 'false precision' exercise in wishful thinking. It underestimated Russian military strength and operational ability and overestimated the capabilities of his own troops and the railroad system's capacity to carry out the plan under the actual stress of war.

The overall impression is that, whatever the quality and importance of the secret military information Redl betrayed, the Austro-Hungarian army was its own worst enemy—its Chief of Staff botched the mobilization, its officers underperformed in combat, military commanders scapegoated each other at every bad turn, and the army was ill-suited for either major offensives or a long war of attrition. Typical of these deficits was that on both fronts (Serbia, Galicia) in August, 1914, men had to march long distances in great heat with a shortage of logistical support (food, water, horses, ammunition stocks) to approach the planned battle fronts. There was no adequate rail transportation for an approach in Serbia, and Conrad changed his mind about de-training locations in Galicia at the last minute, leading to absurd forced marches of men carrying 60-pound loads on their backs. By the time the first shots were fired the army was in a state of exhaustion, soon to be followed by demoralization caused by doomed infantry charges into withering firepower. Losses were so high during the first six months of the war that neither the army nor society in general recovered. Without the periodic infusion of German troops and operational commanders the Austro-Hungarian army would never have lasted until 1918. These negative assessments are made in great detail by historians who have looked at the Redl case within this broader context of Austria's poor pre-war preparation and its actual military performance, e.g., Rothenberg,[35] Herwig,[36] Wawro,[37] and Schindler[38]. Hannes Leidinger's 2014 evaluation of whether or not Redl's treachery contributed significantly to Austro-Hungarian losses early in the war summarizes the above arguments and supports the consensus conclusions: moot in Serbia, nil in Galicia.[39]

In this broader purview, Redl's treason was just one small eddy in a decades-long, downward spiraling current. But such considerations, made fifty to one hundred years after the fact, do not reflect the interwar-era feelings and judgments of Austrians and Germans about who was responsible for the loss of World War I and its dire consequences on their societies. Conservative military and civilian factions in both countries had a persistent view of Redl from 1914 onward: he was "the beast" and "the hangman of the Austrian army", a malefactor who authored cataclysm. Redl's historical importance was over-rated as a result of this convenient scapegoating and the unwillingness of Austria's leadership class to examine the underlying aggressive nationalistic ideals and expand-or-perish economic theories of the era. Actors on the public stage and contemporary historians, many of whom approved nationalist agendas, were even more reluctant to take an objective look at the bad judgment and poor performance of both civilian and military leaders who were still revered after 1918 as heroes[40] (thus the emergence of a postwar 'cult of Conrad', a man who failed miserably and repeatedly, but blamed others for these failures[41]).

Examined in this local Austrian and German light, Redl was of a historical significance that made him a suitable vehicle for artistic treatments of themes of trust, treachery, the precariousness of homosexuality in a society where it was illicit, and the moral ambiguities of the world of espionage. In his play about Redl's final day Kisch had only skimmed the surface of these turbid waters. However, in choosing to reduce his 1924 book to the limited goals of an entertaining cabaret play, his approach sufficed to offer audiences a 'thriller' dealing with moral decay, crime, incompetence in high places, and lethal punishment. The play's comedy also assaulted the privileged position and reputation of public authorities. Most people who entered the theater already knew the supposed drastic consequences of Redl's actions: a lost war, a lost Empire, a lost way of life. But attributing these results to the treacherous Colonel was absurd.

Die Hetzjagd exemplifies the process of turning historical narratives into artistic representations — in this case reportage transformed into melodrama whets historical appetite while taking steps into the realm of fiction. If we take into account typical journalistic mistakes, faulty 'educated guesses' (due to incorrect information received from sources and the insufficiency of available information), and a few inventions in his 1924 book about the Redl case, we can judge its trespasses against historical accuracy as minor. This also applies to the 1926 play, with its limited purview, its fanciful inventions, and its aim to entertain. However, as the Redl story moved to film, stage, and novels throughout the 20th century, fictional inventions and exaggerations became increasingly fantastic. The result was that popular films made between 1925 and 1955 and dramatically excellent and entertaining works of art based on the Redl affair (John Osborne's 1965 play, István Szabó's 1985 film, and Pavel Vilikovský's 1989 novella) thoroughly misrepresented the historical events that inspired them. These later transformations of the story are discussed in Chapter 9 below. After this explication of Kisch's Redl play and its historical background, it is time to turn to his most popular comedy for the stage, *The Ascension of Toni Gallows to Heaven*, taking the reader from considerations of high treason to those of an earthy Prague comedy set in the afterlife.

Chapter 5. The Ascension of Toni Gallows to Heaven

The manuscript used for the play

THE ASCENSION OF TONI GALLOWS TO HEAVEN
A PRAGUE LEGEND IN THREE SCENES

Verily, I say unto you that the
Courtesans and publicans will
Precede you into Heaven
The Gospel of Matthew

[Cast]

The President of the Highest Court

Heaven's court recorder

Hell's court recorder

A policeman from the police-van station called "The Other Side"

Two guards at Heaven's gate

Two guards at the entrance to Hell

The just–deceased Barbara Upejpavá

The just-deceased Mungo Natscheradetz

The just-deceased Antonie Havlová, known as "Tonka Šibenice"*

Mrs. Koutský

Blondie Mirko

The other guests

* Czech for "Toni Gallows"

The just-deceased Miss Upejpavá

Scene I
THE GATHERING PLACE OF SOULS

The sounds of a whip cracking and rumbling wagon wheels are heard. The wind whistles. A police van stops in front of a street-light; an old nag is harnessed to the wagon with white traces. Various graffiti are chalked on the van's side: "This is Green Anthony from Purgatory" and "We're piping out a tune, whistling away our worldly lives" — several letters of "whistling" have been effaced so that it's difficult to read the word at all. A policeman with little white wings on his back climbs down from the driver's seat. He removes the horse's blanket and an excrement bag that was fastened to its hindquarters, allowing it to do its business on the street.

MISS BARBARA UPEJPAVÁ (Her appearance: she's wearing a night-shirt and has a kerchief over her head, fastened at the chin; she has a wreath in one hand, in the other she's holding a lit candle. A squeaky voice; very humble.): Good evening, blessed ones! Here I am, constable, Sir, or guardian angel, Sir, so now we can depart right away and go straight to Heaven. (She wants to get into the van.)

POLICEMAN (from the police-van station nicknamed "The Other Side"): Not so fast — things don't work that way around here.

UPEJPAVÁ: Well, after all, my dear little constable, or dear little guardian angel, I'm going directly to heaven. When I was speaking with that worthiest of worthies, the Holy Ghost, he promised me that, just an hour ago, you know, when he gave me the last rites. "Miss Barbara Upejpavá," he said to me, "Miss Barbara Upejpavá," — that's me, don't you know, (she genuflects) I'm Barbara Upejpavá, proud owner of a laundry mangle – "Miss Barbara Upejpavá, you're going straight to Heaven ..." (she's trying to climb into the van).

112

First it's Purgatory for everybody

POLICEMAN: Nobody goes straight to Heaven. All souls have to go through Purgatory first.

UPEJPAVÁ: But ... but, when the most worthy Holy Ghost spoke he promised me — he was very clear — "Miss Barbara Upejpavá, you're going straight to Heaven."

POLICEMAN: All souls go through Purgatory first, after that they can be transferred from there to Heaven.

UPEJPAVÁ: Well, that'll still be today. So let's get going, why aren't we on the way yet?

POLICEMAN: It's only quarter to twelve. We have to wait until midnight, we're today's last transport. Whoever dies between now and twelve midnight has to go along with us.

UPEJPAVÁ: And then you can finally get a good sleep, my dear little constable, little guardian angel of mine. It must be a very difficult job for you Number Four folks

POLICEMAN: I'm not from Department Four. I'm from Department Five — we're the ones that cover the fifth dimension from the police-van station called "The Other Side". And with our otherworldly natures, we never get tired.

MUNGO NATSCHERADETZ (he enters): Well, good evening, I got here at last, my illustrious lords. Hey, did you have to wait a long time for me, huh? Ah well, a thousand apologies. Are you the conductor? So then, a non-stop ticket straight to heaven, first-class, please, and, if possible, a sleeping compartment. What's it cost?

The coffee-house regulars

POLICEMAN: There's no non-stop straight to Heaven.

NATSCHERADETZ: On my honor, that's fine for you to say, "There's no going straight to Heaven!" That's what you say! You don't seem to have any idea who you're talking to. Well, I'll let you know right now: Tomorrow morning my death-notice will be in the *Prague Daily Paper*,[1] and it'll show up in the *Tribune* too. "We are deeply saddened that a high-class character, a man of superior, excellent qualities has been taken to his home in Heaven ... and so on." OK, now what do you have to say for yourself, Mister Heavenly Chief Conductor? So then, let's get going, let's move it! (He wants to climb into the van).

POLICEMAN: Hold it right there, we still have to wait a bit.

UPEJPAVÁ: We must learn how to acquire heavenly patience.

NATSCHERADETZ: Hey, look, that's Barbara over there with us, huh?

UPEJPAVÁ: My dear Sir, I'm, not acquainted with you ...

NATSCHERADETZ: "I'm not acquainted with you," on my honor, that's a good one! Didn't you use to do some business with me, not all that long ago, when I was still running the Café Melantrich ...

UPEJPAVÁ (terrified): Shhh, don't talk so loud. It's been a very long time since I went to *that* place.

NATSCHERADETZ: Yeah, well, no wonder, you've become an old wretch since then.

Toni Gallows is dead too – – –

UPEJPAVÁ: No, no, that's not why. I haven't been there since the day my bridegroom stole my money and gambled it all away over at your place on Melantrich Alley—like they say, "What's sauce for the goose is sauce for the gander."

NATSCHERADETZ: (terrified): Shhh, don't talk so loud.

ANTONIE HAVLOVÁ, nicknamed TONKA ŠIBENICE (sobbing offstage): Don't you know, little Mother, what kind of dream I had – I saw you up in Heaven ...

NATSCHERADETZ: I know that voice from somewhere.

TONKA (coming on stage): ... There were so many beautiful little angels ... I'd love to go along and be up there with them ... Well then, Mr. Antouschek, open up the Hotel for me, and let's get moving!

POLICEMAN: First you've got to quiet down, you get me?

TONKA: Don't get too excited, Mr. District Chief Inspector, Sir! I'm so happy that I finally made my way out of Department C and most of all out of your whole damned crummy Valley of Tears, that you can't spoil things for me with your bad mood and your snotty official's attitude. Thank God that I'm going to Heaven now. I don't need a reservation or a season's ticket, just so long as things have been checked by the supervisors, week by week, do you want to see my little black book?

UPEJPAVÁ (talking to Natscheradetz): That one over there, that's Toni Gallows, the one who over at your place ...

− − − and she doesn't want to wait

NATSCHERADETZ: What, you want me to admit that I know Toni Gallows? On my honor, that's a good one! When I was still running the Café Melantrich, I wouldn't let her into the bar at all. I had the porter spritz her with coffee and drag her out of the place.

UPEJPAVÁ (giggling): And now she wants to get into Heaven!

NATSCHERADETZ: Wants to get into Heaven, on my honor, that's a good one!

TONKA: So then, what's the "Green Anthony" still waiting for? Let's get this old barrel organ on the move at last.

POLICEMAN: We have to wait until midnight, whether or not another little soul arrives.

TONKA: Get out of here and go hide in your cab with your "little soul" talk! We're not going to wait here for some old grandma or other from Upper Nowheresville or some happy Hottentot from Italy to turn into another stiff. What am I, some kind of half-wit that I should fade away here until midnight? You don't know me at all, my little darling! Let's get going or I'll start mixing it up right here. I'll trot on over to Milk Street, so you can sort yourselves out here.

NATSCHERADETZ: She wants to get into Heaven with that kind of behavior?

TONKA: Don't you go on the hunt, you old pimp, I know you from over at the old Melantrich Café in Brimstone Alley. Well, you're not in charge of anything here, and if you don't shut up, I'll give you such a nice little shot on your cabbage-head that you'll hear all the angels singing before we even get to heaven. (To the

She's been waiting for 52 years

policeman): Now, what's up, Grandpa, what's going on with our ride? Are we going or aren't we going, huh? I don't want to set up business here, you know? That's not my kind of thing, what's in it for me if I hang around until the whole gang's here? I'm like a happy kid after waiting around for fifty-two years for my trip to Heaven, and now I should stay put here? I've had enough of you worms, every week dealing with that doctor who worked for the cops, Pečirka. And now everything's falling apart again? Is that what you all want, for me to go to pieces too, let's put a stop to that right now, zzzzzip! Well then, dear Lord God of Heaven, You big cop, fix things up so we'll get moving along.

UPEJPAVÁ (she makes the sign of the cross): May Heaven protect us!

NATSCHERADETZ: What kind of rabble is pushing its way into Heaven these days!

TONKA: So, what is it? Do we or don't we? I'll heat things up here like a tiger on the loose, your rickety old crate will be in smithereens, it'll fall apart. (She pounds on the van with her fist.)

POLICEMAN: Don't you threaten us, lady, or else ...

TONKA: Stop making waves with you little wings, Mister. An-touschek! My way-station is Heaven, and they're already waiting for me there.

POLICEMAN: Or maybe it's hell.

NATSCHERADETZ (to the policeman, softly): Outstanding! You really gave it to her. Brilliant!

Threats

TONKA: For all I care you can go pick mushrooms in the Jews' cemetery out in the sticks, you old wooden horse from a merry-go-round. What matters is that we get moving soon! I don't want to freeze my feet off here, that's not my style. If this wagon doesn't take off right away, then I'll have at that gray nag's ass so hard that the stars will start flying apart and you'll have a ringing in your ears from whizzing horse-turds, that's what you should know, my little angel.

POLICEMAN: Well, we'll get you to Purgatory soon enough — that'll improve your behavior and put things in order.

TONKA: You're being far too short-tempered with me. Now listen up, I don't want to cause a riot like you praiseworthy officials have never seen up there. I just want you cloud-pushers to do your duty! What do you plan to do with your heavenly billy-club? You can let the angels suck on it. It doesn't cut any ice with me.

NATSCHERADETZ: This skirt's got a mouth on her like I haven't run into since I died.

UPEJPAVÁ: Lord save me, I'm shaking all over.

TONKA: Have you understood me, Mr. Conductor of this American circus act?

POLICEMAN: I'm a policeman, forever and always.

TONKA: So now you're offended, you old ghost! You've got that heavenly style written all over you, like you made the dawn itself!

The street-walker in the carriage

POLICEMAN: Whoever sows the wind reaps the whirlwind, Toni. God's mill grinds slowly, but it grinds finely.

TONKA: For a heavenly hulk you sound like something out of a daily newspaper, you'd better make sure you're not mixing up your proverbs.

POLICEMAN: I forbid such familiarities with me!

TONKA: Don't worry about that, with you I'd like to make my own good luck. I don't throw myself at every man I meet, you know.

POLICEMAN: Shut your mouth!

TONKA (as she rolls up her sleeves): It's just turned twelve, you can't mess with me ...

(The clock strikes twelve midnight)

POLICEMAN (in the manner of a stationmaster): Please take your seats, climb aboard, ladies and gentlemen, no pushing or shoving.

TONKA (she wants to get in, Natchseradetz tries to squeeze in before her): Don't be so rude. You'll have plenty of time.

NATSCHERADETZ: What, there's no first class here? Do I really have to travel in a carriage with a street-walker?

UPEJPAVÁ: For God's sake, me with such a person, whoever would have told me anything like this in my whole lifetime!

Departure!

TONKA: Stop blowing so much hot air, you beat-up old shooting-gallery tinplate dummy, you should be happy that you're getting to ride in a carriage with an imperially-and-royally licensed Prague prostitute.

UPEJPAVÁ (sharply): I've never ridden in a police van in all my life.

118

TONKA Really? Then take a taxi-cab, you old bag. Or just pitter-patter your way up there with your candle and your bridal wreath, if you think that Mister Natscheradetz can squish you into the van. (Addressing the policeman): Listen up, how about a china chamberpot?

NATSCHERADETZ (as he eyes the van skeptically): Don't you have a real carriage? If only this whole thing doesn't fall apart!

TONKA: What else can happen to you, you're already a dead Jew.

POLICEMAN: All aboard, take your seats, move a little faster.

(They all squeeze themselves into the van)

TONKA (She's the last one in—she waves her handkerchief and calls out): Adieu, you goddamned saloon they call earth, Toni's getting out and won't be strolling around here again. Now Toni Gallows is a nice little angel, Ye Gods! Now that I'm dead nobody can pester me anymore, men won't be able to ...

POLICEMAN (He slams the door closed behind her): Departure!

(With the sounds of cracking whips and whistling wind the van takes off)

The officials take a smoke break

Scene II
IN PURGATORY

There are two arched doorways in the background. One is sky-blue and gold and carries the glistening inscription "Heaven". The other is in black and red and is labeled "Hell". To the right and left of each of these entrances there are guard boxes in their corresponding colors. In front of the blue and gold gate a pair of guard-duty angels trots back and forth, palm branches resting on their shoulders; in front of the gate to hell two devils with tails are shivering while they attend to their guard duty — they carry switches. Above the gates the moon glows and the stars shine.

Clouds are hovering everywhere in space. A signboard states: "Smoking is hazardous to your health—it is strictly forbidden." In the foreground is the judge's desk—the President of the Highest Court of Judgment, a man with a long, white beard and big mane of white hair, has fallen asleep there. The court recorders for heaven and hell are busily at work, marking up their tally-books.

HEAVEN'S COURT RECORDER (he's wearing a monocle and twiddling his mustache—he jumps up): Hosanna! The old man's asleep. Damnit, I'm out of cigarettes again.

HELL'S COURT RECORDER: For God's sake, me too!

HELL'S GUARD (tossing a cigarette): Here, have one, Pal.

HELL'S RECORDER: Thanks, Buddy.

HEAVEN'S GUARD (with a reverent bow he extends his pack to Heaven's Recorder): If I may be permitted to do so, I humbly offer the Court's secretary a cigarette.

The Old and the New Regimes

HEAVEN'S RECORDER (as he takes the cigarette): Good, good.

(He trots over to Hell's Recorder, and makes a bow): Does my esteemed colleague have a light?

HELL'S RECORDER: Now, where did we stick those torches? (He opens the door at the gate to hell and lights his cigarette. An alarm sounds.)

HEAVEN'S RECORDER: That's the hell alarm! Shhh! Quiet! Silence here! You bunch of dirty so-and-sos, you wretches!

HELL'S RECORDER (shouting back through the gate): God in heaven, if it's peace and quiet you want, I'll send you a little shower of sulfur. Bunch of damned rascals! (He lights the heavenly recorder's cigarette with his own.)

HEAVEN'S RECORDER: Goddamned Stinkers! I'm already a nervous wreck with all this miserable service time here in Purgatory! It's always the same drawn-out proceedings, and if a man wants to study his Roman Law, then he's got to do it while listening to wailing from hell all day long. What a bunch of whining losers! Those guys should all be put up against the wall.

HELL'S RECORDER: Yours would be a really wonderful democracy. Everyone should be allowed to whimper in his or her own way.

HEAVEN'S RECORDER: Yeah, well, I have to say that I preferred the Old Regime.

HELL'S RECORDER (shouting): Yep, that's good for you and your kind!

Arrival of the transport van

THE PRESIDENT OF THE SUPREME COURT (Awakened by the noise, he sounds the desk-bell): Quiet! I don't recognize any Parties here. I only recognize souls.*

(They all put out their cigarettes and hurriedly resume their service positions. From their left they hear the clattering of a horse's hooves, the rollicking of the van, and the cracking of a whip.)

POLICEMAN: I respectfully report: this is the last of today's transports from earth. Three souls. (He places the protocols listing the deceased in front of the President.)

THE PRESIDENT: Bring the souls forward.

(Meanwhile the litigants, Tonka, Upejpavá, and Natscheradetz, are led in.)

TONKA (talking to Natscheradetz): ... and you had me twice, you old dog of a gourmet.

NATSCHERADETZ: What things we all let happen to ourselves! What's up with you crawling in here in first place? You definitely weren't the first.

* A parody of the famous statement of Kaiser Wilhelm at the outset of the war, "I don't recognize parties anymore, only fellow Germans."

TONKA: Shut up, stop talking to yourself! I've waited fifty-two years for this. (She pushes him out of the way)

UPEJPAVÁ: Oh dear, yes, you get the most with impudence.

TONKA: I'm not going to wait outside, I've already told you that, you bunch of shady gents.

THE PRESIDENT: (ringing his bell): Quiet here in heaven! You souls go and sit down on that bench over there.

Natscheradetz pleads innocent

NATSCHERADETZ: Respectfully allow me to introduce myself. My name is Mungo Natscheradetz, formerly of the Café Melantrich. I respectfully request permission for permanent residence in heaven.

THE PRESIDENT: Wait until you're called.

NATSCHERADETZ: Maybe you can move me up in the line. Right now I'm really in a hurry.

(in a confidential tone): Just let me know how much it'll cost me?

THE PRESIDENT: Just what do you think is going on? Up here we breathe the pure air of heaven.

NATSCHERADETZ: Well, I'm offering a "deal made in heaven" to you.

THE PRESIDENT: Sit yourself down, right now! (reading from the protocol): Barbara Upejpavá!

NATSCHERADETZ: That one's a nasty piece of work!

UPEJPAVÁ: Present!

THE PRESIDENT: Let's see the files. (The policeman brings him the dossier, the President leafs through it.) Do you have anything to say in your own defense?

UPEJPAVÁ: (shocked): In my own defense? I've always led a pious life!

THE PRESIDENT: You've been putting on a show. You're a hypocrite.

The hypocrite sent to Hell

UPEJPAVÁ: But the most worthy Holy Ghost himself told me that I would be going directly to ...

THE PRESIDENT: March yourself into hell, lady!

UPEJPAVÁ (suddenly she becomes argumentative): Into hell? That's a nasty trick! Dirty dogs! I'll show you miserable rabble a thing or two! I'm not letting that happen to me.

(The two devil-guards grab her, scolding and bristling, and trot her over to the door in Hell's gate—the instant it opens a fiery glow flashes.)

THE PRESIDENT (reading from the protocol): Mungo Natscheradetz!

NATSCHERADETZ: How may I be of service to you?

THE PRESIDENT: (to the policeman) The dossier!

TONKA: And I should rot here! How much longer is this farce going to go on?

HEAVEN'S RECORDER: Be quiet and wait your turn.

TONKA: I've waited long enough already. For fifty-two years I've been waiting for my trip to heaven. If I don't get into heaven right now, you'd better watch out, I'll start a brawl right here.

HEAVEN'S RECORDER: Shut your mouth!

Humiliation of the specters from Hell

TONKA: What, shut up for you, you fetch-anything lap-dog?

(Hell's recorder and both guards of hell's gate try to terrify Tonka with gyrations and flicking their tongues): Boo, Boo, Boo!

TONKA (breaking out into laughter): My God in heaven, that's real slop. You all want to scare me to death? You can boo-boo-boo all you like at me, but you're about as scary as a dog's lice. That's what we do to scare babies eating their mush. Tuck in your tails!

(Ashamed of themselves, the three infernal functionaries tuck in their tails and retreat to the guardhouse.)

TONKA (to the policeman): They're trying to get at me with a masquerade like that, what a joke – give me a cigarette.

POLICEMAN (threatens her with his rubber night-stick): Silence!

TONKA: Stick that up your own grape-sucker! I've long outgrown my suckling days. I'd rather have you stick a cigarette in my mouth!

HEAVEN'S RECORDER (jumping up from his seat): Have you lost your mind? In all of the realms of The Other Side smoking is strictly forbidden, no exceptions. It's only permitted for the holy saints in heaven

THE PRESIDENT (softly to Tonka): Quiet down once and for all.

Natscheradetz puts up his defense

TONKA (intimidated): Oh boy! Now I've screwed everything up! It's all over between heaven and me!

THE PRESIDENT (leafing through the pages of Natscheradtez's files): Mungo Natscheradetz, what can you introduce in your own defense?

NATSCHERADETZ: What rigmarole! In my own defense? "Defense", that's really a good one! If I'd known that I needed a defense up here, I would have brought along my Doctor Advocate Bendiener, so that I'd be legally hale and hearty. I ask you, please, Heavenly President, Sir, read through my death notices, they appeared this morning in the *Prague Daily Paper* and the *Tribune*. (he reads them himself in a touching voice): "Deeply saddened, we report the passing away of the very honorable Mungo Natscheradetz" – "very honorable" – That's what I am, if you please—"He was the head chef at the greatly acclaimed Café Melantrich, at number 8 Melantrichová Street in Prague's First District ... "

TONKA: That crappy old beer joint.

NATSCHERADETZ (to Tonka): As I've told you, when you tried to get into the place (he continues reading the death notice): "This evening at eight o'clock a ladies choir will give a concert at number 8 Melantrichová ..."

TONKA: Concert! They'll be plucking on some busted-up old mandolin, just like they're picking lice!

NATSCHERADETZ (to Tonka): What do you know about beautiful chamber music! (reading on): "A man of the highest character"—Please, it's all right there!—

He has to go to hell too

THE PRESIDENT (he takes the newspaper and hands it over to hell's staff): Throw that down into hell too!

HELL'S RECORDER (he takes the paper and tosses it through hell's gate—a red glow comes out): It's just a scrap of trash-paper with special pleading.

NATSCHERADETZ: My very pricey death notice! It cost me five-hundred crowns!

THE PRESIDENT: Well, you get to go to hell for free.

(The guards from hell grab the whining Mungo Natscheradetz and, trotting along, chase him over into hell, from which a red light glows.)

NATSCHERADETZ (now in hell): Ah, Mandelik and Sinaiberger and Roubitschek, you're all here already, huh?

THE PRESIDENT: Antonie Havlová!

TONKA: No, well, at last! What's this all about?

THE PRESIDENT (to the policeman): The files!

(The court recorders for heaven and hell, the two guards from each post, and the policeman lug the files along and place them on the table)

THE PRESIDENT (reading the headings from the big pile of records): "Unlicensed prostitution", "Criminal assault with serious bodily harm", "Public acts of violence", "Disturbing the peace", "Injuries to public morals", "Defilement of public places."

Her nickname – – –

TONKA: No thanks, I don't think so. Don't you have such scrawling on the walls up here too?

THE PRESIDENT (reading the files): Antonie Havlová, you were taken into police custody thirty-two times, and you were convicted in court three, no, four times.

TONKA: And always innocent, Sir, imperial and republican-provincial high judge, always innocent, that's true as long as I live!

HELL'S AND HEAVEN'S RECORDERS (in a state of fright): Live? Who's alive here?

TONKA: Damn it, in all the excitement I forgot that I'm really dead.

THE PRESIDENT: Antonie Havlová ...

TONKA: Yeah, well, that's my name ...

THE PRESIDENT: Perhaps you have another name, right? A nickname?

TONKA: Well, all of us down there in the gang had nicknames.

THE PRESIDENT: So what did they call you?

TONKA: (hesitating): Me ... me – they called me "Toni Gallows".

– – – and how she got it

THE PRESIDENT (as he pushes the file away): And how did this name come about?

TONKA (bursting into speech): That's none of your business! That's my most personal and private concern. That's not in any file, and nobody should get himself mixed up in the matter. You all think it would be better if people stuck their noses in my private affairs — is that the idea? Don't get short with me about it! I'm not giving you any information about it, and if that doesn't fly with you, then you might as well rush me through this dismal waystation right away and have me tossed into Hell and cooked up until turpentine starts running out of my eyes. But I'm not going to let you pester me about it, you can wait forever and you won't get it! People can't harass me, not even police Commissioner Drašner got anywhere with that, not once. I'm not talking about my private affairs, even if you tear me to shreds. So, enough of that!

THE PRESIDENT (looking at her firmly): But, during your life down on earth you told the story many times.

TONKA (more quietly): Well that's something altogether different. When I was in the bar they call "Halánek", if somebody bought me five little glasses of Allasch,* then I'd tell him the story as well as I could. I was paying a tax for the drinks. But I don't let just any old body force it out of me.

THE PRESIDENT (smiling): We certainly don't have any Allasch up here, but you can have a glass of heavenly ether. (He signals, whereupon the clouds part and a bottle floats down.)

TONKA: Take a look at that, won't you! Even the heavenly hosts pour one down the old gullet once in while.

THE PRESIDENT: I don't do that.

HEAVEN'S RECORDER (indignantly): I definitely don't!

* Kummel brandy

Liquor in Purgatory

HELL'S RECORDER: Uh-huh, now I get stuck with it, just as usual. Now all of *us* are supposed to be the big drinkers!

THE PRESIDENT: Give her a glass.

TONKA: What's up with such a tiny little snifter glass? I might swallow the whole thing. It's always better to drink straight from the source. (She drinks out of the bottle)

THE PRESIDENT AND THE TWO RECORDERS (one right after the other): That's enough, enough, enough!

TONKA (she puts down the bottle, then dangles it): Thanks a lot. This stuff really tastes good! I've never had it before. Over at Halánek's they don't have any ether. Can you get this stuff in Hell too?

THE PRESIDENT: No, no you can't. But tell us the story now.

TONKA: All right, high-holy heavenly court. That's all water over the dam by now, it's not even real anymore. It happened in the year 1892, on August the twelfth it was.

THE PRESIDENT: That was thirty years ago.

Memories of a night

TONKA (astonished): Oh my dear soul, thirty years ago to that day. No, can it really be that? (she turns suspicious). Haven't I hashed this out for myself enough back on earth? Do you want me to accuse myself with this story up here? Do you want me to twist up a noose for myself out of this business? What do you really want from me?

THE PRESIDENT: Just tell the story calmly.

TONKA: Alright, so at the time I was employed at Koutský's Salon, a very nice club and bar.

THE PRESIDENT: Yes, the place on Plattner Street, on the corner of Saazer Alley.

TONKA: Look at that, you know the place? Perhaps you were up to something there?

(Everybody laughs)

THE PRESIDENT (looking around severely): Settle down!

TONKA: Swear on your honor and your conscience, Mr. President, Sir, what kind of business was that place, yeah, what was it?

(Everybody laughs)

THE PRESIDENT (coughing lightly, evasively): Oh well, yes − − hmmm − − it was a real ...

TONKA: Well, look here, it really was a very fine, noble establishment. The best people did business with us. You can confirm that for me!

(Everybody laughs)

A success worth pondering

THE PRESIDENT: Silence! (to Tonka): Go on, keep telling the story.

TONKA: So there I was at Koutský's on Plattner Street. I was the most beautiful of all the women there.

(Heaven's Recorder coughs)

TONKA: Stop that coughing over there, before you choke to death. When I say I was the most beautiful of all the women there, you can believe it. Now I'm just an old trollop. What was there about me that I was so praised for my looks, huh? Well, in those days I was "blue Tonka". I had very beautiful blue eyes and I was always flouncing around in a blue satin Empire gown, with the most fashionable, up-to-date stockings and patent leather shoes. When I came down into the Salon there were already five or six fine gentlemen guests waiting for me, and even at four in the afternoon, before the evening's festivities were on, they'd hang around in front of my room like they were lined up for a Polanaise, a whole line snaking around out there, that's for sure. What a stylish creature I was. All the girls − you know, my colleagues − envied me.

THE PRESIDENT: Uh-huh, and what about the twelfth of August in 1892?

TONKA: Yeah, so on August twelfth all of us girls were sitting in the kitchen, eating our evening meal, when Detective-Inspector Lederer[2] comes in with one of the men from the criminal court, you know, a prison warden, and old Lederer and Mrs. Koutský are whispering to each other. We could hear the old lady was getting excited, and Lederer says that he's fed up with huffing and

The condemned man

puffing from one brothel to the next, and if Koutský makes things difficult for him, well then soon enough the police are going to make things difficult for her. Naturally the old lady doesn't want to start up anything with the cops, so she comes up on us from behind with Lederer, and he asks if any one of us girls wouldn't like to go along to the prison, to see Ferdinand Prokupek. Mrs. Koutský says that she'll throw in ten extra crowns. Of course nobody reports in for duty.

THE PRESIDENT: Someone did volunteer.

TONKA: No, high-holy judge, nobody volunteered. Everybody in Prague knew that Prokupek was going to hang the next morning, because he had strangled three women. One over at Brandeis, one near Krtsch and the last one he wrapped up over in the little woods near Hodkovitschka. He strangled all three and then he dismembered their bodies. A horrible, disgusting man! And he looked even worse in the pictures of him, the ones they showed in the *Prague Illustrated Courier*, he was an old tramp with a chewed-up face, it gave you chills just to see his photograph — yuck, a real devil! (She picks up the bottle) With your permission. (She takes a drink) Detective-Inspector Lederer needed a woman to go along with him to Prokupek over at Charles Square because the mug requested a woman, and when a man is going to be put to death, you're supposed to grant him his last wish.

HEAVEN'S RECORDER (deferentially): Mr. President, Sir, you know, it's the old scortum scorto.*

THE PRESIDENT: It's right out of Roman Law.

* Latin saying, roughly meaning "whores for those who go whoring".

Nobody wants to go — — —

TONKA: That stuff you're blabbing about is a real beauty of a pig's mess. And it didn't cut any ice with us. Besides, nobody volunteered.

THE PRESIDENT: Someone did volunteer.

TONKA: No, high holy judge, I know that better than you, nobody volunteered. Not even Ludmilla wanted to go, "not even for a thousand crowns," she said. And Ludmilla was really the crummiest of all of us.

THE PRESIDENT: Go on, go on.

TONKA: Because none of the girls wanted to go over to Prokupek, Mrs. Koutský told Olga Petřiková that she should get dressed and go along with the warden to the prison. Now at the time Olga Petřiková—you should know this—was only working as a household servant at the place, nine months earlier she had been one of the girls, but then she fell sick, and when she got back to us from Janovský hospital, she looked so old and ugly that she couldn't possibly work as a Salon girl any more. She had hollow cheeks flecked with spots, her eyes were red, her hair was falling out, and she rasped, it was just dreadful! (She takes a drink) Koutský didn't want to take her back, but that Olga, she nagged her so much that we let her sleep on the sofa in the Doctor's chamber and fed her too. In return for that she had to keep the place tidy and we didn't call her Olga anymore, but Mrs. Petřiková. Because none of us girls wanted to go to Prokupek, Olga should have been the one to go. She clapped her hands against her head and was screaming and screaming till she lost her voice. She'd rather throw herself into the Moldau, she said, and she was shaking like a piece of jelly ...

That's when it suddenly came to me to speak up, so I said, "I'll go to Prokupek ..."

– – – so Tonka goes

THE PRESIDENT (showing interest): Aha, and so?

TONKA: Well, so then I went marching off with the prison warden until we got to the Karlsturm overpass. It was the first time I'd been there. In the reception office there's a couple of jailers, and the two dopes bleat out, "Miss, we wish you a pleasant entertainment," and then they grope me, like maybe I'm bringing along a knife or a rope for Prokupek—they were worried that I might spoil their little hanging party. And then a young jailer says to me, with a real sad face, "Such a beautiful young woman, aren't you ashamed of yourself." He thinks I'm doing this for a couple of crowns—I didn't explain it to him, I just thought to myself, I don't give a damn what he thinks. Well, then they led me to Prokupek's cell. I already knew him from his photo in the *Courier*, I think I already told you about that. He's like the picture in the paper, but even worse. He's got the greasy jailhouse cracks and a stubble-beard and warts all over his face. (She takes a long slug from the bottle.) As soon as I saw him I thought to myself, if only I was already out of this place! But I didn't make any remarks about that —if I'm already here, well then he should go ahead and enjoy himself with me. I know what we're guilty of in our profession. So right I away I said to him, "I saw your photo in the *Courier*, and then it occurred to me that just on account of that I should come to you." Then he said something very low and vulgar to me, that I should ...

THE PRESIDENT (interrupting her in a guarded manner): ... that you should climb up onto his "little mountain" ...

TONKA: Oh no, something much nastier, I hope you already understand, high judge, that there's no need to go on about that, that would be very embarrassing for me. After half an hour he

Her colleagues jeer at her −

told me, "You can go now." I was very happy, I was so afraid that he might strangle me like he did the three young women, but when I offered him a handshake, he suddenly apologized to me. And then I thought to myself, tomorrow morning hangman Wohschläger will grab him ...

HEAVEN'S RECORDER (to the President): Hoc est nomen carnificis pragensis.*

TONKA: Oh no, not for that reason, you're making a big mistake there. When it comes to it I've had lots of other customers. They were more stylish and a thousand-times better situated in life. But he made a real apology to me, so I said to him, "I'd like to hang around a little bit longer." Well then, he started to growl again like he did before, you already know ...

THE PRESIDENT: Yes, yes, you needn't repeat yourself.

TONKA: No, I'm not going to repeat myself, I only mention that he said something really disgusting to me again. And yet it made him very happy that I'd made that remark to him. Well, around two o'clock in the morning I scurried back home and soon as I got to my room I wanted to lie down and go to sleep. Then I noticed that my colleagues—those filthy swine—had made a cardboard gallows and stuck it on my night-stand. That's no joke if you do that, don't you agree, high judge? I tore it up and went to sleep. When I went down to eat breakfast towards noon, all the girls had read about the hanging in the newspaper, and they were razzing me: "She's gotten very stuck-up since her private parts were ennobled!" And: "You should have stayed with him until the last minute when he was being strung up, then ..." ; "Hey you, that was a real shy one, that Prokupek, he let himself be hanged"; "I heard that you're going to settle down over in Ropemakers' Alley as a mark of your new piety."; "Don't make a big deal out of it

---

* Literally, "the name of the renderer of flesh in Prague", a Latin tag for a well-known hangman from Prague named Wohschläger.[3]

– and denounce her

that not everybody can go for a ride up in the air."; "Don't give birth to any little Prokupek in the house here, he might grow up and strangle us all ...", and the angrier I got the more those old cows razzed me. I ran back up to my room in a rage. When I came back down in the evening in my blue Empire gown that suited me so well ... You remember the rest, right?

THE PRESIDENT: Yes, yes.

TONKA: ... then the mudslingers started up to razz me all over again. "Toni Gallows!" and so on. And just think about this, the vileness of it – they told the customers the story too. That's what I call unfair competition! My old suitors wouldn't even look at me. (Then weeping) Around one in the morning the blondie, Mirko, showed up, he'd been my real lover for the last nine months, I was so fond of that poor little rascal, never again did I like anyone as much as him, no doubt you remember him, Sir High Judge, he always sat down at the middle table, with his yellow handkerchief and yellow silk tie, a real distinguished gent! – – So, I wanted to sit next to him, when he cried out so loud you could hear it through the whole club, "Before the executioner shows up at my door, I'll have you make a call!" (She starts sobbing). And then he went to a room upstairs with the Polish girl, Wanda. He should never have done that to me, not that, no, not that!

THE PRESIDENT: Calm down, Tonka, and go on with the story.

TONKA: On the next day I left Plattner Street. Over in Klarov they took me in at the "Blue Noodle"

THE PRESIDENT: Blue Noodle?

The devil knows all about it

TONKA: You wouldn't know anything about that place, it's a little whore-house over across the street from the Institute for the Blind.

HELL'S RECORDER: But I know all about it.

TONKA: Yeah, you *would* know all about it. Dear God, you can't compare it at all to Koutský's place. There I didn't have a blue Empire gown, I didn't have fashionable stockings, and I didn't have patent leather shoes. And what I missed most of all—do you know what I missed most of all.

THE PRESIDENT: No, what was it?

TONKA: The gramophone. You remember the big gramophone over at Koutský's, don't you?

THE PRESIDENT: Yes, yes.

TONKA: I loved to dance so much whenever it played ...

You are my Racajda,

Little Racajda, Racajda ...

(They all join in singing, making the same motions, while the clouds begin to sway too)

You are my Racajda,

Raca ...

THE PRESIDENT (recovering himself): Shhh! Quiet! (they all quiet down, while the President gives a withering look to the guards and those on the benches) Scandalous! (then, to Tonka): Go on!

Gramophone and flight

TONKA (she starts singing again): Little Racajda, Racajda ...

THE PRESIDENT: Silence! Have you lost your mind?

TONKA: But you told me to go on.

THE PRESIDENT: You're supposed to be getting on with your story.

TONKA: Oh that, sure. Yes, like I said, I really missed that gramophone. And no, Koutský's and the Blue Noodle, that was like day and night, High Judge, Sir. You could make up a catchy song out of the difference between those two places. But I was only there for three nights — on the third night a customer came in, he'd known me over at Koutský's, and that cabbage-head spilled out the whole story right away. The girls there got very snotty about me, because I was the new one and had the best-looking figure, so right away it's "Toni Gallows!" That was something for them to feast on, "Toni Gallows". It's really hard to work in one of the clubs under conditions like that, I think you can see that. So now I'm away from the Blue Noodle and off to the streets. Yeah, well, what's left for me except to do what we call "walking the line"? So for thirty years I went on like that. Even being exhausted is no excuse to skip walking the line. And, thank the good Lord, every night I found at least one client.

HEAVEN'S RECORDER (with irony): Nulla dies sine linea.*

TONKA: What's that stuff supposed to mean?

* Latin saying about Apelles, the Greek painter: "Not a single day without painting a line" or, in Toni's case, "Not a day without walking the line in search of clients".

The sorrows of the street

THE PRESIDENT: It means, not a day without walking the line looking for clients.

TONKA: But really now! First I went over to the Walstatt area, then I was in Zeltner Alley up to the gunpowder tower, ten years there. Well, then I was on the corner of Moat Street and Wenceslaus Square. A couple of weeks before that my pimp even promised to get me a fur wrap (she pantomimes), so that I could also work Ferdinand Street and the nice coffee-houses. (Now she's agitated). But I didn't get to do that. Isn't it marvelous — the streets are the most wretched place there is. What stuff you have to put with from the cops and the flophouse landladies! Every day somebody is messing around with you over something or other and every day they're tightening the screws on your purse. And you have to get through what happens to you every day all on your own and you worry every day about where you're going to sleep that night. And if you want to go out and buy something — a hat, a blouse, some saucy underwear—you can't go running around in flannels—then the salesmen swindle you. Everybody thinks they should exploit girls like us. And just where does that come from? Is it because of our profession's bad reputation?

THE PRESIDENT: Well, where do you think it comes from?

TONKA: I can tell you that, exactly! It comes from the young ladies on the Promenade, from those little sluts. They're such snot-nosed little brats who haven't learned anything and can't learn anything, they think that if they go for a stroll, then they're already real whores. They're just crap! And just look at this—they don't keep themselves clean, they don't go the public health services, and then they spread around all kinds of diseases. But these fish-brains get the most customers. And my kind, we have to walk the line for hours and hours before we get a client. In the

Conflict with Stuttering Betty

wet, in the cold, it's terrible to have to always walk the line. That's not the way it is in a Salon, where all of your worries are taken care of and where you're being served right and left. Oh, a nice brothel is the best thing going! (She sighs) Well, that's all in the past. At least nobody on the street knew about me, and all that stuff about "Toni Gallows" came to an end.

THE PRESIDENT (he rummages around in the files): Came to an end forever?

TONKA: No, not forever. People are such a bad lot! (She takes a drink) Once we were sitting around at the place called "The Old Gentleman", where early in the morning you can get the best tripe soup—it was so thick a spoon would stand straight up in it. I was with an old drunk who schlepped around with me the whole night, and I still wanted to hook him. A couple of floozies were there who hadn't gotten any clients yet, and at the table next to them was Stuttering Betty, who knew me from the Blue Noodle. The old carcass knew that I'd been wandering around all night with my mark, yet I was still making lovey-dovey eyes at him and chatting him up. Well, I wasn't going to let myself get pushed out of a job. I called out to her from the toilet and said, "You're not up to doing anything anymore." Then she said, "Go out to the sticks yourself, I'm not interested in making it with potato farmers." As soon as we sat down back in the bar-room, the whole show started up again. Now the old mug really wanted to pick her up, so I made things very clear to her—"If this farce doesn't stop soon, you little sewer-ditch, I'm going to slam this chair into your snout so hard that your teeth will march right out in two rows, you filthy old sow!" Once I said that, she thought to herself how nasty she could get. "Go along to your clients in the jail, get along to the murderers!" So now when everybody was asking what she meant

She really doesn't know!

by that, what could she be talking about, the dirty old pile of cow-shit starts braying, "That's the one they call Toni Gallows, whenever they're going to hang somebody the cops take her to the man, so he can have one more thrill." Everybody laughed, but I was in such a black-eyed fury that I jumped up (here she drums on the desk so hard that the files fall to the ground) and slugged her so hard four or five times on her coconut that marmalade was running out of her nose. Then I tackled her by her legs and smashed her around so much that they had to call for the first-aid workers. (Pointing at the files on the ground): You can find that right away in the files. Ever since then Stuttering Betty, little shark that she is, makes a wide circle whenever she sees me. And the word got around about it. Well, in the end it's all the same to me, and if somebody treats me to five snifters of Allasch at Halánek's — that's my tax, you know all about that —then he can get me to tell the whole story, how I wound up in Prokupek's cell and all the other details. (In a confidential tone): And if he ...

THE PRESIDENT: Antonie Havlová, will you just answer one more question for me?

TONKA: Sure, why not. I'll answer ten questions. You're such a friendly, likable old paprika! Just ask away quietly about anything that interests you.

THE PRESIDENT: Antonie Havlová, tell me, at that moment why did you go to see the murderer Ferdinand Prokupek?

TONKA (pondering): I have no idea why I did it.

THE PRESIDENT (he gets up and rings a bell)

(As it darkens only a glowing key lights the scene. Organs and chimes play)

To each his or her own Heaven

Scene III
In Paradise

(The sky brightens, and the guard-posts, entrances, and devils have disappeared. In the background you can see several round tables with the typical paraphernalia of a brothel; there are prostitutes and clients. Clouds are floating above.)

TONKA (she looks youthful again, dressed in her blue Empire gown, with big feathered wings on her; she claps her hands): Oh, how lovely! I'm back at Mrs. Koutský's again.

THE CUSTOMERS: Aha, it's blue Tonka!

MRS. KOUTSKÝ (wearing a low-necked dress, well made-up): You want a cigarette?

TONKA (lighting one up): Oh, it's really beautiful here!

BLONDIE MIRKO (He's at the middle table, wearing his loud yellow gloves and tie): Ah, my little golden girl, are you really here?

TONKA: Blondie Mirko! I'm so happy!

HEAVEN'S RECORDER (speaking to the President): Once again, President, Sir, you've done honor to your basic principles: to each

and every man and woman his or her own heaven. You've fulfilled this woman's desires flawlessly.

Simply infallible!

THE PRESIDENT (enjoying the moment): You think so?

HEAVEN'S RECORDER: Oh yes, obviously so! Mr. President, Sir,
you're simply infallible!

THE PRESIDENT (to Tonka): Are you really happy?

TONKA: Very happy!

THE PRESIDENT: Tonka, do you have one more wish?

TONKA: Yes. More than anything I'd like to hear the gramophone
playing again.

THE PRESIDENT (He makes a sign, and the gramophone begins
to play the song "Racajda".)

TONKA (A cigarette in her mouth, she listens rapturously, then
she grabs blondie Mirko and dances the Schlapak with him)

Chapter 6. Toni Gallows, a Real Prague Legend: Feuilleton into Comic Fantasy

Kisch was extremely fond of the Tonka Šibenice (Galgentoni) story, perhaps feeling that it captured the essence of that time in his life when he explored the dives of Prague (he called them *Spelunken*, literally "caves"). These were the years between his adolescence and his departure from his native city for Berlin in mid-June, 1913, when he terminated his position at *Bohemia* after two weeks of reporting on the Redl espionage scandal. Like his reconsiderations of the Redl affair, he came back to the Toni Gallows story, which first appeared in 1921, over and over. He reworked it in several formats: twice as a feuilleton, three times as different versions of the play's German text (one published in a weekly journal and two in different collections of reportage and essays), and, finally, as a reminiscence in his memoirs, where it was embedded in a description of Prague's vice district. He was also involved in producing performance texts of the play in Czech, co-written with Emil Artur Longen, who was instrumental in persuading Kisch to turn the story into a work for the stage.

A depiction of prostitution as part of his native city's underworld was central to Kisch's 1914 novel, *Der Mädchenhirt* (The Pimp). The novel portrayed a layer of society that was populated by both Czechs and Germans, describing the social phenomenon of prostitution and limning its practitioners (whores and pimps), patrons, regulation by the police, and punishment by the courts. Though it has a dramatic story intertwining the fates of several individuals, it is also an artfully disguised 'sociological survey' and critique. In an analysis of the 1919 German film version of Kisch's novel Russell Campbell wrote that Kisch was as interested in the psychology and morals of its protagonist (Jara Chaprot), a young man who somewhat reluctantly turns to pimping, as he was in contrasting the moral character and behavior of two of Chaprot's "girls".[1] Campbell also noted that:

> Where *Der Mädchenhirt* differs ideologically from the norm is in assigning responsibility for corruption not to the pimp but to the representative of respectable patriarchal authority, his [biological] father [a police inspector named Duschnitz].[2]

He goes on to associate *Der Mädchenhirt* with other films that "portray the evil of prostitution as endemic to capitalist society."[3] Kisch would have probably agreed with this characterization.

Stories set in Prague's demi-monde and criminal underworld formed a substantial part of Kisch's first two collections of articles gathered from his newspaper reporting and published in book form, *Aus Prager Gassen und Nächten* and *Prager Kinder*. His 1920 book, *Die Abenteuer in Prag* went over some of this ground as well, though it included mostly new material, much of it historical and autobiographical. A colorful and amusing story about prostitutes, *Magdalenheim*, appeared in his 1913 collection, *Prager Kinder*,[4] having been first published as a feuilleton in *Bohemia*. Kisch rewrote many of these 1906-1913 Prague vignettes and news-reports as reminiscences in his memoirs, in which he included an edited and expanded version of *Magdalenheim*, available in an English translation by Harold Segel.[5] This version, reprised below, has the interesting framing device of Kisch's ironic commentary on the story's odd 'second life', when a plagiarized version won a Nazi literary award. Because of the kinship of its narrative material to that of *Galgentoni*, a brief digression on *Magdalenheim* is in order.

It begins with Kisch's efforts to win approval for a visit to Prague's Magdalen Home, a Roman Catholic facility dedicated to reforming prostitutes through imposing regular hours and meals, prayer, discipline, and training in the craft of sewing. He sends a letter of inquiry to the Mother Superior, who is immediately nervous about allowing a reporter to inspect and write about the institution. He reassures her of his benign intentions, emphasizing that publicity about the Home's good works should be welcomed, not feared. The board of directors, all well-off, middle-aged matrons, agrees to his proposal. At the outset of his visit he is introduced to a priest who gives him a long lecture on vice, the sins of the flesh, the necessity of a daily "prayer and work" routine, and the innate sinfulness of the young women who have chosen this "voluptuous, sensual" path in life rather than working as domestic servants or factory-hands. After this sermon the board's Madame President gives Kisch a tour of the premises. When she takes him to the sewing workroom he recognizes several prostitutes from his journalistic raids on the underworld. They are all delighted to see him, hailing him by his first name, bantering with him about their old haunts and clients, and imploring him for cigarettes. This shocks and dismays his official escort, who abruptly ends his visit.

This later version of the story as retold in Kisch's memoirs differs in many details from the 1913 version and is framed by an account of how a writer named Hanns ut Hamm plagiarized Kisch's piece and won a contest sponsored by the city of Hamburg, which had offered a cash prize for a story best illustrating "the indigenous humor and wit of the German seacoast."[6] Hamm copied *Magdalenheim* almost verbatim, but transposed it to Hamburg, changing names, using local slang, and, including himself in the story as a participant-observer (i.e., as an ersatz Kisch). When the fraud was discovered there was an uproar in the National Socialist Party. An SS newspaper spearheaded the attack against Hamm for using the degenerate work of a banned Jewish guttersnipe to befoul the German sensibility. The prize was rescinded. This farce took place in 1939, indicating that, halfway through the period of Nazi cultural domination, there were still many 'Aryans' who had read and probably enjoyed Kisch's writing before 1933 (including Hamm). Official policy in the Third Reich could ban writers and burn their work, but it hardly had control over the memories of millions of older readers familiar with pre-1933 writing in Germany and Austria. A minor irony of this affair is that Kisch himself had transposed his best-known tale about Prague's demi-monde, the Toni Gallows story, from his native city to Hamburg and Berlin in a republished feuilleton and two published versions of the play's text.

Magdalenheim is almost pure low-key comedy, ironically disdainful of the authorities and only lightly touched by thoughts on the truly pathetic fate of the women in the story. Kisch had changed by the time he wrote about Toni Gallows, so the personally pathetic and socially disturbing aspects of prostitution – lacking in the 1913 piece—are intertwined with its comedy; these aspects of prostitution predominate in his novel. The Toni story does not appear in his Prague-miscellany collections of 1912, 1913, and 1920. It first came out as a feuilleton in *Prager Tagblatt* in 1921.[7] The feuilleton's story is the core of the play, though, as he reworked the material for the stage between 1921 and 1927, Kisch added more characterization and dialogue for the subsidiary roles of Toni's two companions delivered to the court of judgment, Upejpavá and Natscheradetz. These enhancements involve comical colloquial speech that also points up the religious hypocrisy of Toni's fellow travelers, who assume heaven is ready and waiting for them.

Kisch ended the 1921 feuilleton with Toni's final request to the High Judge, i.e., "... *man möge das alles dem Egon e. k. telefonieren, damit ganz Prag davon erfahre*" (" ... maybe somebody might call Egon E. K. and let him know everything, so that all of Prague would hear about it").[8] This is an odd (almost postmodernist) note to end the story on, introducing the author as a mediator between the spirit world and the real one, pointing to the fact that though he is a journalist, in this instance Kisch wants the reader to acknowledge that he is transforming a real downfallen woman into a fictional-fantasy vehicle for making his observations about life on the margins of society. Or perhaps it was just a piece of raillery at his own expense, written to amuse his Prague readers (as in, "Kisch has lots of contacts everywhere, even among the deceased").

In the play the physical setting and the accoutrements of heavenly and hellish officials are also more developed along comic lines, with the angel of the 1921 feuilleton becoming a temperamental policeman sporting tiny wings and the devils depicted in the traditional fashion used to frighten children and superstitious adults. There is a fair amount of jocular and carping verbal byplay between heaven's and hell's bureaucrats, mostly on the subject of smoking, which boredom and exasperation with their jobs drive them to during their work-breaks. One clerk complains of his inability to study Roman Law as he is distracted by the constant hubbub and the shrieks of the damned in the Hall of Judgment (which a devilish clerk deems as betokening an "undemocratic" attitude toward the deceased, to be expected from the snooty heavenly side of things). Other details are changed as well: the names of several earthly locations; the length of the dialogue between Toni and Heaven's High Judge (now the story's major section); and even her favorite song, which in the feuilleton is a melody played by an orchestrion, a song from "The Bartered Bride" about how God has graced us with life and health (basically, "we're lucky to be alive"). In the play it becomes a sentimental love song played on the gramophone at Koutsky's brothel. With such additions and enhancements Kisch filled out a story-line that was simple and linear in the feuilleton version, giving himself enough new material to build a three-scene cabaret play and allow more conversational back-and-forth among a broader case of characters.

Unlike the Redl melodrama, *Die Himmelfahrt der Tonka Šibenice* is not structured in the manner of a traditional multi-act play, in which conflicts are presented and resolved in one way or another after a crucial event takes place. Instead, it comprises three vignettes: the last daily round-up of deceased souls in Prague; a description of the court of heavenly judgment, followed by the recitation of Toni's life story as it is elicited by the court's President; and, the brief epiphany that in the afterlife the divine policy is "to each his or her own appropriate reward". That is, heaven replicates one's most cherished environment on earth, a place where one was at ease among friends. For Toni this is Koutsky's "classy" brothel. Redemption awaits Toni at the end of the road, but it is redemption of a kind bound to infuriate traditional morality and middle-class beliefs, though a cabaret audience is more likely to have responded to the idea as a good joke. In fact, this very brief scene is akin to the punch-line of a long and tortuous joke

From the moment of her entry onto the stage in Scene I, Toni is an arresting character, by virtue of her attitude and speech, a mixture of idioms, metaphors, and curses delivered telegraphically, with abrupt digressions relating striking episodes from her troubled life. At first she is fearless and enthusiastic about her future fate, expecting that heaven is her due, a well-earned reward for a hellish thirty years as a street-walker, an occupation that doesn't strike her as evil or immoral, but rather as necessary, given her lack of other opportunities in life. As the President of the court comments on her extensive police file, her confidence in heavenly reward wanes rapidly, though a few glasses of heavenly ether keep her tongue fluid. The fatalism of the underclass is deeply ingrained in her—you play the cards life deals you. If you come from the lower strata of society, that hand is likely to be a bad one, but you brace yourself and get through the day, finding fleeting moments of pleasure when and where you can (a warm bowl of tripe soup, a glass of schnapps, a nice client, i.e., one who is generous and not too rough).

The above raises the question of 'agency', a critical-theoretical term that has diminishing analytical and explanatory power the more reflexively it is used to make generalizations. Contemporary ideas about agency originate in the substrata of radical individualism and self-creation ('identity-construction'). One approach to this is through the practice of specific psychological and behavioral routines designed to lead to physical and mental self-improvement. The other is more social, based on collective efforts to remediate or 'normalize' one's minority status (be it based on race, ethnicity, religion, gender, or sexual orientation). A more historically meaningful way to look at agency is through a sociological lens. Then it seems to mean the range of freedom of action that various individuals have, based on their membership in one class or another. We all know from experience that wealthy and powerful people have more freedom of action (though they cannot escape biological constraints, and, if careless, legal repercussions in response to their doings). Related to this is the diminishing freedom of action of those who are poor, socially isolated, or members of persecuted minorities. Existentialism's 'philosophy of living' would not deny such people freedom of choice, noting that one can always make a bold 'existential' move if one is willing to accept the consequences (or is clever enough to escape them), e.g., by choosing to be a criminal, a political rebel putting oneself at risk, or, even a sexual freebooter unconcerned with society's reactions to one's choices while yielding to an 'authentic inner self' (as in Sartre's portrayal of Jean Genet as an 'existentialist saint' and role model). It would be fair to say that for most people whose freedom of action is thoroughly regulated and controlled by traditional systems of belief and the legal and cultural powers of the authorities that enforce them, such intellectual approaches to agency and everyday behavior are remote, abstract, and, for the most part, irrelevant.

Having observed and reported on life among the urban lower classes, Kisch knew how restricted their choices were and how their lack of education and financial means made escape from their milieu almost impossible. It was his hope that socialist (or communist) politics would at first ameliorate this situation and eventually totally overcome it by abolishing poverty through redistribution of wealth, accompanied by vast improvements in educational, cultural, and medical services for all members of society. Therefore, while she has a dim awareness of the social reasons for her dismal existence, Toni has no real critical understanding of why things are the way they are. She can chafe, carp, and insult, but she seems to have been powerless to effect a thoroughgoing change in her way of life. Still, she is a heroine, based on her defiant attitude toward traditional authority (an attitude shared by Kisch).

On a related point, when one takes into account the prevailing attitudes of an earlier era (which is one of an historian's basic responsibilities), it is also fair to say that neither Kisch nor his creation, Toni Gallows, were feminists *avant la lettre*. Kisch often chose female characters to present his various social messages because he understood that women (especially poor women) were doubly-damned as politically impotent and objects of disdain by men; as a counterweight to this impotence they were, however, less susceptible to accepting the rationales and justifications for behavior that issues from dominance contests among males (i.e., women were more realistic about life and more critical of male beliefs about what is 'necessary' or 'serious'). Kisch admired this kind of practical everyday wisdom in his own mother. He also assumed that communism would establish a state in which the everyday lives and political status of women would be vastly improved (goals common to most feminist movements).

The preceding social detour allows the reader of the play to sidestep anachronistic theoretical constructs and focus on the depiction of Toni's character and behavior, noting that Kisch was always attracted to colorful characters and urban eccentrics; Toni is certainly both. I say "reader" rather than "viewer", because viewers were going into the theater with a specific set of expectations about cabaret shows, which included a wide variety of sensory experiences, genres, and styles of performance. The liveliness and eccentricity of a cabaret-play character like Toni had high appeal in this popular entertainment setting (and entertainment it was, with no dismissive connotation being attached to the word or the thing).

Her cursive, irregular street language and fractured grammar, bordering on a stream-of-consciousness presentation (though spoken aloud rather than in an inner voice), make her an unseemly candidate for heaven; this is compounded by her disdain of her companions and the officials of the afterlife. As to Upejpavá and Natscheradetz, she sees through them and expresses contempt for their efforts to make a good showing in the Hall of Judgment. She knows Upejpavá, a former prostitute, is a feigner of piety and that Natscheradetz is the kind of egotistic man who imagines his success as a saloon-keeper and his ability to pay for a laudatory newspaper obituary notice in advance will impress God and his legal staff. From scraps of information gleaned from their conversation it is clear that neither of them was given to charitable impulses. Upejpavá has led a pinched life on the defensive, while Natscheradetz has exercised his small-man's authority over those even less fortunate in his seedy milieu. The President of the High Court of Judgment, seeing into their souls, doesn't hesitate to condemn them. Indignant and protesting, they are shuffled off to hell without much ado.

Toni is not impressed by the apparatus of divine judgment and its executors, whether on heaven's or hell's 'team'. The policeman-angel and desk clerks get tongue-lashings for officiousness and dragging things out, while devils who put on a show to frighten her are considered buffoons whose antics are suitable for scaring small children. However, there is one exception to her omnidirectional wrath and skepticism, the dignified, bearded President, the only one present who can subdue her ranting. He is touchy about protocol, yet patient and curious, not rushing to judgment, even after he has read a bill of indictment tallying Toni's offenses against peace and public order (that is, her Prague police file). She pleads not guilty on all counts, declaring that her various brawls and public demonstrations were occasioned by disrespectful behavior on the part of her companion prostitutes, which leads the play to its crux.

She had once been happy as the "princess" at Koutsky's Salon (a brothel), well-dressed, well-housed and fed, and sought by numerous clients, who called her the "beautiful, blue-eyed Tanya". Why the sudden turnabout in her fate and what occasioned it? The President probes gently about Toni's nickname, which has everything to do with the sudden downward turn her life took. At first she resists revealing the origins of "Toni Gallows", perhaps out of shame, though she puts it otherwise, declaring that the story is one of her innermost possessions and not to be bandied about (which it certainly was during her time on earth — she has become a "Prague legend" willing to tell the story in exchange for drinks, as is represented in the final scenes of the 1930 film adaptation of her story discussed in the next chapter). Slowly but deftly the President coaxes her to give her account of how she came to sexually service the despicable serial murderer and mutilator of women, Prokupek, on the eve of his hanging. The sad but grimly amusing story leads to her persecution and mockery by prostitutes and their clients at her beloved Koutsky's and the next brothel she moves to, forcing her to become a street-walker and resulting in several vivid catfights (here, in the dingy streets of Prague's vice district, we get a taste of a Hobbesian social and psychological 'war of all against all').

As she goes on with her tale of woe the President intervenes to pose a simple question: "Why did you do it?" Her answer is the crux of the story —as she looks inward she can only weakly state that she never really understood why she made this impulsive decision. But the President sees deeper and recognizes her unseemly choice as an act of charity, both toward the most down-and-out woman at Koutsky's brothel (a sickly derelict nominated for the job in order to keep the police happy) and the condemned man himself, whom she treats with great kindness in the face of her own revulsion at his appearance and crimes. These simple good deeds, surprising to Toni herself, earn her admission into heaven. The final brief Scene III brings us back to a combination of social comedy (heaven as a 'classy' brothel) and a bit of sentimentality about Toni and her cherished, small world.

The question raised by one of Kisch's biographers, Dieter Schlenstedt, intrudes itself here. Did the raucous comedy of the play overwhelm its intended social message about the causes of misery among the underclass? This is a difficult question to answer with any certainty, as it depends on how audiences responded to the play, noting that audiences differ greatly from professional reviewers and theater critics. While left-wing reviewers of the play praised it for its implicit criticism of the society that created conditions allowing prostitution to flourish and granted police and censorious municipal officials the power to oversee morality, a cabaret attendee could have easily taken away an altogether different message (or no message at all beyond "that was a good show"). Specific styles of performance affected audience and critical reaction as well, as Viera Glosíková discovered when examining reviews of the play—in Prague Xena Longenová emphasized the pathetic side of Toni's tale, while in Berlin and on the road Rosa Valetti was praised for her rambunctious interpretation that highlighted Toni's fiery temperament (Glosikova's observations are summarized in Chapter 7). Readers of the play will come away with their own impressions of the balance between pathos and comedy achieved in *Die Himmelfahrt der Tonka Šibenice.*

The constituent elements of the play's comedy do not differ greatly from those of the Redl play, though their bite is sharper and more vulgar. Where we have bumbling, argumentative detectives and a fatuous Archduke in *Die Hetzjagd*, in *Tonka Šibenice* we see clownish clerks of the afterlife's bureaucracy and an officious assistant to the High Judge. In the Redl play the dialogues be-

150

tween the detectives are of the give-and-take or mutual misunder-standing variety, often seen in comedy-duo skits highlighting temperamental differences between members of the pair. There is some of this in Toni's exchanges with her companions on the journey to Purgatory and with officialdom as well, but a good deal of the comedy is linguistic and carried by Toni herself in mono-logues, which (as characterized by Glosíková) are also "implicit dialogues" with all those responsible for her sad life. A few of the comedic touches are of a personal nature (e.g., "Sinaiberger", who is already in hell, alludes to the name of a lifelong friend of Kisch and his family, Hugo Sinaiberger; smoking as an activity reserved for those admitted to heaven reflects Kisch's lifelong habit of chain-smoking). To some members of the audience these may have been perceived as 'in-jokes'.

Schlenstedt's remarks on the vitiating effect of comedy on a work's more serious social message applies to both plays, but the serious portions of the Redl play are separated by the particular sequence of acts: serious; comic (as a foil to a serious discussion); comic; serious (again with comic notes as a foil); and deadly seri-ous. In *Tonka Šibenice* comedy prevails in Scene I, based on Toni's verbal abuse of her companions and mockery of the officiousness of a heavenly policeman-angel. The play's major section, Scene II, has comedy and pathos thoroughly intertwined once Toni begins to recite her life story. Scene III is very short and has its 'one good joke' (heaven as a brothel). Audience reactions to such mixtures of comedy and pathos are likely to be individual and unpredictable.

It is also likely that a theatrical piece performed as a cabaret play, with an adventurous audience that was small, was more lim-ited in its public impact than that of a full-length play by a well-known playwright performed for the kind of middle-class audi-ence that patronized large urban or town theaters; Germany abounded with such audiences and venues. This limitation could be overcome to a certain extent by publicity about and critical re-views of a 'progressive' or 'revolutionary' play, but such an ampli-fying effect depended on the seriousness (and popularity) of the cultural sections of newspapers affiliated with organizations like the Social-Democratic and Communist parties of Germany and

Austria. While the Social Democratic parties advocated reforms that would improve the lives of their working-class members, they were seldom, if ever, revolutionary in their goals or even their rhetoric, having accepted the necessity (and desirability) of working within parliamentary institutions. Their cautious politics often carried over into the cultural realm.

As Deborah Holmes has shown, the editors of Vienna's Social Democratic newspaper, *Arbeiter Zeitung*, were uncertain of what the standards for feuilletons should be, coming down on the side of the proposition that publishing 'good writing' according to traditional criteria was more worthwhile than printing pieces that were obviously fraught with a left-wing political message (e.g., they were skeptical about 'proletarian writing' or naïve submissions from party members who were not professional writers). When it came to the feuilleton column and the arts section of the paper, 'improving the taste' of its readers, including familiarizing them with the 19th century classics, had a higher priority than printing fiction or essays that had clear, directed political content.[9] As Holmes noted, there was an even more fundamental debate among Austrian social democracy's leaders about the significance of the arts in general and literature in particular, with Friedrich Adler judging that they were irrelevant to the goals and programs of the party. The implication of this judgment is, "print anything you want in the cultural section of the paper, it won't matter."

One can see how this cultural controversy within the precincts of the left played out with the republication of Kisch's Toni Gallow's story as a feuilleton in the Communist paper, *Die Rote Fahne* in 1928.[10] In this revision of the 1921 feuilleton Kisch relocated the Toni story to Berlin (there is no mention of Hamburg). As in his alternate versions of the play; she is now Galgentoni rather than Tonka Šibenice. Though he edited and rewrote many paragraphs, he did not alter the gist of the story or the flow of the narrative as it appeared in the 1921 feuilleton in *Prager Tagblatt*. The full-inside-page version of the story in the 1928 New Year's Day Sunday supplement of Vienna's *Rote Fahne* (a 12-page broadsheet issue with numerous political and cultural columns) is accompanied by drawings that illustrate the story's comical aspects, hardly the equivalent of biting, satirical cartoons fraught with critical content; in contrast, imagine George Grosz's assaultive sketches and prints depicting the world of prostitutes and their clients.[11] Kisch also dropped the original last line of the 1921 story, with its reference to himself as journalistic intermediary. Despite the communist venue and an opportunity to revise the story in a political direction, Kisch submitted a recycled feuilleton that was more lighthearted than probing.

Republishing a slightly altered version of the Toni Gallows feuilleton may not have been important to Kisch at this point in his career, though it allowed him to express his solidarity with left-wing politics, as represented by *Die Rote Fahne*. By now Kisch was well-known in general as *der rasende Reporter* and admired on the political left. This combination seems to have been sufficient for the editors to publish the piece without worrying about its lack of a directly stated political message. Besides, Kisch was a frequent contributor to the Berlin edition of *Die Rote Fahne* — between 1926 and 1932 the newspaper published 60 of his pieces.[12] While the majority deal with current events and politics examined from a left-wing perspective, several discuss cultural topics and oddities often encountered in feuilletons (e.g., a piece titled "The first detective's ruse in world literature—a Sherlock-Holmesiad in Voltaire").

The 1928 republication of the Toni Gallows tale in feuilleton form (its fifth time in print) probably reflects Kischs's fondness for the story itself, which he came back to for a final re-telling in his memoirs.[13] The memoirs' version starts with a retrospective tour of "the dives of Prague", limning the area housing the city's vegetable and meat markets, where night-people (drinkers, journalists, typesetters, the homeless, prostitutes) roam about while dawn-people (market-stall workers, delivery boys, farmers hauling produce) begin their day as most of Prague still sleeps. Kisch describes a cluster of seedy bars (To Hell, Green Frog, Mimosa, Battalion, Café Melantrich) in the neighborhood and tells tales of legendary historical events, drinking bouts, and brawls that took place in several of them across the centuries. Toni is introduced to the reader as a typical creature of this milieu, one whom Kisch stumbles upon when he witnesses her in a wild fight with a prostitute named Stuttering Betty. Overhearing Toni's nickname piques his curiosity, but he loses sight of her when she is arrested for disturbing the peace. Eventually he encounters her again in a narrow passageway leading to the Café Melantrich, where the owner (Isidor "Mungo" Natscheradetz) deigns to serve customers too unsightly or foul to admit to the indoor premises. Kisch buys her a drink, then agrees to a series of meetings in her dark and dirty rented room in order to get the full story of her life and how she acquired her nickname. After several of these sessions he can't find her in her old haunts and learns that she has died in a local hospital. He has already noted that after a few glasses of schnapps Toni would begin to address an imaginary judge in order to explain that her obstreperous behavior is the fault of those who persecute her on account of the infamous deed of servicing a murderer in jail on the eve of his execution. "Toni Gallows" is her scarlet letter for this transgression that offended her fellow prostitutes and former clients.

At this point during his reminiscence Kisch goes over to the fantasy of how Toni's imaginary pleadings with authority figures would play out in the afterlife, and the reader gets the story of Toni at the gates of heaven and hell. This is an extended narrative version of the text of his Tonka Šibenice play, but, with the passage of almost two decades, changes in the details of the story abound. A third-person narration of Toni's experience in the Hall of Judgment (which is compared in its plain appearance to Prague's Court of Common Pleas) flows smoothly in Guy Endore's 1941 English translation, as if the reader were hearing a good anecdotal recitation in a bar, with the commentary of a seasoned observer glossing the action described. The cast of characters is now a mixed roster of Czech and German names, and, once again Toni's favorite song is a new one, *"Karlinnen komm"* ("Carlotta, you oughta" etc.). The benign character of the Presiding Judge is still apparent, and after hearing the story of her miserable life, he resolves the matter in her favor, while Kisch as raconteur points to the suppressed disapproval of his chief clerk.

Jocular remarks about Jews, indicative of the tropes of popular anti-Semitism, vary across the Tonka texts. In the 1922 version of the play set in Hamburg-Berlin, Mesertizer (in the Prague setting, Natchscheradetz) greets three old friends with obviously Jewish names (Schlesinger, Salomon, and Silberstein) who are already in hell, as if it were the most natural thing in the world to find them there. In the 1926 play's text these three companions become Mandelik, Sinaiberger, and Roubitschek. The republished (1927) Hamburg-Berlin version of the play reintroduces Schlesinger et al. In the 1941 prose re-telling of the memoirs in translation - presumably reflecting Kisch's German text at the time—he companions in hell are now Sinaiberger and Schlesinger (both, in fact, old friends of Kisch). Toni's insult about Natscheradetz being "already a dead Jew" (implying nothing worse could happen to anyone) reflects the casual, vernacular anti-Semitism of Kisch's youth, a combination of social snobbery and inherited religious prejudice. At the time such verbal insults would have hardly raised anyone's eyebrows, especially in the mean streets Kisch describes. By war's end things were different, and the 1947 edition of the memoirs omits the Jewish names, substituting "old friends". Kisch himself harbored no anti-Semitic sentiments. While in no sense religious, he was not ashamed of his Jewish origins, wrote about various communities of Jews with as much objectivity as he could muster and decried anti-Semitism (e.g., as in *Tales from Seven Ghettos*). As noted previously, he warmed to the Zionist project of establishing a Jewish state in Israel after he learned the full horrors of the Holocaust (while earlier in life he had argued that Zionism was another instance of nationalism and imperialism, to which he was opposed).

The foregoing discussion adheres to the structure and themes of the play, while the particulars of its performance history and critical responses to the play are given in Chapter 7. But, there is one more matter about Kisch's narrative in *Sensation Fair* that raises questions about his sources, journalistic practices, and desire to have the Toni story interpreted in a way that makes a real woman a representative of the urban underclass. Part of the problem is due to the time-frame of the story. In the first feuilleton version

(February 20, 1921) Toni and her judges remark that the day of her death was exactly thirty years after the night she went to Prokupek's cell in 1891; the feuilleton appeared on this 30th anniversary date. The slightly revised feuilleton that appeared in the Communist newspaper *Rote Fahne* on January 1, 1928 keeps the dayof judgment as thirty years after her night with the killer, which is dated to December 10, 1897. Each of these dates makes his tale "timely', with her imaginary judgment in Purgatory taking place in the weeks just preceding the publication and republication of the story. In the versions of the play that were published in 1922, 1926, and 1927 the date of her fateful night is stated as August 12, 1892, so we conclude that her day of judgment was on the same day in 1922 (around the time the first Hamburg-Berlin version of the play came out). So the dates of the crucial earthly event and its heavenly judgment shift appropriately in a way that is coordinated with publication dates, though Kisch did not bother to adjust the dates in this fashion when he had the text of play republished in his 1926 and 1927 collections ("timeliness" would be irrelevant in such book-form treatments).

How do these dates align with Kisch's years in Prague, especially as recalled later in his memoirs? The time frame of the memoirs is specific. They give an account of his childhood awareness of local popular history, his adolescent explorations of his native city (ca. 1898–1903), and his prowling of Prague's demimonde and working-class neighborhoods as a journalist between 1906 and 1913 (resulting in three "Prague books" between 1912 and 1920). The memoirs end with brief passages set in the first year of World War I. Kisch lived in Prague again during 1920 and early 1921, while also sending in stories to Prague and Brno newspapers and magazines after resettling in Berlin in 1921. The Toni Gallows story told in the memoirs devolves from a description of Kisch's excursions to the "dives of Prague" and their surrounding streets and squares, as described in detail above. In the memoirs' recounting of the story, Toni and her Purgatorial inquisitors remark that her day of judgment is exactly thirty years after the night of her servicing the killer (Prokupek), and that night is given as August 12, 1881. This allows readers to infer that Kisch's encounters with Toni were sometime during 1911, which fits in very well with his journalistic activities in Prague at the time.

The varying dates of her earthly experience and her appearance before the divine court of justice are easily explained if one assumes that Kisch thought readers of the feuilleton and stage versions of the tale would naturally interpret the story as being "split in time", i.e., they would know the milieu of the Toni story is based on his experience as a local-color and crime journalist before 1914, while the date of Toni's death given in the fantasy portion made it timely for newspaper readers in 1921 and 1928 and viewers and readers of the play in 1922. A clue to this idea of 'a split time-frame' comes from Toni herself, who, in the 1926 play addresses the High Judge at one point as both an "imperial and a republican-provincial" official. In Toni's mind the judge was a Habsburg official at the time of Prokupek's execution and is, as it were, an official of the newly established Czech Republic at the time of her judgment. I point out here that these varying dates are not a product of Kisch's inattention or inconsistency but rather an artifact of examining six texts in a way that would have been irrelevant to contemporary readers and playgoers (i.e., an artifact of research into details of variant texts published over a seven-year period).

But the bigger question is: Did Kisch meet Toni Gallows sometime around 1911? Fritz Hofmann cited testimony from an older reporter who knew Kisch at the outset of his career that the story of Toni Gallows, which seems to have circulated as an 'urban legend' in pre-war Prague, had no real prototype and that the gruesome liaison with a murderer had no basis in fact (i.e., there was no serial killer of women whose last request for sexual satisfaction was honored by the police recruiting a prostitute for the task and no hanging of such a person in Prague during 1881 or 1891, as given in Kisch's versions of the story, including his memoirs).[14] The reporter, Josef Vejvara,[15] said he had "taken [the naïve young] Kisch for a ride" with this tale in 1906. So it is possible that the character of Toni is entirely imaginary. Such considerations are of little consequence in a feuilleton or cabaret play not intended to be historical records. But accurate historical intention is (or should be) part and parcel of a memoir, and in *Sensation Fair* Kisch claimed to be giving an unvarnished record of his encounters with Antonie Havlová. Hofmann's remarks undermine an informed, present-day reader's confidence in the accuracy of the earthly side of the story about his meetings with Toni in Prague, if they in fact took place. These considerations do not apply to the heavenly side of the story, which is obviously a clever, funny, and at times touching fantasy. If Hofmann is correct on this point, then did Kisch fictionalize his experience in Prague's twilight world in order to achieve a particular literary or political-polemical goal? This seems likely, though no one knows the definitive answer to this question. Although Kisch undoubtedly had encounters with colorful Prague prostitutes during his years at *Bohemia*, the life-story and character of Toni *may* be fictional through and through, while still accurately representing the underside of life in Prague, as intended by her creator.

In the end the reader has the play, now but a textual aid to the imagination of those who can put themselves in the shoes of a 1920s cabaret theater attendee. As a piece of cabaret "critical comedy" (discussed in Chapter 8), *Die Himmelfahrt der Tonka Šibenice* seems effective enough, evidenced by its performance history in several cities throughout the 1920s. By virtue of its willingness to delve into the unpleasant side of life the Prague version is a 'late Habsburg period piece' that differs from the standard 'waltz-and-schmaltz' depictions that have dominated fictional and cinematic representations of the era. The Hamburg-Berlin version fits well into the gritty realism of mid-Weimar-era art works depicting life's seamier side. Though Kisch called the play a bagatelle, he couldn't let go of the story—its environs were too much a part of his adventurous youth, which was abruptly terminated by the onset of World War I, and it continued to exercise a grip on his imagination.

Like the Redl story, the tale of Toni Gallows had enough dramatic and entertainment value to soon undergo a film adaptation, migrating to a medium that was the true popular art of the twentieth century. As the Redl story went from book to stage to screen its fictional quotient increased, drifting far from the historical basis of the affair. Given its feuilleton origins, such considerations are mostly irrelevant to the Toni Gallows story, though the film and later television versions of the story take us away from Kisch's original journalistic and theatrical intentions and goals, going so far in this direction as to eliminate the 'comedy of the afterlife' as they introduce themes not encountered in Kisch's rough-and-tumble approach to this material. Eventually there was a return to Kisch's original framing device for the story in a 1989 adaptation of the play. While it reduced the cast to two characters and altered the substance of 1926's dialogues, this adaptation of the story for stage and television in Prague returned the audience to the play's posthumous setting. The stage, cinematic, and television departures from the narrative of Kisch's Toni Gallows play are discussed in detail in Chapter 10.

Chapter 7. Kisch's Career as Playwright

Like many young men of his background and education, Kisch had aspirations to be a writer, of the prestigious type known as 'a man of letters'. A slender volume of poetry was often the first step on this path, and, with the help of a subsidy from his mother, he took this step in 1905,[1] following it up with a book of short stories a year later.[2] In his memoirs he disavowed his poetry as sentimental juvenilia that expressed his self-centered adolescent sensibilities without offering readers anything of real interest about the world in which they lived. Spector has analyzed Kisch's rough drafts, published poems, and letters about them and interprets this early work as indicative of Kisch's liberal-German attempt to find a role for himself as the needed mediator who might reconcile Bohemian Germans to a developing culture that would acknowledge their place in a revived Czech polity.[3] If Spector's parsing of this early work is accurate, then perhaps Kisch was trying to bury his youthful ideas about such matters when he dismissed this phase of his writing, i.e. he later found these ideas to be politically incorrect (or unachievable) from a socialist perspective.

His sole novel, *Der Mädchenhirt* (The Pimp), published in Berlin in 1914 and discussed above, was a moderate success with readers and critics, especially considering that he was a new man on the very competitive Berlin literary scene, but he never returned to the form. Looking back at his youth, he wrote that the conditions of life — no radio, no films, no automobiles for quick and easy trips to the countryside — elevated theater and theatrical criticism to a high- and popular-cultural prominence they never regained after 1914.[4] During his secondary school days (roughly from 1898 to 1903) he and his schoolmates were fanatical theatergoers. Each season they would adopt new mannerisms based on their favorite heroes on the stage and argue over the merits of plays, actors, actresses, local newspaper reviewers, and nationally prominent critics. He described this in passages of his 1920 book, *Die Abenteuer in Prag*, noting that over the years he and his friends lost their fascination with the theater—they had undergone new experiences (including a world war) and acquired new responsibilities and interests.[5]

While working as a journalist between 1906 and 1913 Kisch also made the rounds of cafés, bars, cabaret theaters, and other haunts patronized by Prague artists and bohemians (the Café Central, Café Continental, and Café Arco being favorite meeting places). His own age-group of writers in Prague included several men whose reputations blossomed at different times during the coming decades. They discussed their literary elders and found them unappealing on account of their conservative and overly nationalistic 'high-culture' approach to the novel and theater. They argued over the merits and pitfalls of various waves of modernism. In Prague Kisch was one of the few who engaged in these windy conversations in the separate Czech and German literary circles of the city, befriending fellow German-speakers and also men who later became prominent in the new post-1918 world of Czech arts and letters (Jaroslav Hašek, František Langer, Emil Artur Longen). Langer's career as a (Jewish) Czech writer, embracing journalism, highly-regarded plays, short stories, and novels, was somewhat similar to Kisch's, and he wrote many a tale about crime and criminals, though his meditative point of view about guilt and redemption was closer to Čapek's than Kisch's.[6] But his profession during the interwar years could not have been more different than that of his old acquaintance—he was a medical officer in the Czech army for almost two decades and a cabinet member as well. His brother Jiří took an even more unusual path in life, converting himself to being an "*Ostjude*" (Eastern Jew) on his way to Zionism.

As a self-appointed spokesman for this age-cohort of Bohemian-German writers, Max Brod referred to them as 'the Prague circle', many of whom were Jews who affiliated themselves with German culture and wrote in German, an increasingly unsatisfactory and anxiety-generating choice, given the prevalence of anti-Semitism, which reached into professional criticism in all of the arts as well as into political life. In his memoirs Kisch gave capsule summaries of the perspectives and pre-occupations of his local peers and competitors:

The younger generation was united not only by their opposition to the despotic cultural clique, but also by their hatred of national sectarianisms, even though in their turn they were divided by many literary currents. There was for example the satirical demonist, Paul Leppin; the Catholic neo-romanticist, René (later Rainer) Maria Rilke; the ethical eroticist, Max Brod; the mystic realist, Franz Kafka; the philosopher, Hugo Bergmann, follower of Brentano; and an equally varied group that was gathered around Franz Werfel, who at that time was still in college.[7]

This is an interesting characterization of a diverse group of writers, some of whom are now forgotten by all but specialists and others who moved onto fame or fortune. Kafka achieved his broader literary pre-eminence posthumously, and Kisch's "mystic realist" is a pithy, insightful characterization of his work. About the same group the admired and reviled Viennese scold and 'anti-journalist', Karl Kraus, referred to them as 'the Arconauts' and wrote, somewhat caustically, "*Es werfelt und brodelt und kafkat und kischt*" (an almost untranslatable statement, depending on puns based on turning each assailed author's name into a verb).[8] Also common to members of this informal group was a desire to escape Prague, which they found culturally confining—Vienna, Munich, and, above all, Berlin beckoned. Kafka's well-known characterization of Prague as a "little mother with claws" highlights the intertwining of the comforts of an artist remaining in his native city (offering the possibility of becoming a 'big fish in a small pond') with its restrictive grip on one's habits and imagination.

In spite of Kisch's 1920 valediction to the theater in *Die Abenteuer in Prag*, he had not really relinquished theatrical aspirations. His 1914 opportunity to enter the Berlin theatrical scene as dramaturge and playwright for a socially progressive theater had been quashed by his being called to arms in July of that year. But, after his return to Prague in 1920, where E. A. Longen coaxed him to write for the stage, and resettlement in Berlin in 1921, he made a serious effort to turn himself into a dramatist while maintaining his profession as a journalist. This resulted in Kisch writing a good deal for the stage, though no one ever thought of him primarily in this connection, given the publicity that surrounded his reportage and his political activism. In addition to his long discussion of the *Galgentoni* play, Marcus Patka lists six other plays written by

Kisch during this period: *Die gestohlene Stadt*; *Die Hetzjagd*; *Piccaver im Salon Goldschmied*; *Die Sensation des Journalisten* (*Die Mutter des Mörders*); *Letzte Nacht in Castans Panoptikum*; and *Pasáci, Pasáci*.[9] Except for the first play in the list, a full-length historical comedy set during the Seven Years War, these were short or medium-length works intended for cabaret or revue stages, being adaptations of various reportages and feuilletons that also reappear as stylized reminiscences in his memoirs. He co-wrote several other plays, including one in collaboration with Jaroslav Hašek, *Die Reise um Europa in 365 Tagen*. The play was based on Kisch's reportage about his experience as a crewman on a freighter that made a ludicrous 'circumcontinental' passage of Europe in order to travel the short distance between Prague and Bratislava, which have no direct riverine connection. A summary of Viera Glosíková's detailed discussion of this co-written play, his solo full-length play, and his short works (including one not on Patka's list) follows below, after a discussion of how biographers treated the playwriting phase of his life.

Kisch's four major biographers took different approaches to evaluating his fictional and dramatic works, though it is fair to say that all of them view these works as playing an ancillary role in his life as a journalist. Even Patka, with his mission to establish Kisch as an underappreciated "poet of everyday life", finds this poetry in his reportage, feuilletons, and essays rather than in his novel or plays. Patka's predecessors as biographers, Dieter Schlenstedt and Fritz Hofmann, writing from within the post-war communist state of East Germany, placed Kisch's works firmly in the tradition of left-wing journalism that not only represented reality in the most desirable way, but also advanced the goals of the Communist Party. This characterization is not accurate. Kisch himself lived only his last three months in a communist state and had undertaken almost all of his reportage on the basis of his independent interests and literary inclinations—as Patka wrote, "Auch ist explizit von Kommunismus in seinen Büchern nichts zu hören"[10] ("In his books one hears nothing explicit about Communism"). However, readers encountered overt politically leftist statements in short, polemical pieces that Kisch wrote for newspapers and magazines during the late 1920s and the 1930s. Kisch's own ideas about 'legitimate reportage' imply that it would naturally lead to progressive or socialist political conclusions, making it palatable to communist cultural commissars of the interwar era, especially when they were part of the effort to seek a 'united front' against Europe's fascist states. While not entirely dismissing Kisch's works for the stage, Schlenstedt and Hofmann relegated them to a minor supporting role in the development of his reportage methods and his ideas about writing.

In a brief section ("Arbeit für das Theater") of his Kisch biography,[11] Schlenstedt remarked of the Redl and Tonka plays that, although they had an implicit social-critical message, this was masked by the very effective comedy and "grotesqueries" of the two pieces, making them only marginal in typifying Kisch's eventual role as a social critic of capitalism and conservatism. Surprisingly, he found Kisch's anti-militarist and pro-common man message more openly brought to the fore in his historical comedy, *Die gestohlene Stadt* (The Stolen City). By "grotesqueries" Schlenstedt was referring to the exaggerated farcical elements that appear in the Redl and Toni Gallows plays. In the former this is restricted to the comedy of the two detectives arguing with each other and the portrait of a fatuous Habsburg archduke. In *Tonka Šibenice* this element is seen throughout the whole play—the only character who rises above farcical banter, hypocritical self-promotion, or wounded declarations is the heavenly court's High Judge, who in his calmness and fairness takes on the lineaments of an idealized fatherly figure of authority, an unusual characterization on Kisch's part.

Hofmann's discussion of 'Kisch as playwright' has more detail than Schlenstedt's. Much of it describes Kisch's relations with his Czech collaborators, who were associated with E. A. Longen and his Revolutionary Stage in Prague, discussed in more detail below. In late 1921 this led to a flurry of three productions put on by Longen and his troupe: an adaptation of Kisch's recent Toni Gallows newspaper feuilleton; a play based on excerpts from his 1914 novel; and the first iteration of the play based on Kisch's time as a deckhand on the "A Lanna 8", co-written with Jaroslav

Hašek. Later the same group put on German and Czech versions of *Die gestohlene Stadt* for the first time as well, presenting them in Prague's Rokoko Theater.[12] In a 1924 Rokoko production the Longen group had a short-run success with another Kisch 'play-let', *Piccaver in Salon Goldschmied*, as well as mounting the Czech version of the Redl play,[13] which was performed at least 175 times at the Rokoko. Hofmann found it to be "one of his most effective works", based on his agreement with the judgment of many of Kisch's contemporaries that its combination of an exciting crime story with an indictment of the Old Regime in general and militarism in particular constituted a needed retrospective view of the preceding decade's turbulent and consequential history. During these early 1920s years they also mounted a more finished version of the Tonka Šibenice play, which seems to have been a sell-out whenever it was performed in Prague. To this point Hofmann cites the *Prager Tagblatt* opinion that Kisch was "our world's geographer and the historian of the present." He also cites a similar assessment of the Redl book and play by a prominent left-wing writer and critic of the era, Kurt Tucholsky, even though Tucholsky doubted the accuracy of Kisch's 1924 Redl book, with respect to both the events it described and the sources it cited.[14]

Two of Kisch's minor biographers, Michael Horowitz and Klaus Haupt, should be mentioned briefly here. Horowitz's *Ein Leben für die Zeitung* came out in 1985, taking its title from a short Kisch piece published in 1928.[15] Its concise biography is followed by photographs of Kisch in a wide variety of settings, interviews of the Czech critic, Eduard Goldstücker, and the Austrian-American film director, Billy Wilder (who knew Kisch in Berlin), eight critical essays on Kisch's writing, representative Kisch reportages and feuilletons, and anecdotes about Kisch. Thus it is a 'Kisch miscellany' in which the author provides a portrait of Kisch as an engaging personality and a prolific reporter who was "dedicated to depicting reality without compromising the truth." He confines his remarks about Kisch's efforts as a playwright to three short paragraphs, giving cursory descriptions of four of his plays. Regarding the Toni Gallows play he states that the story originated in Berlin as a "local legend" and was conceived as a tribute to a

Berlin actress, Toni Pelzer – a canard that confuses a role with a person.[16] No one else reports this, and it disregards the first newspaper version of the story, set in Prague, as well as Kisch's account in his memoirs.[17] It seems to be a garbling of either the 1922 or 1927 published version's plot line and cast names with inaccurate information about the sources of the story. Haupt's remarks about Kisch's writing for the stage are neglible, though his biography sheds some light Kisch's character and personality.[18]

A decade after Hofmann's biography appeared, Marcus Patka synthesized almost seventy years' worth of writing about Kisch in his 1997 critical biography, which had the goal of not only documenting his subject's life and work but also reclaiming him for German letters as the unsung poetic chronicler of everyday life and an important (and symptomatic) representative of the interwar era in German writing. Given political events of the 1920s and 30s, this would also make Kisch of great relevance in understanding the culture of the Weimar era in Germany. As noted in Chapter 1, John Willett had done this latter service for English readers in his book, *Art and Politics in the Weimar Period.*

Patka treated Kisch's playwriting efforts in a narrow manner: descriptive, with minimal critical judgments about the quality of his writing for the stage, though he quoted both negative and positive reviews of Kisch's plays by Czech, Austrian, and German critics of the 1920s. Noting Kisch's sympathy with the aims of the Weimar era's experimental 'proletarian revolutionary theater' projects, he remarks that Kisch did not avail himself of any of this movement's formal techniques such as chanting or speaking background choruses of workers, agitational propaganda, or open didacticism. His sub-chapter, *"Theater und Zensur"*, approaches Kisch's playwriting with an emphasis on the censorship battles provoked by plans to mount several of his plays in cities where authorities who regulated the press, films, and theater intervened.[19]

The battles, and their accompanying newspaper wars between pro- and anti-Kisch reviewers, took place in Vienna, Prague, and Brno (Brünn), and focused primarily on his play about Toni Gallows, though *Die Hetzjagd* also came under fire in Austria.

A play co-written with Longen and Vlasta Burian, *Die Schwestern Teige* (The Teige Sisters), was banned in Prague—no copy of its text survives. The struggle over *Galgentoni* went through three rounds of futile attempts to mount the play in Vienna between 1922 and 1924. Police authorities and civilian bureaucrats in both the city's and the Lower Austrian provincial government were part of the campaign to suppress the play. Not only was the language of a street prostitute deemed unacceptable, the play's depiction of Toni's 'personalized heaven' as a comfortable brothel was deemed offensive to public morals and to the religious beliefs of a majority of its citizens. Disrespect for Habsburg officialdom was also noted as objectionable (as it was for the Redl play as well). Patka remarked that works of art that showed 'the good old days' (i.e., the pre-war years) in a bad light offended the proprieties and nostalgic fixations of many Austrians, and that the censorship policies of the new Austrian Republic took this into account. Officials based their principles for banning works on laws that had been extant during the late Habsburg years. Pro-Kisch critics ridiculed these policies as antiquated and overly protective, noting that they did not have a counterpart in Weimar Germany. They believed the public had a right to see and hear works dealing with the unseemly side of contemporary urban life, and a few of them even argued that the High Judge's decision on Toni's behalf represented 'true Christian values' better than the punitive attitudes of a church-state alliance, where the church obsessed over moral contamination and the state thought artworks might jeopardize public law and order.

Wishing to avoid another round of 'media wars' the Viennese authorities relented in June, 1924, allowing the Toni Gallows play to be mounted. The popular actress Rosa Valetti, who had played Toni in more than 200 performances at the cabaret theater *Rakete* (Rocket) in Berlin, starred in the role of Toni. Kisch's works encountered no censorship in Berlin. Berlin newspaper reviewers and critics, of course, could be as vindictive and negative as they wished. Conservative critics who detested either 'socialist' or experimental theatrical works abounded in Germany. Making the point about the broad official tolerance of the Weimar Republic, the two most controversial, sexually-charged works of Frank Wedekind and Arthur Schnitzler, *Frühlingserwachen* (Spring Awakening) and *Reigen* (La Ronde), debuted on Weimar stages three decades after their creation and their prohibition in prewar Germany and Austria. Compared to the deep moral turbidity of these two plays (and the queasiness they were bound to arouse in audiences), Kisch's irreverent japes at the expense of the vanished authorities and middle-class mores must have seemed like venial sins, not mortal offenses. In general the federal authorities of the Weimar Republic had a hands-off policy when it came to censorship. Still, specific city magistracies might attempt to ban works; the growing encroachments of municipal police forces as theater and film censors was noted by William Grange in his *Cultural Chronicle of the Weimar Republic*.[20] Exemplifying this, the first German film to openly treat a homosexual theme, 1919's *Anders als die Anderen* (Different from the Others), was banned "for public viewing, but permitted for viewing among psychologists, social workers, and clergyman."[21]

Aside from a blow-by-blow account of these censorship battles, Patka's only other remarks on Kisch's theatrical works were that his Redl play was successful in the lands that had formerly been part of the Dual Monarchy and that the premiere performance of Kisch's full-length play, *Die gestohlene Stadt*, in Teplitz-Schönau in late 1924 received a savagely negative review in a national newspaper. He closed his sub-chapter with the observation that after 1925 Kisch's only involvement with theatrical matters had to do with several lawsuits based on unacknowledged authorship (disregard of 'conceptual credits'), unauthorized use of his work, and plagiarism.

In his Kisch Bio-Anthology, also published in 1997, Harold Segel dealt with Kisch's playwriting ventures with even more dispatch than Patka had, though he was willing to offer his own critical judgment about the value of his subject's theatrical work and the role it played in his career. Here is his summary verdict:

> Although Kisch was glad to see his few original plays and dramatizations of his sketches performed in Prague, it was obvious that he was not going

to take the Berlin stage by storm and that that was no real future for him in the theater. His dramatic works are of uneven quality, mostly fair to good comedies, and assume an importance in his overall creativity only insofar as the lessons he learned from playwriting about dialogue and dramatic structure were put to far more effective use in his reportage.[22]

Segel's view is judicious, but is shortsighted on several matters: first, the intensity of Kisch's efforts to be recognized as a playwright in the years between 1920 and 1925, indicating its importance in his own mind; second, Kisch's belief (identical with the thinking of his Czech partner in these endeavors, E. A. Longen) that socially-critical theater was much needed at the time; third, it overlooks an aspect of Kisch's plays that offers historians and the general reader of Central European history more than either a once-relevant social critique or the pleasures of topical comedies, i.e., his plays provide an imaginative common-man's window into the late Habsburg era that is often missing from political chronicles and cultural surveys; and fourth, the newspaper wars between pro- and anti-Kisch reviewers of the plays flesh out the ongoing cultural struggles of the era with specific examples of clashing standards used to either praise or damn works of art.

Kisch's works for the stage were examined in great detail by two Prague Germanists, Viera Glosiková and Josef Polaček, who have written numerous articles about the different phases of Kisch's life. In a long two-part essay on "Kisch as dramatist" published in 1985[23] and 1986[24] in the Czech academic journal, *Philologica Pragensis*, Glosiková scrutinized all of Kisch's writing for the stage with several goals in mind: establishing an exact chronology of the prose sources of his plays and the variant texts of several of them in both Czech and German versions; documenting the performance histories of these different versions of his plays and critical responses to them; giving synopses of their narratives; and making her own assessment of the merits and occasional inadequacies of the plays. The first half of her essay was undertaken as a contribution to a Kisch-themed issue brought out by the journal during the centenary year of his birth.

Glosiková constructed her overall view of Kisch's writing for the theater on the foundation of his relationship with E. A.

Longen, his circle in Prague, and the announced goals of their 'movement'.[25] Their friendship went back to the pre-1914 years when Kisch worked as a reporter. During the war both men became radicalized in their political and cultural beliefs. By the time Kisch moved back to Prague in 1920 he was eager to affiliate his efforts to become a playwright with the Revolutionary Stage that Longen had established. When this venue was closed the Rokoko Theater succeeded it as an outlet for plays directed or produced by Longen. They agreed that both journalism and theater had an obligation to be 'social' (even socialist) in their concerns and viewpoint, making them adversarial; for plays, looser formal construction in comparison to traditional forms was acceptable, even encouraged. Longen argued that contemporary theatrical art demanded stridency in depicting the lives of men and women to whom bourgeois taste, morality, and political orientation were indifferent, at best, and, worse, often punitive. Kisch agreed. Longen's own view about censorship and negative critical reactions to Kisch's work (especially his Tonka Šibenice play) was that it was motivated not by revulsion over vulgarity but by an understanding that these plays challenged middle-class morality and entrenched authority in an unwelcome way. It was their close association in bringing new works to the stage (and not only Kisch's) that conformed to this ideal of a socially relevant, leftist theater that led to almost all of Kisch's comedies and dramas being performed in Czech before they moved onto German and Austrian stages. In the Czech versions of Kisch's plays the lead roles were often taken by Longen, his wife Xena Longenová, and Vlasta Burian, well-known actors on Prague's socially-progressive stages during the 1920s (Longen and Burian were also very active as writers, directors, and producers). The profusely illustrated 1998 'Kisch miscellany' edited by Patka gives the reader an opportunity to glimpse sketches and photographs bearing on his theatrical career and circle of Prague collaborators.[26]

Kisch and Longen's first theatrical collaboration was the Toni Gallows story, a version of which appeared on Prague's Revolutionary Stage in October, 1921. Remarks on the structure and themes of the play, as well as the present author's critical reaction

to it are given in Chapter 6 above. Kisch and Longen's second col-
laborative effort was based on their joint adaptation of episodes
from his 1914 novel, *Der Mädchenhirt*. This appeared on the Revolutionary Stage as *Pasaci, pasaci* (named after a popular ballad
about pimps) in November, 1921.[27] The subtitle of its billing tells
all about the milieu depicted: *Ein Bild aus dem Leben der Prager ge-
fallenen Existenzen in 15 Bildern* (A Portrait based on the Life of
Prague's Downfallen Souls in 15 Sketches). In a scene where the
prostitute Betka is in police custody, she "holds the mirror up to
bourgeois society" (the social stratum from which many of her clients come) in a way that impressed local reviewers and critics,
who were more receptive to *Pasaci* than they were to Longen's recently mounted adaptation of scenes from Hašek's big novel, *The
Good Soldier Schweik* (*Švejk*). Longen wished to have a scene from
Pasaci, "*Abteilung C*" ("Department C", a venereal-disease hospital
ward supervised by the police vice squad), put on in Brno, but it
was blocked by local censors. *Abteilung C*'s text received a back-
translation from Czech into German by Josef Poláček.[28] Longen's
revised production of the complete *Pasaci* play under the title
Pasák holek was performed in Vlasta Burian's Theater in Prague in
1925, receiving praise from the communist and left-wing press,
who were happy to see working-class protagonists and a realistic
representation of their dreary lives brought to the public's attention.

   The third and final play to be presented on the Revolutionary
Stage was the co-written piece, *Z Karlina do Bratislavy parnikem "A
Lanna 8" za 365 dni* (From Karlin to Bratislava with the Steamer *A
Lanna 8* in 365 Days). Kisch's portion of the writing credits for this
play were based on a story that came out in two stages. The first
was a short report, "*Kde wacht am Rhein*" ("Who's guarding the
Rhine"), published in November, 1920, in *Prager Tagblatt*.[29] This
was followed up by a much longer narrative that appeared as a
chapter in *Der rasende Reporter* ("*Die Weltumsegelung des A Lanna 6*"
or "The Circumnavigation of the *A Lanna 6*").[30] His notes for this
second, six-scene story treatment were the basis for the play,
though he and Hašek transformed them so much through fictional
inventions that these reportages should be considered only a 'gen-

eral map' of what was to come. The earlier 1920 story appears, in altered form, as one of the six scenes in this later story.

The 1920 article had little comedic or dramatic potential, being a factual account of large Czech communities living in the heavy-industrial areas of the northern stretch of the Rhine. This was embedded in a description of the social and economic domination of the river's major cities and famous scenic stretches by English and French troops and bureaucrats of the Allied Control Commission. The Czech first word (*kde*, literally "where") of the the story's title ironically alters the German nationalist anthem *Die Wacht am Rhein*, taking into account that in 1920 over a hundred thousand Czechs were living and working along an industrialized stretch of the river; it may also be an allusion to the Czech national anthem, *Kde domov můj* (Where Is My Home). Meanwhile the 'guardians' of the river—hallowed as an ages-old touchstone of Germanic myth, lore, and history—were tens of thousands of foreign soldiers. The version of the story in *Der rasende Reporter* comprised six episodes in the long, troubled, and ridiculous voyage of a cargo ship that departed from Prague's port neighborhood (Karlin, Holešovice) for Bratislava, which required a circuitous Moldau-Elbe-North Sea-Rhine-Main-canal-Danube route to cover the short distance between the two cities (in fact the journey ended in Frankfurt, though the crew makes it to Vienna in the play).

Longen recruited Jaroslav Hašek, who was amused by the story, to adapt it for his theater, resulting in its first iteration as a series of fourteen loosely connected scenes, with an emphasis on chaos and comedy.[31] At this point in his career Kisch had no difficulties in writing his portions in Czech. This version of the work premiered on December 30, 1921. After Hašek's death in 1923 Longen and Kisch came back to the play, rewriting it extensively, reducing it to eight scenes, and introducing a new major character as a mouthpiece. This version premiered in Prague in December, 1924. Though in Czech once more, the textual changes and restructuring of the play were done mostly by Kisch. Eventually Kisch's German text for another revised version was published in 1930 as *Die Reise um Europa in 365 Tagen*[32] (The Journey around Europe in 365 Days), in which he still identified Hašek as a co-author, in spite of the fact that Kisch was now the main writer. For this final version Kisch reconstructed the play again, building it back up to fifteen scenes, four of which were identical with its first Czech script. It premiered on the stage in Berlin in 1930, where reviews were not as favorable as they had been in Czechoslovakia. Glosiková agrees with the positive assessment of Czech critics in the 1920s, who liked the vibrancy, comedy, and command of vernacular language displayed in the Czech version of the play, though they also questioned its loose, episodic construction, i.e., was it really a play or a just an entertaining concatenation of comedic sketches with no strong element of continuity?

Kisch's biographers ignored, merely listed titles, or gave very brief descriptions of his one-act plays (*Einakter*), a form that was a staple of Longen's theater and cabaret venues. In contrast, Glosiková gives synopses of their plots, cites critical reviews, documents their performance histories, explains how they evolved from Kisch's newspaper sketches, feuilletons, and reportages, and unravels who wrote what in the Czech versions of these works. Her background information and commentary make the four plays in question intelligible: *Letzte Nacht in Castans Panoptikum, Piccaver im Salon Goldschmied, Die Mutter des Mörders,* and a play about a Prague eccentric named Ferda Mestek (the long, involved title of which is given below). Her summaries of the plays' narratives make it clear why Prague's cabaret audiences and reviewers responded positively to these short works ignored by later commentators, often because of the inaccessibility of their texts before the revised 1992-93 edition of the *Gesammelte Werke* was published.

In early 1922 Longen traveled to Berlin with his wife in an effort to co-ordinate with Kisch about passing along the approach of the Revolutionary Stage to a producer-director associated with the *Wilde Bühne* (Wild Stage) in Berlin. Kisch and Longen thought that a work in development with a limited speaking role for the female character would be suitable for Xena Longenová, whose German was rudimentary. This was *Castans Panoptikum,* based on a 1922 auction of the contents of a well-known wax museum in Berlin. Here is my synopsis. In the play a Rothschild bank agent wishes to acquire the wax figure of (Maier) Anselm Rothschild, the founder of the family dynasty, without bidding. He also wishes, for "the honor of the House of Rothschild", that it should be publicized that the piece fetched the highest price at the auction (he has no intention of actually paying it), stipulating that the owner of Castan's should make the bid of 30,000 marks (60 American dollars during this period of inflation) and the agent will then reimburse him. Kisch interwove this with the story of a woman who was the proprietor of a Berlin restaurant, *Die fesche Böhmin* ("stylish woman from Bohemia"). During her youth she had an affair with England's Prince of Wales (later King Edward VII) in Marienbad. She buys his wax figure as a sentimental (and snobbish) memento to be placed next to her bed and shown to her guests to impress them with her former "social circle". The chicanery involved in surreptitious bribes and deals between the auctioneer and these two bidders is comical, yet indicative of corruption.

Before the rigged auction takes place there is an interlude when the sale-hall is closed for the night and four celebrity wax figures—Rothschild, King Edward, Goethe, and a once-famous serial killer, Sternickel—engage in conversation, wondering what their sale prices will be. A status contest takes place, as each figure fears that he may go for small change in order to be turned into ingredients for a soap-maker. Their dialogues are colloquial, heavy with idioms and regional and ethnic accents, and salted with English phrases from King Edward. There is a 'social-structure' debate about the obligations of the wealthy to the poor, and well-known scraps of Goethe's poetry are quoted in comedic context. In the event even the serial killer's wax figure is more highly valued than Goethe's, indicating lamentable taste among the bidders.

The production was never realized on the Berlin stage, but was performed as *Kdo koupí Rothschilda* (Who's buying Rothschild) in July 1923 at the Rokoko in Prague.[33] Local reviews were cool to negative. The German text of the play was included as *Versteigerung von Castans Panoptikum* in Kisch's 1925 best-selling collection of reportage, *Der rasende Reporter*.[34] The source of the story was Kisch's Czech newspaper report on the auction, "*Vladaři a lu-*

piči"("Rulers and Robbers"), which appeared in the Brno journal *Lidové noviny* in March 1922. The report is framed in both tongue-in-cheek and ironic fashion. In 1985 Josef Poláček back-translated the story from Czech into German as *"Herrscher und Räuber"*, allowing a comparison between the German text of the play and the newspaper piece on which it was based.[35]

The comparison shows how Kisch fictionally embellished reportages and feuilletons when he converted their materials into plays. In reality the wax figure of Rothschild went for 11,000 marks publicly (knocked down to less than half that in the behind-the-scenes payoff by the agent from Rothschild's). The woman depicted in the play as the "stylish young Bohemian" got the figure of Austria's last Emperor, Karl I, for 420 marks; she owned a wine bar in Berlin. She announced she would place him in her bedroom as a reminder of the good old days, when she had been present as "one of the girls" at Goldschmied's Nightclub in Prague when the young Archduke Karl visited this 'high-class' brothel (see below for more on Goldschmied's). Though Kisch names many a foreign potentate among the museum's collection, King Edward VII is not one of them. Kisch may have substituted Edward for Karl in order to avoid censorship or hostile reviews, but, as Glosiková reports, the Czech government banned the use of Edward's name in the play, presumably out of deferemce to the sensibilities of the English, whose leaders had co-operated in the establishment of the First Czech Republic before and during the 1919 negotiations at Versailles. Sternickel is only one of a hundred or so famous criminals, jurists, and executioners, who, along with a historical collection of the implements of judicial torture, occupied the fourth floor of Castan's museum. As a 'connoisseur of crime' Kisch had probably made many a visit to this collection. From such meager materials, Kisch made his play, imaginatively adding the colloquy among the wax figures to enliven the occasion and expand its horizons.

The story of Piccaver concerns efforts of the theatrical eminence, Angelo Neumann, and his operatic counterpart, Vyzmětal, to recruit a famous American tenor, Alfred Piccaver, for the ensemble of the German National Theater in Prague. Their efforts succeed with the help a prostitute named Gisa. In his Prague newspaper pieces, and much later in his memoirs, Kisch wrote about Neumann as an impresario who dominated the German theater in Prague and could make or break productions and careers. His intention with this one-act play was to produce a light-hearted 'period sketch' reflecting the atmosphere of Prague theater and its public in the 'golden days' of the 1890s and the early 1900s. The piece premiered (in Czech) as *Piccaver v Salonu Goldschmied* at the Rokoko at the end of 1923.[36]

A prose version of the story came out in 1926's *Hetzjagd durch die Zeit*.[37] This piece, *Die Geheimnisse des Salons Goldschmied* ("The Secrets of Goldschmied's Salon") is an 18-page article that opens with a historical survey of prostitution, brothels, and city ordinances covering this illegal but always tolerated activity in Prague as it existed over five centuries. Goldschmied's brothel, established in the 1860s, was large and 'classy' (harboring private rooms, 'Turkish' and 'Japanese' salons, and dining facilities). It drew clients from the higher reaches of government, the army, and the arts (some of them named by Kisch). Its nickname among its international clientele was "Gogo". The Piccaver incident is only one among dozens of colorful tales Kisch tells about the institution and its clients, both famous and obscure. In this telling Piccaver arrives in Prague in 1907, goes carousing with two friends, and winds up in Goldschmied's where he takes a fancy to one of the girls, Mizzi, whom he serenades with famous love songs from operas. His passion is seemingly reciprocated by the smitten lady of the night. The Director of the (German) Opera, Trummer, is on the scene and informs Piccaver of Neumann's desire to speak with him. Piccaver misses the appointment, instead going back to Goldschmied's. Suddenly Neumann ("he who would never patronize a coffee house because it was beneath his dignity") shows up with Trummer in tow and they sign Piccaver to a one-year contract as a member of the German National Theater's ensemble, emphasizing that this will allow the singer to continue his affair (Piccaver has no idea that Mizzi is already on Neumann's payroll). Once again, from a one-page sketch in a long, variegated piece Kisch teased out a cabaret play through fictional embellishments.

In Volume 12 of the reissued Kisch *GW*, there is a text of the play that was back-translated from Czech into German.[38]

Another short play, comprising two scenes ("On the Street" and "In the Bar") was based on Kisch's reportage, *"Die Mutter des Mörders und der Reporter"* ("The Mother of the Murderer and the Reporter"). This heartfelt tale recounts the story of Mrs. Polanski, a washer-woman who is thrown into despair by the police detention of her son as a suspect in a burglary-murder case. "The reporter" (Kisch), who is a participant-observer in the story, interviews her and she suddenly expresses a willingness to take full responsibility for the way her son has turned out, to "take his sins on herself", as it were, claiming that in her youth her own heart was filled with hate and the desire to murder her child's father and the child himself. In her mind she is a worse 'murderer' than her son. Given her poverty and the harshness of her life hitherto, her willingness to accept blame for his actions is not merited by the circumstances, but her overpowering desire to protect her son drives her 'confession'. Even the happy ending of a son returning home (and demanding a meal!) after the police find the real murderer is not enough to assuage her guilt and despair.

Like the monologues of other similar characters in Kisch's stage works, Glosiková considers her speeches to be monologues in form, but dialogues in function. The absent parties are those in power who are implicitly indicted for creating the kind of conditions that overwhelm society's downtrodden. The Czech version of the play premiered at the Rokoko in November, 1924, under the title *Sensace Žurnalisty*. It was reviewed favorably in the Prague press and the play moved on to Brno, again eliciting a positive critical response. On this latter point Glosiková writes that Kisch was "overdoing it" when he claimed to be slighted by reviewers who raved about Longenová in the title role and the overall high quality of the production, while ignoring his authorship.[39] The prose version of the story was included in *Der rasende Reporter*[40] and was also returned to in Kisch's memoirs.[41] Poláček's back-translated text of the play (under the title *Sensationen eines Journalisten*) from Czech into German is in the reissued *GW*.[42]

The last theatrical work of Kisch's to premier on a Czech stage in the interwar era concerned the comical adventures of an eccentric whom Kisch had befriended in pre-war Prague, a man with the mellifluous name of Ferda Mestek de Podskal. In 1914 Mestek gave Kisch a bundle of dirty papers that were a memoir about his exploits as a dancing teacher, street merchant, and impresario of the flea circus, wondering if he could turn it into an article. Kisch did that and more. In 1920's *Die Abenteuer in Prag* Kisch wrote of Mestek in a humorous section titled *Dramaturgie des Flohtheaters* (Dramaturgy of the Flea Circus).[43] In 1925 he told Mestek's life story in serialized installments in *Lidové noviny*. He then reworked the material into a play, which was mounted in the Rokoko in March, 1925, appearing under the title *Jak si obšlap Ferda Mestek de Podskal na bleší divadlo,* followed by an even longer subtitle. The amplified title comes over into English as "How Ferda Mestek de Podskal got his concession for the flea circus — A grotesque historical Prague tale from the era of martial law in the 1890s." To build his play Kisch used scenes from Mestek's memoir which revolve around the man himself, his fiancé, his prospective father-in-law, and the city's governor (*Statthalter*) from whom the 'family team' is trying to win approval for his exotic (and highly questionable) commercial venture. Glosiková notes its inventive use of local dialect and its amusing anecdotal character, which allowed it to have a run appealing to Prague cabaret attendees for sentimental reasons, but cites the writer-critic Vladimir Ryba's review that the episodes should have been fleshed out and supplied with more continuity. Once again the cast featured Longen, Longenová, and Burian, always popular with audiences.[44] Such was the stuff and fate of Kisch's one-act plays.

As to his only solo full-length play, *Die gestohlene Stadt,* Glosiková tends to agree with the generally favorable reviews published in Prague and other Czech venues, where the play was performed both in German and Czech. The narrative line deals with an episode in the Seven Years War that brought Prussia's King Frederick the Great into contact with Prague's 'king of thieves', Käsebier, whom Frederick employed as a spy within the city. The two 'kings' engage in dialogues with comical elements that show the local rogue holding his own in conversation with the glorious war-lord and patron of high culture. This diminution of Frederick's stature might be accepted in some quarters in old Austria-Hungary, where the view of the Prussian monarch was generally negative: an ambitious, aggressive man who had stolen Upper Silesia from the Habsburg dynast, Queen Maria Theresa. But playing in this fashion with the character of such a national icon was bound to fuel negative criticism in Germany, as will be seen in discussing Josef Poláček's writing about the play. Even in Prague reviews of the play clashed, not so much on aesthetic merits as on Czech self-perceptions of how their land was being depicted. The respected novelist and critic Vladimir Vančura hailed it as "witty and adroit", while Jindřich Vodák thought the play was uncomplimentary to the city and the nation because "[Kisch] eagerly celebrates the Prussian king while portraying Prague as a city of prostitutes, spies, and Jews," coming to the opposite conclusion of German reviewers.[45]

Like the majority of Czech reviewers and critics in the 1920s, Glosiková approves of the play's anti-militarist message. In this connection she notes a rhetorical strand that appears in at least five of Kisch's plays, i.e., selecting a female character to voice Kisch's views on the state, social class, and warfare. Here the character Margit becomes a spokesperson for the common man and woman who must suffer and die by the thousands in a senseless war undertaken for the sole purpose of expanding the power and glory of the Prussian king.

Margit's pronouncements are consistent with the way Kisch uses the voices of women as social critics in his other works for the stage: Betka the prostitute in the play based on *The Pimp*; Toni Gallows through the recitation of her miserable life and suspicion of all authority; Franzi, the fiancé of Redl's protégé in *Die Hetzjagd*, who assails the morals and behavior of men of high position and status like Redl and his military and civilian colleagues; and the "mother of the murderer", Frau Polanski, on whom society has inflicted burdens beyond bearing. Is this feminism in the broadest sense of the word? Probably not, but Kisch does not seem to have engaged in any of the misogynistic conceits of his era, either those of the patriarchal bourgeois world or expressed in numerous works of art, traditional and modern, from the mediocre to the 'great'. Rather than feminism these allocations of social criticism to female characters may reflect Kisch's appreciation of the fact that women, along with children and the large mass of people without power or wealth, often suffer and have their lives rearranged in negative ways by those who exercise power and influence in everyone's everyday affairs: armies, the police, the judicial system, the wealthy, government officials, all in all, 'the authorities' who dominate society. Unfortunately the same patriarchal-punitive institutions often flourished in the communist societies that Kisch hoped would replace existing regimes.

In Czechoslovakia the German version of the play premiered in June, 1923, at Prague's New German Theater to overwhelmingly positive reviews and then moved on to productions in Brno and Olomouc, where it was equally well-received. Within a year the play had been translated into Czech and mounted on the stage of Prague's Apollo Theater as *Ukradená Praha* (Stolen Prague). A second series of performances started in late 1924, when Longen edited the play (making cuts and "tightening it up") and also directed it at the Rokoko under another title change, *Král zlodějů* (The King of Thieves).[46] Its performance history and reception in Germany are discussed below in a summary of Polaček's remarks on how the play fared in that country. The original prose narrative from which the play was later developed appeared as a three-page newspaper historical essay, *"Der Erzfilou Käsebier vor Prag"* ("The Scoundrel Käsebier at The Gates of Prague"), in *Prager Tagblatt* in March, 1921.[47] Kisch came back to the story again, rewriting it almost completely as *"Käsebier und Fridericus Rex"*, published in his 1931 collection of pieces, *Prager Pitaval*.[48]

Like other writers who have treated the plays about Toni Gallows and Colonel Alfred Redl, Glosiková notes the broad popularity of and positive critical response to these two works. *Tonka Šibenice* was hailed as a robust presentation of the experiences of society's marginal people, while *Die Hetzjagd* was seen to effectively present the case against militarism and the dereliction of Habsburg society's most privileged members. Having translations of the two plays above, the reader does not require a synopsis of either work. Chapters 4 and 6 above give the reader information on the sources of the plays in Kisch's feuilletons and books, while Josef Polacek's additional remarks about the variant versions of the stories are given below.

Regarding performance histories and critical reactions to the two plays, Glosiková is typically thorough and even-handed.[50] Within ten months after his newspaper sketch of Toni Gallows, Kisch, at the urging of Longen, had worked the materials into a Czech script for a play. It premiered at the Revolutionary Stage under the title *Tonka Šibenice na onom světě* in October, 1921. Xena Longenová played Tonka. Reviews in Prague were favorable. In mid-1923 Longen took the play to Brno, where an uncooperative local theater ensemble and sharply hostile critical reactions quickly terminated its run. Back in Prague Longen re-presented the play at the Rokoko, where he had become the theater's "leading personality" who promised productions of high dramatic quality. A prominent Czech critic complained that Toni's monologue dominated the play to the extent of reducing other characters to meaningless roles. As noted above, Glosiková made the observation that Toni's monologues were conceived as "implicit dialogues" in which an oppressive society and middle-class culture were silent voices. The first German version of the play was put on in October, 1922 at Berlin's *Die Rampe* Theater, starring Rosa Valetti, who moved, along with the play, to the *Rakete*. Glosiková continues her discussion of the play's long afterlife with an account of an early 1930s lawsuit in Prague, in which Kisch took on the producers of a musical version of the Tonka story that totally transformed her character, the nature of the role, and the play's message. She ends with remarks about the 1930 film adaptation of the play and a proposed new film for which Karel Čapek was hired as screenwriter (an eight-page typescript text of his treatment exists). This last effort to revive 'a real Prague legend' came to naught after the dire events of September-October, 1938 eventuated in Czechoslovakia's final dismemberment by Germany six months later (Čapek himself died in December, 1938). However, parts of Čapek's treatment influenced a 1978 revival of the play in East Germany, which is discussed in Chapter 10 below.

The Czech version of Kisch's "famous and often-performed" play about Redl's final day premiered at the Rokoko in January, 1924, under the title *Vyzvědačská aféra obstra Redla*. The production featured Longen as Redl (a role he repeated in the Czech-language release of the 1931 Redl film), Longenová as his protégé's fiancé, Franzi, and Vlasta Burian as Archduke Viktor Salvator (a suitable role for an actor the Czechs called "the king of comedy"). The comic role of the Archduke embodied, as Longen opined, "The mindlessness of Austrian militarism" and "the degenerate idiocy of a man accorded the highest honors". This version of the play ran 175 times in Prague and 120 times in other Czech venues. Glosiková notes the appearance of the German text of the play, *Die Hetzjagd*, in Kisch's 1926 book but makes no mention of when and where it was performed in Germany and Austria during the mid- or late 1920s; its 1930 revival in Berlin is discussed below. She deems the Czech and German versions of the play's narrative line to be virtually identical. The play's very effective comic dialogues, inflected by irony and sarcasm, are emphasized as contributing to its popularity. Its anti-military and anti-monarchical sentiments are clear, as is its depiction of Redl as a high-ranking representative of Austrian society who abuses his power for his own ends. This, of course, is what most audiences and critics took away from the play.[51]

The second Prague Germanist who examined a subset of three of Kisch's plays is Josef Poláček, who edited the last four of twelve volumes that comprise the reissued Kisch Collected Works and also co-wrote many of their Introductions and Afterwords with Kisch's biographer, Fritz Hofmann.[52] In the final two volumes of the *GW*, he back-translated numerous pieces written by Kisch that first appeared in several other languages (mostly Czech, but also Slovak, Russian and English) into German.[53] Poláček's earliest research findings about particular Kisch works came out in the 1960s. Of relevance to the factual story behind *Die Hetzjagd* is his reporting of mistakes and misrepresentations in Kisch's 1924 book about the Redl case, discussed in Chapter 4 above. In his 1991 article about Kisch's involvement with theater in Berlin over the years, he focused his attention on *Galgentoni*, *Die gestohlene Stadt*, and *Die Hetzjagd*, noting that the historical record can establish definitively that only two other of his plays were performed in German, the cabaret piece, *Letzte Nacht in Castans Panoptikum*, and the full-length play co-written with Hašek, *Die Reise um Europa in 365 Tagen.*[54]

In dealing with the Toni Gallows play, Poláček unraveled its complicated textual variations, where different versions of the plays were put on, and what the basis and results of censorship attempts were.[55] As discussed in Chapter 6, there were four long variants of the narrative in German, published between 1922 and 1942, three as play-texts and one as a prose reminiscence. The first version of the play is set in Hamburg and Berlin. Berlin enters the story after Toni leaves a small Hamburg brothel, the "Blue Ape", fleeing harassment by other prostitutes. She returns to her "sweet hometown", Berlin, to walk its mean streets for the next thirty years. The Berlin passages account for only a small part of the text, and were probably inserted to give Berlin playgoers a touch of local color; in this version Toni is a native Berliner, so her dialect and slang are those of the capital city (Chapter 2 provides the reader with details on the textual sources of the play's several versions).[56] The second published text of the play, set in Prague and translated in Chapter 5 above, is lengthened by new dialogues among several parties, some for purposes of deepening characterizations, others to add Prague local-color touches. In the next version that came out in 1927's collection, *Wagnisse in aller Welt*, the slightly edited text of the 1922 play was re-published, returning the scene to Hamburg and Berlin.[57] Appropriately, since it appeared in his 1941-42 memoirs, the final version is a prose retelling of the story set in Prague; with the exception of one subsidiary character, names are again in Czech.[58] As he reworked material from one variant to the next Kisch rewrote sentences and paragraphs, deleted elements of earlier versions, and added some new episodes and dialogue; however, the overall narrative, the flow of the story, and the principal episodes in Toni's earthly life remain the same throughout. The characterizations of Toni, her companions, and the divine judge and his assistants are also consistent in the different versions, though in the 1926 text the President of the divine court of judgment is sketched in a more dignified fashion. In all German variants of the play he is the only character who speaks without using slang and with a proper accent.

Poláček notes that extant performance records and reviews do not allow a completely clear picture of which variant text was used for performances in some cities. As to the three versions for the stage just cited, one should realize these refer to published texts and not necessarily to actors' scripts used for the numerous performances that took place in different locations over a period of seven or eight years. Kisch's willingness to transform "a real Prague legend" into a Hamburg-Berlin story shows his opportunism and constant search for new audiences (and revenues), something he could do with cabaret-play texts but not with reportages that he rewrote.

Poláček records the largely enthusiastic responses of a number of both local and prominent national critics and literary men to the play and quotes their fulsome praise of two actresses who excelled in portraying Toni. In Prague Xena Longenová was lauded for her affecting interpretation of the character ("full of genuine pathos"). In Berlin and Vienna Rosa Valetti impressed the audience with the defiant storminess of her performance. Valetti, who 'took the show on the road', claimed that the conservative Roman Catholic citizens of Cologne reacted positively to the play, in spite of local critics tarring it as blasphemous. She thought the audience correctly perceived its underlying message of Christian charity. Poláček also quotes from several extremely negative reviews — among the latter are the observations of a Viennese critic that in a performance in that city the cast had used a veritable mish-mash of accents and dialects that made the play misfire in its attempt to add 'local color' to the piece.[59] Poláček also included Kisch's own reactions to the critical furor over the play, quoting his responses to questions posed in a 1922 Viennese newspaper interview. Kisch remarked that while some German, Austrian, and Czech critics found smuttiness in the play, it was also often praised for its ethical-social message by local critics and well-known actors and actresses in several cities, a fact in which he took pride. Furthermore, critical reactions in Paris and Milan (where the play was put on in translation) never even raised these points as issues. Besides, Kisch noted, in spite of his intended critical social message, the play was a "bagatelle" that should hardly have aroused anyone's fury.[60]

Unlike Kisch's willingness to accept the Galgentoni play as a successful piece of popular entertainment, his ambition for *Die gestohlene Stadt*, as noted by Poláček, was that it would establish his reputation as a substantial dramatist, more than just an occasionally successful dabbler in the cabaret-play and one-act forms. It was not to be, at least not in Germany. The play's text was published in 1922. The panned 1924 debut performance in Teplitz-Schönau, mentioned above, resulted in a very short run. Glosiková characterized *Der Tag*, the paper that published the damning review of the Teplitz production and spearheaded a campaign against Kisch and the play, as "fascist in its orientation".[61] It was withdrawn and withheld from production until Kisch could secure a theater in Stuttgart that was willing to include it in a proposed program bringing new playwrights to the public's attention. The overwhelming critical reaction to the few Stuttgart performances in July, 1925, was that the play fell between being a poorly thought-out mediocrity and a disaster. Especially negative were the repeated critical comments about Kisch's handling of one of its two main characters, King Frederick the Great, who is brought into melodramatic and comedic contrast (and implied equality) with Käsebier, a Prague rogue who controls criminal forces in the city and is employed as a spy by Frederick.

Frederick was a German icon and idol (though not an Austrian one), and not just among extreme nationalists. Given the long history of German literary and dramatic treatments of the King's life, the critics thought Kisch shed no new or alternative light on him—they found the play lacking an "inner necessity" (in contrast to *Galgentoni* or *Die Hetzjagd*) and his dialogues boring, clumsy, and implausible. In early 1926 Dr. Jo Lherman, who had directed the play in Stuttgart, planned to mount it again in Berlin. Erich Reiss, Kisch's publisher, intervened. Based on his belief that

Lherman's casting was shoddy and his scheduling of only mat-
inees would harm Kisch's reputation and purse, Reiss stated in the
press that, as holder of both the copyright and the stage rights, he
would legally enjoin the production. Kisch was absent in Russia
and not embroiled in what proved to be a fiasco, amply covered
by the local newspapers, with Lherman abruptly vanishing from
the scene and the play never again being revived.[62]

Poláček confined his remarks about *Die Hetzjagd* to the political and cultural climate of Berlin when, after a performance hiatus
of several years, the play was mounted in that city's *Kaberett der
Komiker* in November, 1930. The immediate context, on everyone's
mind, was the large nationwide Nazi gain of Reichstag seats after
a recent election, ominous to those on the left of the political spectrum. Critical opinion in the Berlin press was divided on this
point. Liberals and those farther to the left hailed the play as an
antidote to renascent militarism and chauvinism expressed in the
election result. Others thought Kisch's play was by this time out-
dated.[63] They may have had a good point. While *Die Hetzjagd's*
explicit anti-militarism and implicit criticism of a class-based system of rule still had purchase in the present, these messages were
embedded in an Austrian anti-monarchist viewpoint that was no
longer relevant (and, as Schlenstedt pointed out, its comedy vitiat-
ed its more serious messages).

When one acknowledges the differences between Vienna in
1913 and Berlin in 1930, the critique of a faulty or overdrawn historical comparison is strengthened. In Berlin people were faced
with the possible takeover of the State by a fringe party that was
becoming mainstream, with a growing popular belief that the exotic specimen, Adolf Hitler, might prove to be a 'national savior'
(economically and socially, and as the paragon of protest against
the Versailles settlement of 1919). In Vienna in 1913 there was
widespread anxiety over the Balkan wars and the strident nationalism that threatened to destabilize the Dual Monarchy, while
Conrad von Hötzendorf viewed himself as a national savior too
(though he had formidable foes in the cabinet, War Ministry, and
at court). But Conrad's proposed means of salvation was limited
to "quick, clean wars" (as he imagined them) against Serbia or Ita-

ly, a far less grandiose program than Hitler's. It took the assassination at Sarajevo to turn the minds of Austria's leadership in Conrad's direction, leading to a near-hysterical abandonment of diplomatic caution. In fact, the problems of late Habsburg society might have been remedied through incremental changes and concessions.

In contrast, in the minds of an increasing number of Germans, the problems of Depression-era Germany required a drastic solution, one in which they were willing to sacrifice their own freedom of action to the right 'strongman'. A doctrinaire communist interpretation of the 1930s would attempt to make the Wilhelmine and late Habsburg era and the advent of Hitler into a sort of seamless strain of anti-progressive political forces unfolding on the 'dialectical stage of History'; this is barely an analytical approach at all, resting on critical terms resistant to empirical findings. On the other hand, a cabaret play is just that, an entertainment of limited public penetration, whether its political implications are deemed by critics to be relevant or not. The interpretation of the Berlin revival of *Die Hetzjagd* as a weathervane of German political winds seems therefore overdawn.

As to critical judgments of these three plays, Poláček did not express his own opinion; rather he bundled together positive and negative reviews and commentary from the years 1921-1930, letting the preponderant tendency of reviewers speak for itself. Thus *Galgentoni* (or *Tonka*) is indirectly evaluated as a successful comedic drama based on its long runs in several cities, the praise of its lead actresses, and the critical consensus that it dealt with unseemly matters (the life of a member of the demi-monde) in a modern, sympathetic, and socially relevant manner. Poláček did not contest the overwhelming majority (German) opinion of *Die gestohlene Stadt* as a lackluster failure. And, other than his politically-framed remarks about the revived Redl play, he was willing to let the findings and commentary of his former pupil, Viera Glosiková, stand as a more comprehensive critical look at the play than he himself undertook.

One other aspect of Kisch's writing in general, including works for the stage, should be mentioned here: the question of his relationship with German-language readers who were living in three very different political and cultural environments during the late-Habsburg and interwar years. In *Edge of Irony* Marjorie Perloff examined one aspect of this question, i.e., the distinctive mentality of Austrian writers who had matured during the final decades of the Dual Monarchy, as opposed to the outlook of Wilhelmine-era German authors. As she contends, 'Austro-modernism' of the interwar era was quite different from its German counterpart—Austrian and German writers had very different cultural inheritances, experiences, and affective responses to the postwar world.[64] Kisch had 'migrated' from the Austrian to the German milieu, but tried to keep a foot in each camp. Like most writers, he wished for as large a readership as possible. Yet at times he had to tailor his writing to more limited audiences or forego specific audiences altogether. Such constraining conditions also applied to his plays, both as theatrical performances and as texts published in various collections. In short—just like writers—readers in Germany, Austria, and Czechoslovakia did not have identical taste, interests, and biases. While his German audience was large and diverse enough to embrace readers with a critical attitude about contemporary German and Austrian political and cultural life, Kisch's flippancy about the 'good old days' of the Dual Monarchy met with critical resistance in Austria.

As to his readership in Czechoslovakia, it was bound to be influenced by the ages-old rivalry between Czechs and Germans who, after 1918, resided in the new First Republic. Kisch himself had written about the increasing self-segregation of the two ethnic and linguistic communities in Prague.[65] Regarding this piece ("Czechs and Germans"), in *The Coasts of Bohemia* Derek Sayer amended Kisch's somewhat misleading account of the socio-economic class composition of the Prague German community.[66] (Kisch wrote that Prague had no German working class—it did, and it was more integrated into Czech society than the German middle class and Bohemian-German intellectuals or literati.) The broad context of this strife between the two nationalities had its roots in 19th century political and cultural trends that are well-described in Gary Cohen's *The Politics of Ethnic Survival*.[67] Cohen also notes the struggle's dire implications for the city's Jews, many of whom felt themselves stranded between Czechs and Germans, neither of which welcomed them as allies, much less as members of their own 'national communities'. Nonetheless, many Jews opted to join one side or the other or, like Kisch, imagined they might somehow mediate between them.[68] Spector analyzed Kisch and his fellow Prague German-Jewish writers in terms of their beliefs and writing as measured by three "axial" features that mapped their position with respect to German-Czech identity conflicts and how Jews fit into this struggle: nation or ethnicity (*Volk*), cultural affiliation ("language"), and territory (homeland or *Heimat*).[69] Kisch's solution to these conflicts was twofold: as a writer he chose to use German and Czech everyday language to depict common men and women (vibrant 'low culture'); as a citizen and activist he committed to international socialist politics that would presumably eradicate ethnic strife and the identity problems generating it and derived from it.

Kisch, of course, was one of the potentially isolated 'men in the middle', but he had several advantages over most postwar German citizens of Czechoslovakia or Czech Jews who had identified with German culture and language. While Germans were declining in number and influence in cities like Prague and Brno, there were still large numbers of older Czechs who spoke and read German and thought of Kisch as a local celebrity who had done well in the wider world; they were part of his readership. However, his supportive attitude about the new Czechoslovakian Republic would have lost him many German readers in that country, especially among their largest grouping, the 'Sudetenland Germans', who longed for absorption by Germany and had little interest in being guided toward compromise by German liberals or their offspring, who were centered in Prague. Kisch also kept a professional foothold in Czechoslovakia through continuing translation of his books into Czech by well-disposed publishers[70], his own writing in Czech (mostly articles for Brno's *Lidové noviny*[71]), and his involvement with Longen's theatrical circle.

In discussing Kisch's 'hybrid' status with respect to new Czech artistic developments, the simplest and most straightfor-

ward way to state it is: in his first decade as a journalist (and novelist) Kisch was on the margins of liberal Bohemian-German culture, with which the 'Prague circle' had both a dependent and adversarial relationship. A further qualifier to this is that, although
he was Jewish, Kisch had a temperament, a background of daily
experience, and literary aims that did not align with the anxious
viewpoint and artistic goals common to the 'Jewish contingent' of
this German-oriented milieu (i.e., he was less introspective and
had stronger everyday ties to Czech society and culture than Kafka, Brod, or Werfel). The present author has written about Kisch's
views on 'Jewish identity self-construction', as seen in an amusing
story in which he paints a portrait of a Prague working-class Jew
who professes respect for all religious sentiments, yet resorts to
fisticuffs whenever disparaged on account of his ethnicity.[72]

As far as the generational outlook of his Czech age-mates is
concerned, this has been exceptionally well-characterized by
Thomas Ort in his book, *Art and Life in Modernist Prague*. In Ort's
terms (though he does not mention Kisch), during his youth Kisch
shared the attitudes about art and society held by his confident,
forward-looking Czech counterparts in 'the Čapek generation', a
group-designation that Ort (like Čapek himself) believes to be at
times accurate, at times misleading.[73] With respect to postwar developments, Kisch's reaction to the disaster of the war was less
cultural and more political. His views aligned with those of the
nascent Czech communists of the 1920s, whose dogmatic 'revolutionary' beliefs were advanced by the *Devětsil* group and 'program'.[74] While he was equally smitten with the 'new man' and the
'new life' in the USSR, Kisch was seldom as inflexible as his Czech
counterparts, and his writing of the 1930s illustrates a wide range
of interests beyond the normal left-vs.-right terms of debate.

Kisch's reputation as a leftist activist lost him conservative
readers in Germany and Austria, but his increasing fame as a colorful, adventurous journalist appealed to many readers regardless
of their political orientation. All of these subtle distinctions among
various groups of German-language readers became meaningless
after the 1933 ban of his works in Nazi Germany. Now his German audience was truly reduced, though he managed to find pub-

lishers in cities like Amsterdam, Paris, New York, Moscow, and Mexico City. An interesting example of just how thoroughly he had vanished from the minds of younger German readers can be found in an article by Max von der Grün, a man of the Hitler-Youth generation who first encountered Kisch's writing while in a prisoner-of-war camp in Louisiana.[75] It was only after 1945 that Kisch could re-establish a larger German readership and also cultivate a whole generation of younger Germans who had no access to his work during the twelve years of the Third Reich.

Returning from Kisch's 'readership problems' that stemmed from cultural, political, and economic ('market') factors, it is appropriate to sum up the foregoing discussion of his plays. Excepting the co-written *Die Schwestern Teige*, about which information is difficult to obtain, this chapter includes descriptions of all of Kisch's plays, most of what can be known about their performance histories, and an account of critical responses to them. It is not exhaustive, but it does summarize the research and commentary of Kisch's four major biographers (three German, one American) and two Czech specialists who devoted attention to this aspect of his writing. While the preceding discussion deals with the content of Kisch's plays and critical reactions to them, the plays were being performed in a context of competing works, some by outstanding playwrights, others by writers who enjoyed brief vogues and several years of success, and yet others by writers who are all but unknown today. This broader literary and theatrical context is examined in the next chapter.

Chapter 8. Theatrical Context:
German Playwrights and Weimar Comedy and Cabaret

When Kisch embarked upon his several years of close involvement with E. A. Longen's Revolutionary Stage in Prague, he was entering a theatrical world that had well-defined conventions but was also being re-organized (and disrupted) by ambitious producers, directors and playwrights who wished to take theater in new directions. The middle-class drama, repeatedly handling the old themes of romantic love, marriage, family conflicts, and (occasionally) the strivings of heroic individuals who wished to set themselves apart from contemporary social constraints, could still find an audience, though it had to take into account current background social conditions and attitudes (i.e., 'modernity' influenced all aspects of life). The heroic nationalist drama, which had blossomed on theatrical and operatic stages as part of movements for political and cultural autonomy during the nineteenth century, seemed either pompous or politically unnecessary on account of the results of World War I. Before the war these older types of play already had competitors, as seen in the works of powerful dramatists such as Chekov, Strindberg, Ibsen, and Hauptmann. Their departures involved neither the settings of plays (parlor, home, country estate) nor the social niche of depicted characters, but rather the intensity of their psychological scrutiny.

In Austria and Germany during the years immediately preceding and following the war Arthur Schnitzler and Frank Wedekind come to mind as playwrights whose works can be used as a standard of comparison for their peers and successors. While they shared several decades of Late Habsburg-era experience with Kisch, they were a generation older, exposing them to a rapidly changing set of conditions that had led to the world Kisch knew during his first three decades of life. The 1860s–1870s yielded the failure of liberalism, the rapid growth of separatist nationalism, increasingly strident anti-Semitism, and the emergence of the first

inklings of modernism in all the arts. By the 1890s the consolida-
tion of socialism as a parliamentary force had also taken
place—these were the new conditions of life when Kisch was
growing up and commenced his career. Admittedly, looking at the
works of these two dramatists is a highly selective or even forced
basis for comparison, but they can stand in for the larger cohort of
writers who conducted their careers as playwrights ambitiously
and earnestly, which Kisch might have once thought of doing, but
in fact never did.

Both of these dramatists looked at existing social fissures and
sexual behavior in a frank manner (which their critics called
"coarse", "brutal" or "pornographic"). Their most adventurous
works for the stage (Schnitzler's *Reigen*, better known as *La Ronde*,
and Wedekind's *"Lulu"* plays in both early and late versions) were
censored before 1918 and not performed in Germany or Austria
until the 1920s. Schnitzler's novels and novellas had also been assailed by conservative critics for their unseemly dwelling on sexual relations and for their critical appraisal of the damaging absurd-
ities of accepted and admired Austrian social conventions. In a
new stream-of-consciousness style (before James Joyce, one
should mention), his novella *Leutnant Gustl* depicted the mental
life of a typical Viennese professional military man in extremely
unflattering terms: the protagonist, "Little August", was narcissis-
tic, vain, arrogant, childish, and thoroughly irresponsible. Conservative middle-class critics considered the story an assault on
the honor of the Austro-Hungarian army, resulting in Schnitzler
being stripped of his commission as a reserve officer. Earlier in his
career he had raised eyebrows with his presentation of intertwined issues of anti-Semitism and progressive medicine in his
play *Professor Bernhardi*, based on the difficulties his physician father had encountered during his professional life.

Other Jewish artists dealt with similar themes, with some notable exceptions, primarily Franz Kafka, who transformed his anxieties over being a Jew in Europe into allegorical stories (often
blackly comic) that never once mentioned the word "Jew"; however, his notebooks, diaries, and letters brought the discussion
back to earth in this respect. In contrast, in his 1908 novel *Der Weg*

ins Freie (*The Road to the Open*, understood as "the path to freedom from prejudice") Schnitzler examined every intellectual stance, social behavior, and 'escape route' available to middle-class Jews: cultural assimilation, religious conversion, extreme Orthodoxy, 'cultural Zionism', emigrationist political Zionism, and pan-German chauvinism. He came to the conclusion that none were viable as a response to the era's prevalent anti-Semitism, though many an Austrian, German or Czech Jew pursued such alternate paths. The novel could just as well have been titled "No Exit" (for Jews, that is). The Gentile character at the center of the narrative, Baron Georg von Wergenthin was there to point out that exits from negative social judgments were available to others, but not Jews. Wergenthin finds an easy escape from his personal and ethical problems by moving from Vienna to Germany and taking up a professional position in a city where no one need know of his past indiscretions and questionable behavior (he is a self-absorbed aesthete who misinterprets his own experience—his social anxiety about the opinion of others outweighs any guilt he feels about his failed affair, illicit offspring, and the consequences of his actions). But none of his Jewish friends and acquaintances can escape their social dilemmas—they will be damned if they do something in particular and equally damned if they don't do it, with the remark, "that's just like a Jew".

This is the kind of absurd generalization and broad stereotyping that enabled a later generation to believe that Jews were 'international criminals' responsible for both the sins of capitalism and those of its fiercest enemy, Bolshevism. Both of these vast modern social forces were alleged to be prongs of an evil 'Jewish conspiracy' to control the world (as in that supreme fantasy of forgery, *The Protocols of the Elders of Zion*). In comparison, as a journalist and essayist Kisch wrote a fair number of pieces that addressed the era's anti-Semitism, but he never produced anything as panoptic and penetrating as Schnitzler's novel about this subject. While Kisch believed political programs would eliminate anti-Semitism, artists like Schnitzler were more pessimistic, based on their understanding of the dark underside of human consciousness.

When it came to sexuality, Wedekind and Schnitzler not only dealt with it openly, thereby violating bourgeois taboos, but also addressed its importance in human social relations, probing its insistent compulsions, its attractions, and its ability to elicit repulsion in both heterosexual and homosexual variants. Kisch's Redl play displays benign neutrality about homosexuality. His Toni Gallows story sticks to the surface of what it means to be a prostitute, while implicitly criticizing official and middle-class censoriousness about a phenomenon in which these conservative elements of society were effectively collaborators. However, these plays lack the depth of insight into sexuality achieved by Schnitzler and Wedekind. For example, Kisch's neutrality about sexuality, including homosexuality, does not probe the inner conflicts or social harm and ostracism that specific sexual behaviors might bring about, in contrast to Schnitzler's and Wedekind's treatments of this fraught topic. As Wedekind eventually concluded, unconstrained sexual activity, initially believed to be liberating, can lead to misery and self-destruction (which, in his suicide note, the real Redl acknowledged too).

A close contemporary of Kisch's, Robert Musil, had also gone down the path of 'depth psychology' when writing about sexual relations in *The Confusions of Young Törless* and in *The Man without Qualities*. In the former, adolescent homosexual pairings were the product of forced segregation of the sexes (the military school environment) and the efforts of several characters to achieve and exert dominance over their fellow pupils, i.e., 'power plays'. In the latter Musil ruminated on many areas of life where intimate personal experience intersected with a social milieu characterized in turn by false bravado, anxiety, romantic illusions, and revulsion about sex. He did this through a series of intertwined 'case histories' presenting a spectrum of "psycho-sexual problems": a mentally sluggish, depraved, socially alienated serial killer of women, who attracts a circle of wealthy women seeking excitement by visiting an asylum in order to gawk at the beast himself; an hysterical victim of paternal incest who converts her wild energies into aestheticism and a psychological war against her husband; a well-off matron whose extramarital liaisons are undertaken for reasons of cultural climbing and imagined self-improvement; and the possibility of the aloof protagonist's sexual liaison with his sister, a reciprocal attraction based on mental and emotional compatibility and the idea that each has been missing his and her complementary half (a 'twinning' or 'self-replication' theme). Kisch was not the kind of man or writer who could probe these depths, either in reportage or a stage treatment.

Another standard of comparison for Kisch's writing for the stage can be found in several post-World War I exemplars of inventive Expressionist and social-critical plays (e.g., Ernst Toller and Berthold Brecht, who shared Kisch's left-wing politics). But, just as he was not competing with eminences like Schnitzler and Wedekind, Kisch was not aiming this high either in the realm of experimental theater—he knew, or learned, his own limits (he thought Expressionism was a dead end, but found that his own 'sociological realism' could not compete with works by professional playwrights). In the Redl play he mollified his didactic message about the incompetence and frivolity of Austria-Hungary's leaders with broad, unsophisticated comedy that would appeal to cabaret-theater audiences. While the Toni Gallows play was rougher, it also contained enough farce and verbal comedy to make it as entertaining as it might be thought-provoking with regard to social inequities. Given the modesty of Kisch's theatrical ambitions for these two plays and the nature of his writing for the stage, it makes more sense to consider them in terms of the variety of comedies presented to the 1920s German public, as described and evaluated by William Grange in his book, *Comedy in the Weimar Republic*. Grange's study surveys the field, provides a genealogy of German comedy written for the stage, and describes its variant forms, its economics, and its durability as popular art.[1]

Grange records that during the fourteen years of the Weimar government the stages of Berlin, Hamburg, Munich, Frankfurt, and numerous smaller cities hosted nearly 900 productions of comedies. The vast majority of plays listed in his annual tables from the years starting with the 1918-19 season and running through March, 1933, were premieres, including translations of plays from England, France, and the US.[2] Grange's list for the

1924-1925 season contains Kisch's only full-length play, the historical comedy *Die gestohlene Stadt* (The Stolen City); though he makes no comments on the play, many of Kisch's contemporaries did, as discussed above.[3] Comedy is not a uniform genre, reflected by Grange's comments on descriptive labels for its many different types, each with a peculiar framing, subject matter, and accent (whimsical, satirical, farcical, didactic, etc.):

> Popular comedy was distinguished by various genre labels, such as Lustspiel, Schwank, Komödie, Volkstück, Besserungstück, Zauberstück, Lokalposse, Zauberposse, or simply Posse.[4]

Eminent playwrights also tried their hand at popular and cabaret comedy during stages of their careers when they wanted to broaden their audience or needed a financial success. After a brief flurry of sensational and critically hailed productions in the early 1920s, Expressionist and experimental theater faltered because the (mostly middle-class) play-going German public found it too cerebral, abstract, or didactic.[5] They wanted to see more tried-and-true, less taxing approaches. Therefore, comedy was king on the Weimar Republic's stages.

Upon reflection, the reasons why conventional comedy prevailed are obvious. The years between 1918 and 1923 were turbulent and socially destabilizing: a lost war and the accompanying loss of Germany's border territories to France and Poland; a collapsed monarchy; a Social Democratic government that deployed police, army units, and even right-wing *Freikorps* bands to put down a leftist revolutionary movement (the Sparticists) and subsequent demonstrations; a disgruntled cohort of war veterans; an inflationary spiral of 1921-1923 that robbed millions of their savings and pensions; a thriving black market; the assassination of prominent leaders (Erzberger, Rathenau); the shame and burden of the Versailles treaty, including its 'war-guilt' clause; Allied occupation of the Rhineland; the administration of the Saarland given over to France for fifteen years; and the drain on the economy brought about by mandatory reparations payments (when Germany was unable pay in 1923, French troops occupied the Ruhr industrial basin for almost two years—forcibly exporting coal instead of cash, indicating Germany's impotence). 'Cataclysmic' seems the right word to state the effects of these events upon many German minds. They acted in the manner of an earthquake, shaking up beliefs and the underpinnings of material and mental stability, which had already been degraded by the dire effects World War I had on civilian material welfare and traditional social and cultural values. After a six-year interval of relative recovery, the Depression arrived in 1930, plunging Germany's citizens back into the cauldron of economic uncertainty, mass unemployment, and bitter, adversarial politics, with electoral gains going to the extreme left and right at the expense of centrist parties. And so, off to the theater or the movies to enjoy a good comedy and a few hours of respite from these distressing realities. For similar reasons light-hearted comedies and musicals dominated American theater and film during the Depression of the 1930s.

This superabundance of comic works, many of which were conventional and formulaic, catered to the taste of Germany's large middle-class population, who, under duress, yearned for earlier certainties and stable prospects. Their volume was so great that Grange refers to them as "industrial comedies", i.e., works that were mass-produced by their authors, including famous two-man teams of writers (e.g., Franz Arnold and Ernst Bach, who concocted a succession of annual hits during the Weimar era). These plays relied on theatrical formulas that used popular stereotypes of members of the aristocracy and the middle- and working-classes. Many were farces deploying vanished relatives who suddenly re-appear (e.g., an American cowboy who is the long-lost heir of a German nobleman), bastard children who enter a family's life through sheer chance, bedroom antics with lovers and mistresses, mistaken identities, mutual misunderstandings, sudden reversals of fortune such as the fate of rags-to-riches parvenus who ape their 'betters', marital strife and deception, intergenerational animosity, and the whole panoply of contrived situations and stage devices enabling surprises: characters hiding in closets, exiting while someone enters an eye-blink later, or dropping through trapdoors. Usually they ended in a resolution (reconciliation and 'getting on with life') that allowed the audience to depart in an untroubled mood. The resilience of their protagonists was considered admirable and reassuring.

But there were other kinds of comedies that went beyond the formulaic or that parodied the formulas in such an extreme way that audiences realized that the conventions were being undermined and used ironically, yet in an acceptable (i.e., entertaining) manner. Grange calls these "critical comedies"—their goal was not only to entertain the audience but also to take a critical look at Germany's current social and political realities. Commonplace targets were the corruption of public officials, the remoteness of society's leaders from the lives of most German citizens, the self-imposed social isolation and small horizons of the middle class, the rampant greed that resulted in financial chicanery, get-rich-quick schemes, fraudulent speculators, suave confidence men, and German servility towards authority, especially men in uniform. On the lattermost point the smash hit of the 1930-32 seasons was Carl Zuckmayer's *Der Hauptmann von Köpenick*, based on the real 1906 adventure of a middle-aged shoemaker and occasional jailbird named Wilhelm Voigt. Wearing a Prussian Captain's uniform and simulating a blustering military man, he hijacked a small detachment of troops and looted the town treasury of a Berlin suburb, with the ready acquiescence of the town's mayor and other citizens.[6] Here contemporary life had proved to be as surrealistic and farcical as its portrayal on the stage, all due to unthinking reverence for authority.

Kisch's two best-known works written for cabaret stages, *Die Hetzjagd* and *Die Himmelfahrt der Tonka Šibenice*, can be seen to fit into Grange's characterization of Weimar-era critical comedies. But, in terms of widespread productions and audience response, he could not compete with the dozen or so star playwrights who dominated the German comic stage throughout the Weimar era. Unlike playwrights who were professional theater men from the outset of their careers, often starting out as actors and assuming directorial or production roles, Kisch came from another sector of the popular arts, literary journalism in the form of reportage. Lacking this professional basis, his theatrical works fall in the middle range. Segel described his plays as interesting stories with some good comic dialogue and a nice satirical or ironic edge.[7] This is correct, noting that whatever their merits, Kisch's plays did not win over large audiences and the backing of more substantial theaters that had to pay their way by presenting works that promised broader success. And yet both of these cabaret works were considered interesting enough to undergo film adaptations, reaching larger audiences in a medium that was the true popular art of the twentieth century.

How did cabaret comedies fit into the larger scheme of full-length plays mounted in traditional theaters, the subject of Grange's analysis? Cabaret began in Paris in the 1880s. In the early phases of its development staged plays (or, given the constraint of brevity, 'scenes' or 'sketches') were not the main element of cabaret, and, even after their insertion into playbills, they remained only one ingredient in the nightly fare of cabaret troupes and theaters. Ballads, soulful chansons ('street songs') that often dealt with crime or the miseries of urban life, puppetry, ventriloquism, comedians who commented farcically on current social trends and political events, music (jazz by the 1920s), and dancers all contributed to the type of show presented in cabaret theaters. Stage scenery and props were minimal or impressionistic in design, and there was no attempt to frame scenes or sketches in a way that would encourage the audience to accept that they were viewing a 'natural' or realistic venue. Transparent artifice was more than acceptable, it was progressive and even 'postmodern' in the sense that a performer could directly address the audience with remarks on the artificiality of the enterprise he (or she) and they were engaged in. As to the viability and popularity of cabaret theater during Kisch's play-writing days, Grange, in a note about Rosa Valetti's opening of her theater (*Die Rampe*) in 1922, recorded that at that time there were 37 other cabaret stages operating in Berlin.[8]

In his memoirs Kisch wrote that in 1905, when his volume of adolescent verse was published, he was an admirer of the witty and sarcastic writing of a cabaret troupe in Munich, *Die Elf Scharfrichter* (The Eleven Executioners), whose work was hailed by bohemians and the artistic avant-garde throughout Germany and Austria. Regarding this influence, he wrote:

The cadence of my verse was borrowed from Heine, the content from the Eleven Executioners, a group of Munich artists. Heine is a master of versification, and the Eleven Executioners had a cocky outlook on life, but in the poems of the youth [Kisch] who plundered from them you will find neither of these merits.[9]

A cocky attitude (a mocking questioning of authority) stayed with Kisch up through his middle age until social and political conditions became so menacing that it lost its luster. Using sarcasm, satire, and caricature, the artistic jabs of newspaper pieces or cabaret routines aimed at authority and power were neither sufficient nor effective responses to the likes of Hitler and Stalin, who were real executioners, not metaphorical ones, on a vast scale. But, as a template or role-model, the Executioners' approach was effective on cabaret stages from the time of its inception (ca. 1900) up through the advent of Hitler's regime. Harold Segel's 1987 survey of European cabaret across five decades and numerous cities (Paris, Munich, Berlin, Vienna, Krakow, Moscow, among others) devoted a long half-chapter of his book to the Executioners, giving the reader an idea of the excitement generated by this inventive, experimental-theater group that influenced Kisch's views on the medium.[10] Wedekind had a pre-World War I association with cabaret theater as well— Segel describes his roles as writer, actor, singer,[11] and poet with The Eleven Executioners during the 1901-1902 seasons.[12] Seen in this light, cabaret, whether or not a troupe was staging short plays in any single instance, still belongs to the broader category of theater as understood by both audiences and critics (just as late-Victorian or Edwardian music-hall variety shows and Vaudeville are understood to be forms of theater in its broadest sense).

The variegated nature of the cabaret experience probably affected how audience members reacted to specific plays, because plays were part of a basically unrelated series of performances designed to keep customers amused. This applies more to the rough comedy of the Toni Gallows play than it would to the Redl melodrama with its recent-history component—also, it was long enough to be mounted as a separate work not embedded in cabaret routines. In some venues the 1920s performances of the Toni

Gallows story would have had other enticements: singers, mono-
logists, dancers disporting, perhaps a ventriloquist or puppeteer,
while viewers ate and bottles and glasses clinked and clanked
amid a buzz of conversation, flirtation, and even ripostes to those
on stage.

In fact we know the whole bill of fare at Berlin's *Rakete*
(Rocket) cabaret theater for a specific performance of *Galgentoni*
when it was put on one night in October 1923. Joined by a popular
Munich folksinger named Anita Degen, the (unnamed) daughter
of Hans Hyans, a writer of chansons, sang his songs while a (presumably American) "Negro" smoking a cigar tap-danced furious-
ly, feigned fatigue, then rebounded and rasped like a motor behind the patter of the "straw-blonde" Interlocutor, Helmut
Krüger; Krüger bantered with a petite, witty actress known from
films, Irmgard Bern, and with Hermann Valentin, renowned as a
political satirist; two one-act plays followed, one an adaptation of
a "light-hearted" English piece, the other a "thriller" adapted from
a French play; the night's entertainment came to a conclusion with
Kisch's *Galgentoni* play, starring Rosa Valetti.[13] And then the patrons returned home in the wee hours to think about it the next
morning. Customers fond of such entertainment would probably
have been more than satisfied with the substance of *Tonka Šibenice*
(or *Galgentoni*), though they may not have dwelled on its underlying socially-critical message.

Though many a cabaret play was 'here today, gone tomorrow', even if admired or talked about, Kisch's two works under
discussion made more than a temporary impression, thanks to his
increasing fame as the 'raging reporter' in 1924-1925. Liberal and
left-wing newspaper critics and commentators who reviewed and
discussed these plays also widened public interest in them,
though this interest was often based on discussions of Kisch as a
controversial political figure rather than on the artistic merits of
his work for the stage. While several of Kisch's plays entered the
repertoire of Longen's Revolutionary Stage, this enterprise itself
was fading in importance by the late 1920s, and was not able to
present some works in its repertoire in extended runs; most of its
performances were in Czech, also limiting German exposure to

Kisch's one-act plays. After the 1930 revival of the Redl play in Berlin, the only subsequent performances occurred in one-night runs undertaken in places like London and Mexico in order to honor Kisch by bringing attention to a writer-in-exile known as a prominent anti-Fascist whose works could be used to rally sentiment during World War II (while providing an evening of diversion from the ongoing stress of the war).

Finally, the question of how Kisch evaluated this phase of his life raises itself. His choices and deeds are the indices and record of his judgment. From 1925 onward he turned away from new theatrical involvements. This was the time of his breakthrough into a larger readership and a wider orbit of activity. He made his 'theatrical exit, stage left', as it were, concluding that the widespread popular and critical success of his collection *Der rasende Reporter*, which his contemporaries viewed as the paradigm of reportage and *die neue Sachlichkeit*, showed him a way forward. It was a step onto a path of journalism that would be both socially engaged and politically influential, framed by his progressive, left-wing views of current realities—he now aspired to do this through thematic books, not just newspaper and magazine articles that were republished as collections in book form. At least this was the ideal, if not always the fact—between 1925 and 1947 Kisch continued to write short notices and political polemics, standard-length journalistic reports on current events, and even long essays on historical topics in profusion, hundreds of which were never collected into thematic books of reportage.

As Hofmann noted[14] and Kisch's letters show,[15] in 1925 Kisch went into a frenzy of activity that resulted in a rapid succession of books with titles using words ("raging", "pursuit", "adventures", "exploits") that grabbed the attention of readers and made them think of him as the energetic reporter who uncovered the deeper story everywhere, all the time. (These were the qualities that made Musil and Roth think of him as a gadfly jumping opportunistically from one subject to the next, but in a sense this was a crafted illusion, given how much background research and rewriting Kisch did; still, they admired the stylistic immediacy and social relevance of Kisch's writing[16]). As he developed these projects he took a literal step into the wider world beyond the confines of Prague, Vienna, and Berlin, beginning his two decades of global wandering with a trip to the USSR, where he hoped to find his beliefs validated and his dreams of a better future realized by the new experiment in socialist government. Yet, in his books from the mid-1920s up until the end of his exile (1945), whenever Kisch turned his attention away from survey-type socio-economic information and towards colorful and idiosyncratic people and customs, he put his playwriting apprenticeship to good use, dramatizing mundane encounters, exhibiting a special flair for vernacular speech, and recording (or inventing) wry or comical dialogues. While not a true man of the theater, he had not wasted his time writing plays. He used what he had learned from this experience as he turned himself into 'the raging reporter', a man who was perceived by his liberal and left-wing contemporaries as the journalistic exemplar of the spirit of the age and a prose-poet of everyday reality.

Kisch was extremely fond of the Redl and Toni Gallows stories in their several forms (reportage, feuilletons, plays), coming back to them throughout the 1920s, 1930s, and 1940s. But they also took on a life of their own in the hands of artists who mined their narratives for their own purposes. The numerous re-creations and adaptations of the two stories by others is the subject of the next two chapters, where we encounter the Redl story on film, back on the stage (this time in England), and in a bizarre and entertaining Slovak novel that is a small compendium of Central European twentieth century political and cultural history, as seen in a warped mirror. After that we consider the afterlife of the Toni Gallows story, which also migrated to film, returned to the stage in altered form in Prague, and appeared as four different televised plays in East and West Germany and in the post-1992 Czech Republic.

Chapter 9. Afterlife of the Redl Story: Films, on the English Stage, a Slovak Novel

The post-World War II revival of the Redl story as a topic of popular history began with Robert Asprey's 1959 biography. Properly speaking, the artistic afterlife of the Redl story began with Franz Antel's 1955 film, *Spionage*, made seven years after Kisch's death. However, for the sake of convenience and continuity of discussion of the theme of fictional transformation of historical material, the first three Redl films (made in 1925, 1926, and 1931) will be grouped with the later stage and cinematic adaptations of the story. These three films were contemporaneous with a very busy phase of Kisch's life as an international reporter and political activist. Though he was definitely moving away from involvement with the theater, he was aware of the 1925 and 1926 films—they are among the unauthorized adaptations and plagiarized works that he complained about in his memoirs.[1]

There had been an earlier attempt to capitalize on the story through the rapidly expanding popular medium of film. In April, 1914, Colonel Urbanski was forced at Archduke Franz Ferdinand's insistence into a premature retirement from service. In addition to infuriating the Successor because he had played a major part in the General Staff's cover-up, Urbanski was also accused of selling Redl memorabilia to a film producer,[2] indicating an interest in such a project, though it was not brought to fruition at the time—war and censorship intervened. Interest in the case survived the war's end in 1918, and Kisch was instrumental in unearthing new information and publicizing it.

Within a year of Kisch's 1924 book the first of five Redl films made its appearance. This was *Oberst Redl* (Colonel Redl), directed by Hans Otto Löwenstein, with Robert Valberg playing the Colonel. A silent film, its subtitle was *Eine Tragödie aus der Vorkriegszeit in 7 Akten* (A Pre-war Tragedy in 7 Acts). It was also advertised as *Oberst Redl, Der Totengräber der Monarchie* (Colonel Redl, The Gravedigger of the Monarchy). While the film had restrictions placed upon it by the Berlin police in 1925,[3] it was both an artistic and commercial success.[4] Kisch's book was not mentioned as a source for the screenwriters.[5] The film's subtitle elevated Redl's treachery to a historical significance that it did not merit—the Dual Monarchy had many gravediggers, including its own dynasts and political and military leaders. A German website gives a plot summary of the film:

> The k.u.k. Colonel Redl, constantly in need of money, meets Sonja, a Russian, in Vienna; she becomes a spy in order to bring about her marriage to a nobleman who is an officer in the Czar's army. Sonja seduces Redl, leading him to sell her secret military information about the Austro-Hungarian army. He even steals information from his friend Captain Erdmann, who winds up being imprisoned. After Redl's information loses its value to Sonja, she betrays him. As a result he commits suicide. Erdmann is exculpated, Sonja marries her officer.[6]

This summary is misleading and far too terse to be informative. A viewing of the film allows the following additional remarks to be made.[7] The character Sonja is the mistress of a Russian lieutenant in military intelligence stationed in Warsaw. As a nobleman he cannot jeopardize his career and status through marriage to a commoner. He hatches a plan that will target his lover on anyone high in Austrian military intelligence; if she succeeds in getting valuable information, then the authorities will facilitate their marriage. She meets Redl on a train to Vienna, sizes him up, and starts an affair with him. Soon aware of his indebtedness and ambitions for a more luxurious life-style, she recruits him for Russian military intelligence.

The time-frame is indicated by Redl's rise through the ranks during the film, starting as a Captain on the cusp of promotion to Major and ending as a full Colonel (ca. 1904–1912 in the real Redl's career). During this time he steals the secret construction and deployment plans for troops stationed in the Przemyšl fortress complex from his old friend, Captain Erdmann, and then frames him for the crime. He deviously cajoles Erdmann's daughter to reveal the hidden location of her father's desk-drawer lock, then steals his work documents. This detail is taken from the real Redl's behavior during the controversial Hekailo-Wieckowski-

Acht espionage affair of 1903–1904, discussed above in Chapter 4. Another reflection of this case in the film is the use of the cover name of "Baron Wiechawski" for an Austrian spy working for Russian intelligence out of Warsaw (this may be another of Redl' false identities).

Ultimately Redl betrays two other high-level secret plans to the Russians: the construction schedule for a military railway line to the Russian border, and the current mobilization plan of the k.u.k. army in the case of war with Russia. The chief of Russian intelligence exults in these coups and in information he has received from Wiechawski that the Austrians and Germans are completely misled about Russia's ability to mobilize quickly and are unaware of her hidden reserve of 75 Divisions stationed in Siberia. These 'film-facts' regurgitate retrospective Austrian intelligence evaluations of Redl's treason during 1914–1915 and the immediate post-World War I period, reflecting Kisch's (but not only his own) 'maximalist' interpretation of the consequences of the Colonel's espionage during the opening campaigns of World War I.

In the end Redl's Russian handlers set him up for a fall by having Sonja mail a letter under a pre-agreed code-name to Vienna, "to the usual place", where Redl will pick it up. They make the letter's address and mailing origin suspicious enough to interest the Viennese security police. The ruse works and the post-office trap is arranged. The sole detective on the scene loses his man but gets a taxi-cab license plate number, enabling him to locate the cab's stand and thereby recover evidence (scraps of paper and a pen-knife sheath) used to ensnare Redl at the Hotel Klomser. There is a scene where General Staff officers assemble in dismay and confusion to decide Redl's fate. Conrad is part of this scene, but is not named. The suicide commission is constituted and sent to Redl, who instantly agrees, agonizes for a few hours, then shoots himself through the mouth. Erdmann is exculpated and restored to service after three year's false imprisonment. Sonja and her lover, Lieutenant Jamischewicz, are given license to marry by none other than "little Father", the Czar himself. Thereby two love stories—Erdmann's domestic bliss with wife and daughter, and

Sonja's affair—conclude happily. The third, Redl's deep infatuation with Sonja, leads to infamy and death.

There is no mention of homosexuality as an element of the story, and its narrative strays widely from the known historical facts of the case as they had been presented to the German and Austrian public by Kisch in 1924. Reflecting one of the persistent 1913–1914 rumors about the case, the 1925 film features a Russian female intelligence agent as part of its narrative, a character who appears in the four Redl films made between 1925 and 1955. Kisch had dismissed this particular rumor in his 1924 book. In contrast, Asprey discusses such a "Countess Kobiakov", who failed in her mission to recruit Redl for the Russians, but his sourcing on this point is not stated, though it seems to have come from "Tristan Busch", whose questionable reliability has been discussed above. This character reappears in John Osborne's Redl play as "Countess Delyanoff".

According to the German film website containing the film's plot summary, screenwriting credits were given to the director (as Hans Otto) and to Walter Reisch, while an American film website lists the director and Hans Seeliger as writers.[8] (The sole extant copy of the film has no screenwriting credits.) Seeliger's brother, Emil, was involved in investigating the 1904 Hekailo espionage case in which Redl played an odd (and retrospectively damning) role. An Austrian film website quotes a 1925 press-release for the film that showered praise on Valberg as Redl and stated that the film was both artistically and technically polished, as well as "convincingly plausible" in its content.[9] Given the plot summary, the film is anything but plausible as an accurate representation of the Redl affair. Though Kisch is not cited in the film's credits, it is obvious that elements of its narrative depend on his reporting as well as on widespread pre-war rumors about the case. For example, Colonel Urbanski is portrayed as "Ulmanitztky", based on the name given to this character in Kisch's Redl play ("Umanitzky"). The existing copy of the film is missing a few brief sequences.[10] In technical terms the film is, in fact, polished, though, common to the medium of silent films, facial expressions and melodramatic gestures will appear overwrought to current audiences.

In a silent film directed by Max Neufeld in 1926 Valberg re-prised his role as Redl, while the director starred as Rasputin, and his brother, Eugen Neufeld, played a Russian Grand Prince. There were connections between the films — in Löwenstein's film of the previous year Eugen Neufeld had played "Colonel Ulmanitzky", using Kisch's name for this character. The film's writing credits do not cite Kisch, but Jacques Bachrach.[11] The film's title and subtitle, *Die Brandstifter Europas — Oberst Redls Erben* (Europe's Incendiar-ies — Colonel Redl's Heirs), make Redl an indispensable link be-tween the collapse of the Habsburg Empire and the ascent of the Bolsheviks in Russia; among others the film had roles for Czar Nicholas and Lenin, the chief incendiary.

In *Brandstifter* Redl appears in only the first of six scenes, with his actions setting the stage for his "heirs". As Bernadette Kester has written, *Brandstifter* was one of several Weimar-era films that purported through misleading advertising to address the rankling issue of Germany's 'war-guilt'.[12] In the films she dis-cusses in this connection, it is Russian court and military men who are depicted as provocateurs responsible for creating a situation in which Austria-Hungary and Germany were forced to respond with military mobilization. Kester states that no copies of the film survive, but there was sufficient information in studio records, film-magazine advertisements, and reviews in German newspa-pers to allow a reconstruction of the film's story-line.

Brandstifter did not address the topic of war-guilt directly; ra-ther it was a historical fantasy depicting colorful personalities and featuring a romantic-love theme (this time the female agent has a liaison with a Russian Prince). The story implicating a Russian dynast and Russian military circles as bellicose agents responsible for the war was an interpretation calculated to find favor in Aus-tria and Germany. Such a reaction would have been a natural, self-exculpating one on the part of Germans who knew that the re-sponsibility for the onset of World War I could not be placed squarely on Germany alone, without reference to events in the other Great Powers and Serbia. Though there were bellicose men aplenty in influential Russian diplomatic and military positions, they can be deemed no more (or less) responsible for the war than their mirror-images in Austria-Hungary, Germany, England, and France — fear of encirclement or invasion and the assumption that a pre-emptive knock-out blow could be delivered in the first campaign of the war characterized all of the national leaderships on both sides of the conflict.

The film was Austrian, yet made no mention of Austria's non-negotiable ultimatum to Serbia after the assassination at Sarajevo, thereby avoiding the war-guilt issue with respect to Austria. Nor did the film mention Germany's 'blank check' offering unconditional support to Austria-Hungary in its plan to punish Serbia for the Successor's assassination. Several reviewers of the film, which claimed to be based on "confidential" German and Russian diplomatic documents, pointed out its irrelevance to a serious discussion of the war-guilt issue. However, these critics remained agnostic about the issue because too much classified information had been kept from the public (including filmmakers). In *Brandstifter* Redl is a 'functional malefactor', like a cog-wheel that sets larger machinery in motion. Scenes including the arrival of Lenin in Russia and the murder of Rasputin, both of which herald the demise of the tsarist government, take the film's viewers on a colorful but highly selective view of events preceding and during the war. The real actions of the historical Redl and their consequences have been elided in order to produce a melodramatic narrative pieced together from imaginary, colorful vignettes.

Based on available plot summaries, it is doubtful that the 1925 and 1926 films either reflected or influenced serious thinking about the Redl case or the actual causes of World War I. Nonetheless, because they involved well-known directors,[13] actors and actresses, they had some success with the movie-going public, who would have been interested in espionage skullduggery, the exciting story of Redl's last day, and the presumed consequences of his treason. In the minds of many Austrian and German viewers the idea of Redl as an instrumental felon responsible for the war and its outcome persisted. Today it is obvious that the logic of this causal chain—from Redl's espionage through the fall of the Habsburgs, the Hohenzollerns, and the Romanovs to the rise of Bolshevism — is highly questionable. However, neither logic nor causality is the strength or object of film in particular or the dramatic arts in general, which offer artists considerable license when they transform history into fiction.

A 1931 film with sound, *Der Fall des Generalstabschefs Oberst Redl*, directed by Karl (Karel) Anton, credits Kisch as the ultimate source (but not as a screenwriter) of the story told in the film, and its title is identical to that of his 1924 book. The film was released in German and Czech versions, featuring two different casts of actors and actresses. In the German version Redl is played by Theodor Loos, known for major roles in a series of acclaimed films directed by Fritz Lang. In the Czech version, *Aféra plukovníka Rédla*, Kisch's friend and theatrical collaborator, Emil Artur Longen, plays Redl. Redl's protégé and lover, Stefan Horinka, becomes Lieutenant Stephan Dolan. Conrad von Hötzendorf is represented under his real name, but Colonel Urbanski is played as Colonel Umanitzky, the pseudonym used in Kisch's play. There is also a role in the film for "Marchenko", the Russian military attaché in Vienna who was expelled by the Austrians in 1910 under suspicion of espionage. This is the man whom Redl identifies as his Russian blackmailer in Kisch's 1924 book, his 1926 play, and his 1942 memoirs. Whether or not he blackmailed Redl remains a subject of debate. Anton followed the general outline of Redl's last day as presented in Kisch's book and play (which differ from each other) but made numerous departures from Kisch's version of the larger affair as he told it in 1924, probably in the interest of heightening the narrative's dramatic and romantic quotient. A Czech film anthology gives the following summary of the film's plotline:

> Contents: Alfred Redl, a colonel on the Austrian General Staff, leads an extravagant private life. No one suspects that in reality he is passing information to Russian spies. To obtain further information the Russians station agent Levanzová to him, but Redl resists the temptations of the beautiful woman. Levanzová discovers Redl's passionate letters intended for Lieutenant Dolan. Redl is transferred to Prague and he tries to prevent the lieutenant from marrying. The Russians threaten Redl with making public his letters to Dolan and they force him to give away the plans for an attack in Galicia. Those on the General Staff have been looking for a long time for an informant from within their own ranks. Everyone is shocked when suspi-

cion is directed at Redl. The suspicion is confirmed when he goes to claim the letters that have been deposited a long time already at the main post office. Officers of the staff come to Redl and hand him a gun. Redl shoots himself in a hotel room[14]

This summary[15] omits other cinematic details of interest, including various sub-plots introduced to create a complicated web of relationships among its featured characters. A viewing of the film allows one to gauge how its several narrative strands deviate from Kisch's 1924 book.

Before this discussion of directorial inventions, a few remarks should be made about the dramatic and cinematic qualities of the film. In spite of the superior technical resources available to the film-makers of the 1950s and 1980s who treated the Redl story (discussed below), the 1931 film has its own merits and attractions that make for a more authentic presentation of the Redl story than the later films. By "authentic" I am referring to the film's re-created 1913 atmosphere, not its historical accuracy, which leaves a great deal to be desired, though it is marginally better in this respect than earlier and later films. Most of the people involved in making the film had lived through the events depicted. They were familiar with the styles, the 'normal manner of expression', and the hierarchical social conventions of the late Habsburg era. Although silent films had just been replaced by those with sound in 1931, directors still used long close-up camera shots of facial expressions and gestures to convey emotions, though these elements were not as exaggerated as they had been in films without sound. In short, scenes were performed in a more natural fashion. For instance, toward the end of the film, Loos renders an excellent expressive and gestural performance of a man who realizes he is doomed and then undergoes a mental and emotional collapse; language would have been superfluous in this kind of scene, with the possible exception of a man talking aloud to himself as he agonizes over what he might have done differently to avoid disaster.

Returning to directorial elaborations and alterations of Kisch's material, one notes that the film presents a longer time-line and more locations to the viewer than the stage version of Redl's last day depicted in *Die Hetzjagd*; yet it does not provide the depth of background information about Redl and his career that can be found in Kisch's 1924 book. We see Vienna, Prague, and Russian intelligence headquarters in St. Petersburg, though all are interior scenes, easily filmed on a studio set or in a few appropriate 'period' properties in Prague. Although they used the title of Kisch's 1924 book about the espionage affair for the German-language release of the film, the director and screenwriters invented numerous plot elements that stray far from the story as Kisch told it.

The most important of these inventions is the entirely fictional role of the Russian widow, Countess Nikolayevna, whose relationship with Redl supplies a key narrative element in the 1931 film. Under the cover-name of Countess Levanzová she is assigned to recruit Redl as an agent who should be able to supply the Russians with the Austrian mobilization plan. Though she becomes Redl's "female friend" who accompanies him to cafés and social functions in Vienna and Prague ("all society is talking about them"), she reports to her handlers that her relationship with him is platonic. She soon discovers the reason for this, which will allow blackmail. She pilfers discarded drafts of love-letters from Redl to his protégé, cavalry lieutenant Stephan Dolan, which she passes along to her controller, Colonel Marchenko (who also wishes to establish a romantic connection with her). She has an additional personal motive to engage in espionage on behalf of Russia, which adds drama to the film's plot. Her former husband, executed for selling information to the Austrians, was betrayed by agent "Opernball 13" to Russian intelligence, "ruining her life". Not intuited by her Russian employers, she seeks revenge for this. At the film's outset her Russian handlers are also in the dark about the fact that her target, Redl, and "Opernball 13" are one and the same man (Opernball 13 has gone silent on them, and they are looking for another way into the General Staff). She probes Redl about the identity behind the cipher, while he fends off her inquiries in a manner piquing her suspicions. Until late in the film she remains ignorant that Redl is the man responsible for her husband's death. The interpersonal plot thickens, and, as it does, it drifts farther and farther away from the real Redl case.

Using narrative elements from *Die Hetzjagd,* the film hews to Kisch's incorrect remarks on the letters with cash prominently addressed to "Opernball 13, Poste-Restante, Wien" (in reality they were addressed to Nikon Nizetas). It presents the entirely imaginary meeting of Conrad, Urbanski, and the confabulated Archduke Viktor Salvator as taking place not on the day of Redl's detection (an invention of Kisch's Redl play) but at some intermediate point during the overall time-frame of the film; the scene is designed to show the viewer the technical tricks of the espionage trade at *Evidenzbüro* headquarters, as recounted in Kisch's book and Act II of *Die Hetzjagd.* Taken from the play (and augmented for humorous effect) is the invented portrayal of the two comical detectives who bungle their surveillance, then manage through sheer luck to find their suspect and identify him through a ruse. We see them banter as they play cards and then iron their pants in a back room at the post office, clad in jackets, ties, derbies, and the leggings of their long underwear.

As to mistakes, the film conveys the incorrect information that the Russian military attaché in Vienna was Colonel Marchenko at the time of the events shown (he had, in fact, been expelled from Austria in 1910). This mistake (or deliberate choice, depending on how well Anton was acquainted with the factual background of the case) is made as part of the director's effort to telescope various events in Redl's life into a roughly two-year time period, from 1912 through mid-1913, during which we see him leave Vienna for Prague and move up in rank from Lieutenant Colonel to full Colonel. Another instance of this is to present the complicated 1903–1904 Hekailo-Wieckowski-Acht investigation and espionage trial as a 1912 or 1913 affair in which Redl frames a captain named Garnovský for selling the Russians information on troop dispositions and the Przemyšl fortress complex in Galicia (Redl is the real culprit here, covering his tracks through mastery of counterintelligence techniques).

We have already seen a similar use of this incident in the 1925 film. In the original case Redl played a hide-and-seek game with a suspect's young daughter in order to discover where the man had hidden documents, which his colleagues found distasteful (or retrospectively claimed to). Garnovský's judgment by a military tribunal in the film alludes to this episode and, as in Kisch's 1924 remarks on the matter, is meant to indicate something off-putting about Redl's character and methods, though he still remains above suspicion. While his methods may seem questionable to his fellow officers, their results are not—he is the paragon of a military intelligence professional in their minds. Another scene at the film's outset shows Redl secretly recording a Russian colonel in civilian mufti who is willing to sell the Austrians Russia's mobilization plan. Redl forwards the recording to St. Petersburg, allowing Russian intelligence to grab a traitor in their midst. This scene condenses material from Redl's presumed betrayal of a Russian Colonel (Laikov) working on Austria's behalf, as recounted in Kisch's 1924 book.

The film adheres fairly closely to Kisch's version of Redl's behavior after he evades the trap at the post office, the discovery of his identity at the Klomser Hotel, his attempt thereafter to escape surveillance when he scatters shredded documents on the street, the confirmation of his identity through handwriting samples, and the General Staff's alarmed (and lethal) reaction on May 24th, 1913. It leaves out his meal with his friend, Viktor Pollak. In book, play, and film a delegation of three officers confront Redl, supply him with a pistol, and demand his suicide (Kisch was mistaken about the number of men in the suicide commission, leaving out Redl's old deputy in counterintelligence, Major Max Ronge).

The depiction of "Franzi" (the fiancé of Redl's protégé) in the film is completely different than in the play, where she is a serious mouthpiece for Kisch's criticisms of the General Staff and the upper reaches of Austrian society. In the film she is merely an attractive, somewhat silly, love-besotted young woman, and her inamorata, "Stephan Dolan" (Stefan Horinka in real life) is an equally light-headed character. This portrayal of the pair is a typical cinematic romantic trope, frothy to the point of implausibility; their expressions of infatuation are accompanied by waltz music and a jaunty nightclub song. The originals of this pair may have been far more cynical and manipulative, hoping to cash in on Horinka's relationship with "Uncle Alfred".[16]

Several important aspects of 1924 book are omitted or only briefly alluded to. First, there is nothing about Redl's pre-1912 life and military career (shown in Szabó's film, discussed below, though his version of Redl's childhood and early career is entirely imaginary). Second, the events of the day after Redl's suicide are not covered, while in fact they were important in determining the scope of his treason and could have been handled in a very brief scene. Third, there is no place for a reporter (modeled on Kisch) breaking the story and exposing the General staff's falsehoods about the case. Fourth, there is no indication of the actual consequences of Redl's treason, especially its presumed effect on military campaigns at the outset of World War I—this might have been done by a brief 'postscript scene' after Redl's suicide. Thus, though viewers see enough to judge whether the General Staff was remiss in ignoring aspects of Redl's life that should have deserved more scrutiny, there is no probing of deeper causes and effects. These are the film's major omissions.

And, on a matter that is still unresolved, the Russian management of Redl as an agent is given a new twist. In the film's opening scene the Russians themselves are worried about the recent silence of the star spy they call "Opernball 13", noting that so far he has been immune to the charms of female agents. It is through the wiles of their new "irresistible" agent, Levanzová (Nikolayevna), that they discover Redl's homosexuality. Rather than waiting for Redl's opportunistic choice of secrets to sell them, Marchenko uses the correspondence between Redl and his protégé, stolen by Levanzová, to blackmail him into betraying the current Austrian mobilization plan, the 'holy grail' of secret information. In the film Redl's agonized decision to comply is presented as crossing a psychologically and morally "terrible" (*furchtbar*) line that he has been unwilling to cross hitherto. There is no historical evidence for any of this happening in 1913 (or earlier), and the blackmail aspect of the Redl case remains moot, with historians still debating if and when it happened. Redl's sale of the mobilization plan is also unsupported by documentary evidence, though it may well have happened.

The film's combination of omissions with inventions alters Kisch's 1924 book substantially, while it retains a few sequences that replicate his reporting of the events (some of which are incorrect to begin with, though these aspects of the story were not contradicted or amended by historical researchers until the 1960s and later). Many of the events depicted in the film never happened, and some of its scenes are about matters and motives unknown and probably unknowable, moving the film farther toward fiction than normal artistic license would allow in a more faithful adaptation of Kisch's 1924 book. The viewer gets a potpourri of historical and fictional fragments woven into a dramatic film plot. The factual elements of the case have been doubly transformed: first by Kisch's own fictional embellishments in *Die Hetzjagd*, then by an extra layer of inventions imposed on the story in the 1931 film. The cast of roles in the film uses a mixture of both real and ersatz names for well-known public figures involved in the Redl affair (litigation or the banning of the film are possible reasons for this). However, the film-going public was well-aware of the identities of the film's major characters, due to the publicity about the case throughout the 1920s. Another small point requires mention here. In his 1985 book on the Redl case Georg Markus noted that the 1925 and 1931 films depicted Redl having female lovers, stating that the topic of homosexuality had not yet been broached openly in cinema at the time.[17] The plot elements of Redl's relationship with Levanzová being "platonic" and of purloined love letters from Redl to his protégé in Anton's 1931 film indicate that Markus's remark about this is incorrect.

The sole existing copy of the German version of the film in the Czech national film archive is missing several minutes. These are marked by awkward splices and the duplication of the opening scene. It also lacks the end of a scene headed in a direction not entirely clear to the viewer (i.e., the film's last 90 seconds, during which it appears that Levanzová intends to shoot Redl as he ponders suicide). However, the viewer who understands German can follow the story-line easily in spite of these minor infelicities. No copies of the Czech version of the film have been found, but it is likely that, apart from the language difference, the narrative line and the substance of the dialogues are identical in the film's German and Czech versions.[18] What the viewer misses with the loss of the Czech version of the film is a chance to see E. A. Longen perform as Redl. His contribution is of historical interest on account of his long friendship with Kisch and the important role he played throughout the 1920s in his collaboration with and guidance of Kisch during his years of writing for the theater.

Like the contemplated 1914 film that did not materialize, another 'might-have-been' Redl film was envisioned by the American director Billy Wilder, who had been born in Galicia, grown up in Vienna, and moved to Berlin, where Kisch befriended him during the late 1920s. Just as Kisch did, he left Germany for Paris in 1933, eventually settling in Hollywood in 1935. When interviewed by Michael Horowitz in 1985, Wilder mentioned he had last seen Kisch in 1933 and that his old friend was on his mind in the late 1940s when he proposed making a Redl film, wanting Charles Laughton to play Redl and Horst Buchholz for the role of Stefan Horinka. The project fell through.[19] How a film made within the constraints of the Hollywood studio system would have altered the Redl story for popular consumption by an American audience is anyone's guess. Perhaps a *film noir* that viewed authority with skepticism and the pervasiveness of human corruption with irony (typical Wilder tropes) could have done some justice to the Redl story.

By 1955, when the Austrian director Franz Antel directed the fourth film based on the Redl case, *Spionage*, the perspective of German and Austrian audiences had changed a great deal. They had gone through the turbulent, polarized 1930s, the ascent of Hitler, the *Anschluss* that brought Austria "home into the Reich", and the criminal behavior of the regime during World War II, ending with the devastating loss of the war, Austria's exit from "Greater Germany", the administrative partition and occupation of their homeland by the Allied Powers, and Austria's new status as a minor "neutral" state. Yet, tradition, cultural conservatism, and the urge for self-justification were so strong in Austria that the resulting Redl film seems neither more 'modern' nor more socially or politically critical than the films of the 1920s and 30s.

In *Spionage* Ewald Balser plays Redl and Oskar Werner his protégé-lover under the fictitious name of Leutnant Zeno von Baumgarten. As in Kisch, he is a young man seduced and maintained by Redl, whom he unsettles by expressing his desire to leave the army in order to marry. In Antel's version the sexual relationship between Redl and the lieutenant is hinted at through suggestive, not explicit, scenes. There are name changes for other characters: Urbanski and Conrad von Hötzendorf become Rabansky and von Heymeneck, respectively, while the two detectives who trail Redl use the names in Kisch's 1926 Redl play, Steidl and Strebinger. The film's opening credits announce that while the Redl case was an historical event, the cinematic narrative to follow is "freely imagined" and "any resemblance between the names of the film's characters and living persons is purely coincidental." With the exception of the scene at the post office and the ensuing surveillance, when the detectives discover his dropped penknife sheath and set their trap at the hotel, the film's narrative is entirely fanciful. Even the surveillance scene is not straightforward, introducing a diversion meant to say something about Redl's character—knowing he is under watch, he enters a Catholic church where mass is in progress and, with a troubled expression, he appears to seek forgiveness. The scene has echoes in both John Osborne's Redl play and Szabó's movie, but it is a screenwriter's invention.

The viewer is exposed to a complicated set of relationships built around the love of another (fictitious) young officer in the *Evidenzbüro* ("Captain Angelis") for a Russian baroness residing in Vienna. Her brother ("Baron Korff") is one of Austria's agents conducting espionage against Russia—Redl betrays him to the Russians. Korff is motivated to work against Russia by his desire to "free the Baltic States", an anachronistic and historically implausible motive in 1913, and one inconsistent with Austrian diplomacy, which was wary of how foreign 'freedom fighter' movements might exacerbate its own corrosive minority-nationalism problems. Redl frames Angelis in order to satisfy his superiors that he has finally caught the suspected General Staff officer responsible for selling military information and betraying

Austrian operatives to Russia. The Angelis-Baroness Korff relationship is a peculiar twist of the way earlier films used an invented Russian woman agent as part of the story, allowing it to high-
light the 'Russian connection' in a manner that betrayed current
(1955) West European concerns about the USSR. Or, perhaps it
was just another product of a screenwriters' imagination, alluding
to the fact that there had once been influential communities of Baltic Germans, many of whom served the Tsars and some of whom
would have preferred political and cultural association with Germany. The only accurate part of this plot element is Redl's betrayal of Austrian agents working in Russia, so the imaginary Baron
Korff stands in for all of them.

Earlier in his career Antel had made several light-hearted
comedies and musicals that showed late Habsburg society in positive terms, much to the delight and approval of conservative elements in Austrian society. *Spionage*, however, elicited a very different response from some of Austria's older political and military
figures, men who had survived into the post-World War II era.
They were dismayed by a film that showed the k.u.k. army in a
bad light, even though that light isolated Redl as the army's sole
scoundrel. In a long review of *Spionage* a writer for the German
weekly news magazine *Der Spiegel* noted this negative reaction to
the film (just as he noted the narrative's departures from the established historical record). The reviewer also discussed the Austrian
government's punitive response to the 1925 Redl film, pointing
out similar official reactions that took place in 1955.[20] Conserva-
tives in Austria were over-reacting — except for Redl, the film
casts no aspersions on any element of late Habsburg society. As
Markus reported, *Spionage* had the imprimatur of eminent Austrian generals.[21] The film has Redl selling the Russians information
on the important fortress complex at Przemyśl in Galicia and betraying Austrian intelligence agents to St. Petersburg, but does not
mention the mobilization plans, thus avoiding the sensitive topic
of General Staff dereliction leading to immense losses at the outset
of World War I. Likewise, *Spionage* does not use the names of Conrad, Urbanski, Ronge or other officials involved in the case, as if
historical accuracy about the men who played the most important

roles in the Redl affair and its attempted cover-up would blemish the reputation of the *k.u.k Armee,* Austria's leaders, and the dynasty.

Though entertaining, melodramatic, and successful in re-creating the atmosphere of late Habsburg Vienna, *Spionage* is a romantic period film that hardly does the Redl affair justice. A much later (2013) documentary film about the Redl affair shown on Austrian television used footage from *Spionage,* but only for the purpose of providing background imagery for a discussion of the case by historians and other interested parties.[22]

A discussion of John Osborne's 1965 Redl play, *A Patriot for Me,* is needed here, because it had an influence on the next, best-known (and egregiously ahistorical) film made about the Redl case, István Szabó's 1985 *Oberst Redl* (Colonel Redl*).* Osborne's play came at the end of a decade when he was deemed England's leading playwright, critically acclaimed and commercially successful. Osborne had emerged from obscurity and penury into renown with the success of 1956's *Look Back in Anger,* leading the press to christen him the nominal leader of a cohort of playwrights known as 'the angry young men'. His five 'canonical' plays (*Look Back in Anger, The Entertainer, Luther, Inadmissible Evidence,* and *A Patriot for Me*) all featured protagonists who are defiant individualists at war with family, friends, and society in general, wavering between heroic displays of egotism and collapses into deep troughs of self-doubt and despair. As Osborne's major biographers have shown, each of these protagonists was in some way or other an idealized alter-ego of Osborne himself, a combative man whose greatest triumphs were shadowed by public displays of alcohol-fueled vituperation and petulance, though he could suddenly revert to charm and generosity.

In *Patriot* the viewer sees an Alfred Redl who is not only duplicitous, ambitious, and greedy, but also a man who is a defiant individualist, yet a self-divided one, wavering between anxiety and self-fulfillment at any cost (a sort of 'existentialist hero' in the terminology of the times). Not only do viewers get a typical Osborne protagonist, they also get a well-wrought critique of his surrounding society (i.e., a portrait with a deep social background).

Luc Gilleman made a sound argument that at the time of its first performances *Patriot* was also a "state of the nation play", in which Austria in 1913 was meant to be emblematic of England during the period that ran from 1945 up through the mid-1960s.[23] The point of the comparison is not based on an itemized list of similarities but rather on a general dissatisfaction with aspects of public life and pessimism about the near future in both societies. The parallels of interest to Osborne were: punitive attitudes and laws about divorce and homosexuality; rigid class attitudes and politics; and scandals involving men in high places who were granted cover or immunity by the 'Establishment' (e.g., the treacherous Cambridge spies, the Profumo affair). For his English audience other sources of discontent were the loss of empire, subordination to American foreign policy (similar to Habsburg Austria's relationship with Germany), and nuclear-arms proliferation.

In Osborne's play, the most obvious departure from Kisch's version of the Redl story (which Osborne had learned by reading Asprey's book, discussed below) is its bravura central act, which depicts a flamboyant homosexual ball where many of the participants are dressed in drag. (Osborne heard descriptions of such 'drag-queen' balls in 1930s London from Christopher Isherwood.[24]) As it turns out, however, there is little solidarity among these men who would be shunned or marginalized by society if their sexual lives were known. In its internal divisions of personal enmities, ethnic bigotry, class-consciousness, and self-defense of one's privileges, the homosexual counter-world mirrors the 'official world', seen earlier in the play in a staid Hofburg ball scene. Because of its frank depiction of homosexuality, the play was officially banned by the Lord Chamberlain but was mounted in a theater masquerading as a 'private club', winning a large audience and a major annual theater award, and then moving on to success in the US. Interested readers can read the play itself.[25] Excellent discussions and analyses of *Patriot* are in John Heilpern's[26] and Luc Gilleman's[27] biographies of Osborne.

Though it was a critical success when it debuted, *A Patriot for Me* presents particular challenges and obstacles that prevent revival performances for all but the most financially well-endowed theatrical companies, primarily the elaborate sets and the size of the cast. Nonetheless it was performed in its entirety in major productions in Great Britain and the USA in the 1980s and 1990s. At least two revivals have taken place since 2000, and a new Magyar translation was performed at the National Theater in Budapest during the 2012 season. This production aroused the hostility of Hungary's extremely conservative government, evincing many of the same criticisms that emerged during the play's original production in London. Hungarian government spokesmen and their press allies were offended by its frank treatment of homosexuality and its skepticism about nationalism and established authority.

One other aspect of Osborne's play is of interest in any examination of continuities and departures from the historical record. That is, its indebtedness to Robert Asprey's portrait of Redl. Osborne admitted reading the book and finding its overall story suitable as a vehicle for a narrative exploring identity and social problems raised by homosexuality — but he dismissed it as a "bad biography" (which it was not).[28] The present author has found episodes and dialogues in Asprey's book that were used to build scenes in Osborne's play — they are too numerous to be discounted as coincidences.[29] The point is that Asprey was a little-known writer whose emotionally overwrought prose describing Redl's innermost character was heavy-handed, while Osborne's use of this material was done very stylishly and in sharp, penetrating language (his special gift), and for these artistic transformations Osborne gets the credit due him. In this passing and altering of the story's fact-based episodes (and speculative ones as well) from Asprey to Osborne, Kisch's narrative of Redl's actual career in espionage is further obscured.

Twenty years later István Szabó adapted some of Osborne's material for use in his 1984-85 film *Oberst Redl* (*Redl ezredes* in Magyar), which had an international cast and dialogue in German.[30] During these twenty years Osborne had transformed himself from being an outspoken 'unaffiliated socialist' into something of a conservative 'Little Englander' living as a country squire (he made and spent several fortunes). Meanwhile Szabó had started his career as a film student at a time of extreme turbulence in Hungary's political life. The year of Osborne's sudden ascendancy, 1956, was also the year of England's humiliation in the failed Suez Canal military fiasco, while in Hungary an armed rebellion against Russian control of Hungarian affairs was taking place. The uprising was crushed, and its aftermath was brutal: executions of leaders; imprisonment of thousands; mass (illegal) emigration of people of talent and energy; residual groups of Russian troops functioning as military police; expansion of the Hungarian (secret) political police; and the latter's establishment of a huge network of informers spying and reporting on their fellow citizens. Szabó himself was caught up in this web of deceit and treachery as a student, discussed below. The lost war (World War II), the internal divisions and recriminations that accompanied it, the postwar lingering of fascist sympathies in some quarters, the forceful establishment of a communist dictatorship that attempted to control cultural as well as political life, and the failed revolt against Russian control all produced the sinister and demoralized society of Szabó's formative years.

During the intervening decades between the dire events of 1956 and *Oberst Redl*, Szabó had been involved in more than two dozen films as director, script-writer, and producer. His 1980s films made him well-known internationally, but recent Hungarian history and experience were always on his mind. He could transform this history, he could displace it in time and location, but he couldn't forget it or ignore it. *Oberst Redl* is a film that presents the Hungarian history of Szabó's youth in disguised form, with a strong personal-emotional force that produced willful distortions of Colonel Redl's life and deeds. It is also, I believe, part of a trilogy of 'betrayal films' that includes *Mephisto* and *Hanussen*. In both of these films the protagonists betray their own pasts and former friends and colleagues in order to cultivate the patronage and protection of society's new masters, the Nazis. In contrast, Szabó's Redl detests the very idea of betrayal, yet winds up being betrayed by the institutions that he admires and loves above all.

Before considering Szabo's transformations of the Redl story, I should say a few words about the film's technical and dramatic qualities. The cinematography is superb as the camera roams through the diverse lands of the Dual Monarchy, and the color-palette of scenes is evocative (misty blue-gray in the mountainous Hungarian countryside, bright at the Adriatic seashore, opulent in rich browns, reds, white, and gold in interior scenes representing Habsburg imperial decor). The acting is excellent, with Klaus Maria Brandauer playing Redl and Armin Mueller-Stahl as the sly and sinister Archduke Franz Ferdinand. All supporting actors are skilled professionals. In terms of the film industry's varying standards of 'production values', the film received praise, as it should have. Dramatically it is also compelling, as the viewer is induced to identify with Redl as a talented, passionate man who must conceal his modest origins and his homosexuality in order to advance his career. As the film progresses he becomes sympathetic as the victim of a plot to frame him for treason, initiated by Archduke Franz Ferdinand.

Oberst Redl acknowledged Osborne's *Patriot* as a source (Szabó had seen the 1983-1984 revival of *Patriot*). The opening credits list Szabó and Peter Dobai as the film's writers, followed by a statement that the film is a "free adaptation" of Osborne's play and that it has also been "inspired by the events of our century". While the latter phrase can be construed to refer to the events leading to the First World War, it is also an allusion to very specific Hungarian events of mid-century that are foremost to Szabó's transformations of the material from Osborne and any other sources he may have used, including Kisch and Asprey. Szabó was aware of Kisch, as will be seen below.

The interpretation of *Oberst Redl* as belonging to a group of three 'betrayal' films is neither unique nor original. Yet Szabó maintained that the films in question were not a trilogy at all, having been conceived as independent depictions of men floundering in societies ruled by forces intent on suppressing individuality. Two knowledgeable commentators, David Robinson and Peter Hames, wrote a chapter about Szabó's *Oberst Redl* in Hames's anthology of essays on Central European films.[31] They also link it with *Mephisto* and *Hanussen* in the opening lines of their essay:

Critics have chosen to regard Istvan Szabó's *Mephisto* (1981), *Redl ezredes* (Colonel Redl, 1984) and *Hanussen* (1988) as an integrated trilogy. Each is an impressionistic and speculative biography of a historical figure whose personal ambitions and dilemmas reflect and illuminate aspects of twentieth-century European history.[32]

In the main it is difficult to disagree with anything that Robinson and Hames say about *Oberst Redl* with respect to directorial intentions, dramaturgy, or the way recent history influenced Szabó's thinking. Taking this into account, it is still astonishing to find the following interview quotation from Szabó, until one realizes that the standard theatrical devices of the Stalinist state in framing up inconvenient individuals had permeated his thinking to the extent that his version of Kisch's reporting is at odds with all earlier evidence. The following quotation includes Robinson and Hames's preceding paragraph, followed by Szabó's remarks:

Szabó, however, brought to the Redl affair the skepticism of someone who had grown up under Stalinist socialism and the show trials of the Cold War era. The Redl affair had first been made public by the Prague-born Jewish journalist Egon Erwin Kisch (1885-1948), and the way that Kisch had come by his scoop put Szabó uneasily in mind of later techniques of leaking incriminating evidence:

"It was very peculiar. Kisch was watching a football game in a stadium in Vienna, and next to him was an Austrian officer. He paid no attention to the officer, because he was interested in the football. When the game was ended, the officer had disappeared, but beside Kisch was a sealed package. He assumed that someone had dropped it, and opened it up to try to trace the owner – only to find all the documents about Colonel Redl. Why would these documents land up at a football stadium? And why next to Egon Erwin Kisch, already an important news reporter? Who had the idea of leaking this information to Kisch, knowing that he would be sure to publish it? In such a case one begins to ask, were the documents authentic, or was it a prefabricated affair with manipulated documents?

The story instantly reminded me of the machinery used for the show trials organized by the Stalinists regimes in the USSR, Hungary and Czechoslovakia – the trial of László Rajk in 1949, for example. And then Redl's suicide recalls the 'confessions' and self-incrimination and apparent self-destruction that was part of those trials. The only version we have of his death is that issued by the Austrian War Office ... But did Redl commit suicide? They say he did, of course, but perhaps his last words before shooting himself were, '"Don't shoot!' It was also very significant to me also that Redl was essentially an outsider, coming from one of the many minorities within the Austro-Hungarian empire. The existence of so many minorities caused a lot of confusion in the Austrian army before the First World War. The generals needed to keep the army together; and maybe a scapegoat helped. And if a scapegoat was needed, it was obviously important to find him from a minority."[33]

Based on a supposed need for a "unifying scapegoat from a minority", Szabó's reasoning implies that sinister Austrian powers wished to destroy Redl while risking great embarrassment to themselves. The first mistake is that Redl was from a minority; he was not, being a German-Austrian. Szabó seems to have accepted that he was Ruthenian—or a Ruthenian Jew—without having delved into Redl's biography. The point is moot anyway—a widespread 'spy mania' throughout the Austro-Hungarian lands during 1913-1915 found members of *all* of the Empire's nationalities suitable for prosecution, though most official investigations concentrated on the Ruthenian population of Galicia, which was presumed to be susceptible to Russian subversion.[34] Ironically enough there was a mirror-image spy mania in Russia, including lurid fantasies of who had "sold out" Redl to the Austrians, as described by William C. Fuller in *The Foe Within*.[35] The second mistake concerns the idea of a scapegoat (which Redl became *after* the failures of the Austro-Hungarian army in 1914–1915). The last thing the dynasty wanted in 1913, in the unstable diplomatic atmosphere of the two Balkan Wars, was a show-trial of any high-ranking Austrian official, civilian or military. This would only undermine already shaky confidence in the regime. The partially successful cover-up of the Jandrić espionage case and the attempt to replicate this a month later in the Redl case indicate official anxieties about publicizing crimes committed by military men on behalf of a foreign power. Matters like these were to be handled through closed military tribunals, not highly publicized trials, though leaks to the press about such cases were unavoidable, given the complexity of Austria's factional political life. Redl's forced suicide was chosen as a 'policy option' specifically to avoid such a trial. The public prosecution of a General Staff man for treason was extremely unpalatable to both military and civilian authorities. The General Staff spent a year attempting to stanch every leak about the Redl case and to minimize its likely consequences, pursuing a course of action that is the opposite of a 'frame-up'. Rather, there was a continuously revised cover-up about what had actually happened and, after the military debacles of 1914-1915, an effort to make Redl retroactively responsible for them.

Szabó's paranoia on these points and his distortions of the Redl story are only understandable in the light of his personal experience. As was revealed after the collapse of the communist system, when Szabó was a film student in the 1950s, the Hungarian secret police pressured him to act as an informant on his classmates, a common practice of the system (others would have been informing on Szabó). Like many people who had been put into this uncomfortable position, he stated that he relayed harmless gossip about his friends and colleagues to the police, who expected no more and therefore pursued no 'actionable intelligence' about treasonous activity. While they framed prominent targeted individuals, the security services also wanted to show their political masters they were zealously compiling mountains of files on people from all walks of life. Whatever the truth of his own case, the pervasiveness of informants and Stalin-era scripting of show-trials were deeply embedded in Szabó's psyche. But what about the details of his strange distortions of the actual Redl case?

Where did Szabó get this story of Kisch and the package? He seems to have taken elements from the alleged football match that Wagner missed, leading to Kisch's scoop, and re-arranged all of its elements (e.g., he has Kisch watching a football game in Vienna rather than managing his team in Prague) until they matched his own notion of the appropriate mechanics of a 'frame-up'. He may have been incorrectly recalling a passage from Kisch's memoirs stating that while he was reporting on the case in 1913 two police agents made him an offer to swap military news in return for his revealing his sources of information about the Redl case (an offer he refused).[36] Szabó was aware of Kisch's writing about the case, but has altered it beyond recognition. There's 'history' here, but of a peculiarly twisted kind, displaced by half-a-century and reconfigured by Szabó's personal response to the new anti-human forces that emerged in the USSR's satellite states and intensified to their peak in Hungary during his youth.

The film's narrative expands all earlier film and stage treatments of Redl, starting with a picture of his happy home in the living quarters of a Lemberg railway station where his father is the station-master, moving through his military school days, and arriving at Redl's appointment to the leading position in military intelligence (incorrectly identified as a War Ministry office rather than as a branch of the General Staff). The episodes that comprise these stages in the protagonist's life are invented by Szabó and his screenwriter (Peter Dobai), though the film owes a few scenes to Osborne's treatment, including the ethnic politics of a duel between officers (tinged with anti–Semitism) and the device of two dance balls which are 'mirror–scenes', each reflecting Redl's state of mind at the time.

The ball scenes illustrate the trajectory of Redl's deepest motivating ideal, that of loyalty to the dynasty that has raised him high on the basis of merit as a professional soldier. The lesson that he owes everything he might become to the Imperial House is drummed into him by his mother as he is sent off to a military academy. Redl soon enough comes to believe that his 'real father' (in the broadest social sense of the word) is the benevolent Emperor, Franz Joseph—he even refuses to return home for his own father's funeral so as not to miss the academy's celebration of the Emperor's name day. In the first of the two balls, a provincial affair in Galicia, he comes to blows with his old friend and fellow officer, the Hungarian nobleman Kubinyi, after the latter has insulted the regime and its dynasty as feckless. In an earlier scene in the sitting room of a brothel Kubinyi had angrily raised the red flag of the Habsburg's suppression of Hungary's 1848-1849 revolt ("Arad", and the "butcher and hangman Haynau" are the Pavlovian stimulus-words here, which had been used by Osborne in similar fashion[37]). His resentment is countered by another officer that things worked out well for the Magyars, because the Compromise of 1867 (*Ausgleich*) gave them free rein to abuse their numerous minority subjects. Redl, acting as the adult in the room, calms them down with remarks on the wisdom and necessity of Habsburg policy. For Szabó the Russian army's intervention and victory over the Hungarian rebels at Arad in 1849 prefigure the events of 1956.

However, by the time the second ballroom scene occurs—a masked ball in Vienna—Redl has become as cynical as all of the opportunists and careerists on whose conversations he eavesdrops. Behind a glittering façade there is pervasive self-dealing, corruption, and fear that the dynasty might suddenly collapse, thereby destroying the pleasant life of its leadership class. By this time he believes the dynasty has targeted him for political reasons, fitting him up for a show-trial of a disloyal minority member. Szabó's typically Hungarian preoccupation with the untrustworthiness of the dynasts plays a role in determining how Redl follows a pathway that takes him from a deep loyalty to the Habsburgs (a 'supranational' attitude inculcated in all army officers) to one of despair and emotional rejection of his former love–object.

In all of these scenes Szabó is constructing the identity of a man destined to become a victim of the authorities, as personified by the Successor. His portrait of Franz Ferdinand constitutes his most egregious departure from the historical record, for a variety of reasons discussed below. The Archduke is seen as his most conniving when he interrogates Redl about his nationality and religion, suggesting that Redl should find his own *Doppelgänger* as a suitable subject for a show trial; and when he orchestrates Redl's final entrapment. Szabó accents these scenes with a piquant Habsburg-era flourish, having Franz Ferdinand drily whistle a Strauss waltz to himself as his mind is spinning a web to ensnare Redl, who senses that a fraudulent case might be built against him for strictly political reasons (finding a high-level traitor in order to stimulate public fear and rally patriotic sentiment). He tells Kubinyi's sister, Katalin, that he dreamt he was crushed by his father (symbolizing the dynasty) sitting on his chest. Redl's marriage, arranged by Katalin, is another Szabó invention. Katalin knows Redl is homosexual, though he has had sexual relations with her as a substitute for his real heart's desire, her brother. In reality, like many career officers, Redl was a bachelor, a status that raised no suspicions. The plot against him proceeds.

In a later scene the Successor performs as a 'script-writer' (in the Stalinist sense of outlining a false story to be used against a perceived enemy) at a star–chamber meeting of military officers. The cabal has filmed Redl passing information to his young Italian lover, who has been paid by them to induce him to pass along military secrets. This is not real espionage because Redl intuits that the information will be going back to the Austrians, not the Italians or Russians — he acts out of fatalistic despair at this point. Franz Ferdinand lays out the terms of arrest (choosing Redl's old friend Kubinyi as the messenger bringing the news that he will be prosecuted unless he commits suicide). And the conspirators determine how the press will "discover"their fabricated story — an official at the meeting suggests information should be leaked to a reporter in Prague (this alludes to Kisch, though he is not named). As the plot reaches its fruition Kubinyi faints after delivering the message and Redl paces his room frantically before taking his own life. None of this happened in Vienna in May, 1913. Most unbelievably, Szabo's Redl is not a spy, working for either Russia or Italy — in real life he was paid handsomely by both.[38]

Why is all of this so preposterous? In the first place Franz Ferdinand was not an instigator or organizer of police or military intelligence investigations of minority nationalists suspected of plotting treachery, though Szabó indicts him as the creator of a Stalinist show-trial script. He was wary of nationalist dissent and had ideas for dealing with it if and when he came into power. Like the Emperor and various ministers, he was a recipient of information about treason or espionage cases that were developed by the police and the *Evidenzbüro*, not an originator of such information. Secondly, as noted above, there was no desire for a public show trial of a high-ranking military man, which would only undermine public confidence in the regime. Thirdly, the furious reaction of Franz Ferdinand to the deliberately misleading behavior and perceived irresponsibility of the General Staff in the Redl affair indicated his desire to reduce their influence as an independent executive branch of the government, not to employ them as part of a cabal. But Szabó took advantage of the traditional Hungarian dislike and distrust of the Successor, whose plans for "dis-

ciplining Hungary" and cutting down its political-diplomatic influence (with which Chief of Staff Conrad agreed) when he came
to power were an open secret. His anti-Semitism, dislike of liberals
and journalists, and desire to harness pro-Slavic movements into
the service of the regime were also well-known (Hungarians
feared 'drowning in a sea of Slavs'). In Hungarian eyes he made a
perfect villain. Portraying him as the personification of sinister
government forces came readily to Szabó, who, as a result of his
formative years in a communist system of fraudulent treason trials, may have even believed in the historical accuracy of his own
inventions in this respect.

As to Redl the man, the film sketches him sympathetically
while also creating a false biography. Based on scenes set during
Redl's service time in Galicia, Szabó hints at Redl's allegedly concealed Jewish roots. For instance, while dining in a small-town café, Redl is approached by a friendly Orthodox Jew who invites
him to a Sabbath dinner, leading to a violent fit of temper in Redl,
who feels publicly humiliated. In another scene, after his regimental colleagues ponder the rumor he is a Jew in disguise, he walks
back to the garrison late at night followed by a pack of yelping-
dogs—beset with anxiety, he shoots one of them. In his troubled
mind he fears he is being 'hounded' by forces out to assail his Ruthenian roots and expose his humble origins and his secret homosexual life (but not his double-life as a spy, for in Szabó's representation he is no such thing). In contrast, the real Redl's military records classify him as German and of the Roman Catholic religion.

Redl imagining himself as a man always being hunted by
others is also an aspect of Osborne's construction of his protagonist's character, noted by Gilleman and quite possibly taken over
by Szabó.[39] Thus, while Osborne identified with Redl as a talented
outsider who started out in life with no connections to the high
and mighty, Szabó, Jewish and from Transylvania, identifies with
him somewhat on the basis of ethnicity, and even more so as a victim of the detested Habsburg 'spider's web' of police spying on
their fellow citizens. The idea of the Habsburg Empire as a police
state (or spider's web) goes back to Metternich's time—it is exag-

gerated, and has been undermined by the research of the British historian Alan Sked.[40]

As to how much anxiety over his double life the real Redl experienced, there is no documentary evidence about his state of mind during his years of service, other than love-letters to various men expressing his desire to continue his way of life. As an intelligence officer he was aware of the need to compartment his sexuality from his career and his activities as a spy (he had no 'lover confederates' in espionage). Szabó takes a few well-known incidents such as the Hekailo-Wieckowski-Acht espionage trial (the Ullmann-Worowka affair in the film) and transforms them into elements of the supposed plot masterminded by Franz Ferdinand. He also creates a Redl who is thoroughly professional officer admired by his superiors, but then cross-cuts this with scenes in which fellow officers find Redl distasteful as an ungentlemanly pryer into their lives and also as a possible concealed Jew who cloaks his identity in a military uniform. To repeat, none of this reflects the record of Redl's life or the constant positive evaluations recorded in his personnel files.

Oberst Redl was a joint West German-Austrian-Hungarian project. It had wide European, English and American distribution and drew a positive response from film-goers and critics (it won the 1985 BAFTA award for Best Foreign Language Film and was also nominated in the same category for an Academy Award). Obviously Szabó took major liberties with the story as reported by Kisch and Asprey and dramatized by Osborne. And he took even more liberties with history, viewing it through a very Hungarian lens. Szabó cannot be criticized as a Hungarian chauvinist, many of his films being critical of Hungary's political regimes and cultural climate in the twentieth century. In general he is negative and cautionary about the history of his country, while he also expresses a wistful, nostalgic melancholy about aspects of pre-World War II Hungarian life in several of his films. Nonetheless, in *Oberst Redl* he took advantage of some cherished, hoary Hungarian ideas about the Habsburgs as oppressors in order to construct his linked portraits of Redl and Franz Ferdinand. Ian Armour and John Schindler's remarks represent the view of historians who have considered Szabó's film in the light of the the long historiography of Redl case:

> Why, then, make a film with, as its starting point, a real historical person and real historical events, and deliberately jettison the real for the utterly imaginary? ... The Redl being discussed here, however, is the Redl of Szabo's imagination, not the Redl of history... In appearance, Colonel Redl is a brilliant illumination of the past, a slice of historical life, from which most intelligent viewers probably come away feeling they have learned something about the Habsburg Monarchy, about history. In reality, Szabó's film is nothing but a vast and pointless fiction, which by building its story around the skeleton of real events, gives fantasy the veneer of truth. It is a depressing contribution to the long list of unhistorical films. The extraordinary history of the real Redl deserves better treatment.[41]

And,

> The films are particularly wide of the mark, the worst offender being Szab's [sic] aforementioned 1984 *Colonel Redl*; a magnificent film, it is based on John Osborne's play "A Patriot for Me" and is factual in the very limited sense that there was an Austrian colonel named Alfred Redl: the rest is fantasy.[42]

Drama and film critics, who judge such works on other bases and who are often ignorant of the facts behind such dramatizations as Osborne's play and Szabó's film, will shrug off critical objections based on the idea of bad or implausible history—to them aesthetic standards, compelling drama, and psychological plausibility are primary, with historical accuracy a distant second. While Szabó's film is a cinematically effective work of art, unfortunately it has little to do with Colonel Alfred Redl and his role in Austro-Hungarian history as understood by historians.

So history received a serious stretching from Szabó in order to underscore his anxieties about the coercive pressures of a powerful state authority extant during his own formation as an artist. But, when it comes to artistic adaptation of historical materials, just how elastic is history itself? In 1989, four years after Szabó's film, when once again Central Europe was re-arranged and 're-thought' in response to the sudden and unanticipated political fall of Communism, Pavel Vilikovský, a Slovak novelist, exploded history—as instanced in the life and times of Alfred Redl and as imagined in the works of earlier artists who had turned to his story for their own purposes. Szabó's film ends with images of showers of debris from exploding artillery shells, indicating the onset of World War I in response to the Archduke's assassination by Serbian nationalists. Vilikovský's explosion of the Redl story turns the debris of history into comic fantasy. And, as Szabó's Archduke remarked of Redl's visage, much of the comedy is brutal and sensuous.

While it would seem that there is little left to be artistically extracted from the historical Redl case after Osborne's and Szabó's treatments, Vilikovský has done that and more. After being submerged in a moral atmosphere of murk and doom for eight decades, Alfred Redl's reputation and its metaphorical and allegorical usages assume a very odd and entertaining role in Vilikovksý's novella *Ever Green Is ...* , which, while not exactly light-hearted with respect to the history of the era and the region, uses the looming presence of the Colonel in a comic manner. The significance of the book's title, which appears in its last sentence, is explained in the American edition in a footnote by its gifted translator, Charles Sabatos:

> "ever green is ... [the horse of life]'" This is a parody of Goethe's well-known line from Faust: "Grey is theory and ever green is the tree of life." The 'green horse' may refer to Marcel Aymes' 1933 novel *The Green Mare*, a somewhat magical-realist [surrealist} saga that was popular in Czechoslovakia in the 1960s.[43]

The opening paragraph of Vilikovský's surrealistic comedy introduces the Colonel's specter in a new and condensed nominative form, conjoining his first and family names:

> Beginnings you say, first steps? How good-looking I was then! A pale face, that was the fashion, velvety blond whiskers ... yes, I still didn't shave much; that was when I became the lover of Colonel Alfredl.[44]

The reader will as soon become as confused about who "I" is as he or she is about the role of the Colonel, for the narrator is anonymous and at the same time, protean and ubiquitous on the European map of the twentieth century. The narrator is, of course, an intelligence agent, a spy. But for whom, against whom, and for what purpose he spies remain ambiguous throughout the story, which begins as a scenario of his seduction by Alfredl that is never completed, because the narrator has a wandering mind and suffers from a surfeit of free association. There are other impediments along the way to consummation, such as the Colonel's erotically inconvenient seizure. Moreover, the narrator loves the words of his own and other languages, and he expands words, stock phrases, adages, and metaphors to their improbable literal and figurative conclusions, leading him and us down bizarre and often ridiculous by-ways. Like *Finnegan's Wake* (though more firmly anchored in our everyday reality), the book is a linguistic playground where Vilikovský exhibits acrobatic verbal skills that yield comical puns and identity-shifting semantic equations.

The anonymous narrator's identity and career, and the identities of his patrons and targets, are described without ever being explained — why bother, when they make no rational sense? He undertakes a series of ridiculous espionage adventures in Switzerland, Israel, Romania, Cyprus, and Lebanon, all of which use elements from James Bond movies and other generic spy-thrillers, taken to ludicrous, incredible conclusions. For instance, he runs afoul of "Israel's greatest spy, Jerzy Stummdorfer-Wisniewsky, real name Yehiel Blum", a ski instructor (in Israel!) who snares him and ships him out of the country (which is "full of Jews", to the narrator's surprise and dismay) in a crate labeled "Sauerkraut". "Stummdorfer" is literally "dopey villager", perhaps better Americanized as "stupid hick". He has an affair with Mata Hari, who wishes to settle down with him and run a bicycle shop. Closer to home, when he enters Slovakia as a "Czech tourist" an effort is made to apprehend him as a spy (or perhaps to rob him), which he escapes by becoming inextricably coupled to a Slovak cowherdess with whom he is having sex. Nothing is easy — she suffers from an extreme form of "vaginismus", and, locked together in this touching posture and mounted on the back of a cow, they become an object of tourism themselves. This naturally has an adverse effect on his efforts to spy on the program producing the new Czechoslovakian fuel, *dynalkol*, made from wood spirits; the

Vacuum Oil Company has sent him on this mission—for seekers of historical resonance, let it be known that before his career in the SS, Adolf Eichmann was an Austrian sales-representative for this company whose "territory" included Czechoslovakia..

The above episode is an entry portal into a discussion of relations between Czechs and Slovaks, a topic of intrinsic interest to readers from those countries and one that naturally fascinates Vilikovský. "Czech tourist" is a facetious phrase alluding to relations between the two major nationalities of the new, post-1918 country of Czechoslovakia. The harnessing together of Czechs, Slovaks, half-a-million 'sub-Carpathian Ukrainians' (Ruthenians), 700,000 Hungarians, and approximately 75,000 unhappy Poles of Silesia as a political entity had been a war-time improvisation by agile politicians (the Czechs Masaryk and Beneš, the Slovak Štefánik) who were in exile and lobbied the Western Allies to support their creation. The preceding list of nationalities does not include the approximately three million Germans who lived in border strips and pockets of Bohemia and Moravia, often referred to misleadingly as "the Sudetenland Germans". Problems in dealing with this important and troublesome minority were ultimately the pretext for the forced dissolution of the Czechoslovakian state in 1938-1939.

Slavic fraternity could not overcome basic political problems of the new republic that stemmed from the long history of Czechs having once had their own state, followed by four centuries of rule by Germans, while Slovaks had been a politically weak minority in the very different Hungarian system of rule. After initial enthusiasm for the unification of these related peoples the poor country-cousin Slovaks began to resent their treatment by the more urbanized, wealthier, and better-educated Czechs. In short they felt themselves patronized by the Czechs and the victims of economic and cultural discrimination by the central government, which established the institutions of the First Czechoslovakian Republic during the 1920s. The historian Joseph Rothschild gives the bare statistics that go a long way toward telling this story to the English and American reader: during the 1920s Slovakia was flooded by an influx of about 100,000 Czech bureaucrats (tax-collectors, judges, teachers, police, and military officials) as well as business and professional men; among them there were almost 30,000 Czechs who were now running various aspects of public administration and education in Slovakia.[45] This amounts to one Czech adviser (or 'baby-sitter') for every twenty-five or thirty Slovaks; one can understand the latter's irritation. These events, in which the Czechs who poured into Slovakia are referred to as "tourists" by Vilikovský's narrator, are summarized colorfully in his novella; his statistics[46] are quite close to those given in Rothschild.

As Rothschild also points out, in the polemically important census of 1921, many Slovaks were uncertain of their nationality or what the census-takers were looking for, so they listed "Hungarian"; after all, even if they spoke Magyar poorly or not at all, they had lived in 'Upper Hungary' for almost a millennium.[47] And for every three identifiable Slovaks in the published census, there was still one real Magyar living in the neighborhood, making the latter a substantial and politically sensitive minority in what had been until 1918 the northern precincts of their old 'millennial kingdom'. The first post-war censuses in the successor nations of the former Austro-Hungarian Empire were conducted to maximize the number of indwelling 'co-nationals' and minimize the number of minorities; nobody was fooled. The multiethnic character of many cities in this region can be inferred from the recent history of their names: Bratislava was Pozsony for its Hungarian inhabitants and Pressburg for its Germans; Slovakia's second city, Košice, was called Kassa by its Hungarian majority and Kaschau by its German minority.

Vilikovský's narrative, in the fashion typical of post-modernist novels is constructed to allow ample opportunities for digressions like the above 'treatise' on Czech–Slovak relations (the specific place of *Ever Green Is ...* within Slovak post-modernist literature — a small realm — and its multilingual games as a mirror of the historically fraught relationships between the Czech and Slovak languages has been analyzed by the book's translator in a 2003 essay).[48] These digressions lead the reader all over the map of Europe in the twentieth century, and the information they deliver comprises amusing surveys, 'instructions' to the reader (who is often addressed directly and is in obvious need of instruction), and parodies of the standard elements of spy stories known to the public through adventure books and films. In several chapters Alfredl disappears altogether, yet, as a sort of tutelary spirit of all spies, he has a numinous presence that hovers above the fabulous adventures and droll observations concerning espionage and the routine activities of secret policemen who spy upon their fellow citizens. Alfredl himself is mostly mute, his body entangled in a novel-length embrace by the narrator, who is the character given to digression and wordplay.

With respect to wordplay, examples abound: "It's funny, as a child I thought that a starlet was a baby star and couldn't understand why my uncle said all starlets were whores ... how admirable are the paths of language." Or: "You're an amateur, or greenhorn, as they say — which, I might add, isn't the same as a blues trumpet." In matching wits with his feeble auditor (the constantly insulted reader, "you,") he demonstrates how the second part of a metaphorical comparison is always broader and more vivid than the first part:

> ... all right. Now my turn, and in order to show you my virtuosity, I'll begin from the same starting point: You smell like the broth from the socks of an Olympic marathon champion. Good, isn't it? Your turn. Yes, yes. I smell like shit, that's true. Admirable. Sharp and to the point. One point I envy you, I admit: that flight of fancy.[49]

The ironical insults aimed at the reader go so far as to embrace whole nations, whose traditions and 'greatest cultural achievements' the narrator catalogues, starting with the unloved former masters of Slovakia: "You are as many people as the languages you speak. This common saying has a single regrettable exception: You can speak Hungarian twenty times over, and yet you still won't stop being a Hungarian" (a very dubious compliment). Like the Slovaks, the Poles relish only their own survival as a nation.[50] The achievements of the Romanians can be summarized by two paltry items — a sheep-cheese and the ruins of a castle in Slovakia. Regarding the Swiss: "Just think, a nation that reckons the quality of a cheese according to the number of empty holes in it!" The Germans function merely as a negative exemplar of extremes that others should avoid. The glories of French culture have been reduced to de Gaulle's big nose and advertisements for cologne and condoms. And the once-powerful Austrians? "An eloquent witness to the fall of Austria is the fact that the best school in Vienna is Spanish, and it is attended by horses," an allusion to the popular displays put on by the rigorously trained Lippizaner horses at the Spanish Riding Academy. Before listing the deficiencies of his fellow-Europeans, Vilikovský had mordantly mocked the foibles of his own countrymen: they are described as uneducated, unhygienic (taking advantage of sporadic rainfall to wash), superstitious, given to preposterous wedding customs, and cretinous drinkers of toxic, home-made alcoholic beverages. Is this bestiary of decaying nations intended seriously, or is it meant as a catalog of clichéd stereotypes, the debris of regional history? Probably the latter, with the proviso that stereotypes sometimes skirt uncomfortably close to the truth while they irritate collective self-regard.

Concerning the author's identity-shifting semantic equations, a comical pseudo-historical passage provides an example:

> ... and, back in Colonel Alfredl's embrace, I came up with an idea as simple as the egg that Columbus crushed to make it stand on end. I was truly on the ball ... to be specific, the lower one on the left. I don't know if you realize that in view of its weight, the left testicle is the bearer of fertility and virility ... and may even produce identical twins, who grow from a single egg – that's having your egg in one basket, so to speak.[51]

He continues in this vein to discuss the legend that Hitler suffered from this condition (monorchidism) after Ernst Röhm accidentally crushed one of his testicles with an iron boot when they were scurrying to escape the Munich police in 1923 during the failed *Putsch*. So we go from the equations of a legendary egg (as a metaphorical terrestrial ball) with balls as testicles and testicles as eggs and eggs as embryos and back to metaphorical eggs and wind up in a realm where 'history'—fictitious episodes in the lives of Hitler and Columbus, who allegedly used an egg to demonstrate the earth's sphericity —is nothing but a tall tale.

Buried within these free-association passages and stories are oblique criticisms of both the chauvinistic and communist societies in which Vilikovský had spent his whole life up until 1989. For instance, the above-mentioned adventure of the narrator's literal sexual entrapment by the unwashed Slovak cowherdess has a surprising sequel. This fetching creature is named "Stella II", and later in life, despite her mute bovinity, she becomes an exemplary model of a "Slovak woman professor". This nasty comment may reflect realities of the educational system in which Vilikovský grew up, with academic appointments and titles given to unqualified dunces for political reasons. The most egregious incident of this practice in the communist bloc were the sham "chemistry professor" credentials awarded to Romania's Elena Ceauşescu, who was apparently unaware of the chemical composition of water.

The various episodes describe the fantastic life of the narrator, whose mind wanders through them as he is embraced by Alfredl, the supreme spy. Often the infamous Colonel is only a convenient springboard from which the narrator launches his verbal assaults. In fact "Alfredl" is but a fleeting presence in the narrator's mind in Chapters 6 and 7, which deal with a fantastic, but strangely credible, treatment of police interrogation. The emphasis here is on how one should behave as an ideal subject of interrogation. Above all one should create a story that not only entertains one's interrogator but also flatters him; this is a sort of etiquette manual of victimology. As for the interrogators, forget fancy new gadgets and psychological techniques, all they need to know is "how to kick the shit" out of people—the old ways are the best ways. The event that brings on these meditations (and connects them to Alfredl, who has already asked the narrator the standard interrogator's question, "who are you and who sent you?") is the narrator's capture by the Romanian security police, who ask him this same question after placing him naked upon a slender beam of ice—where he worries about getting diaper rash—which is suspended above a tub of sulfuric acid, a scene that has faint and preposterous echoes of Kafka's infernal torture machine in his story *In the Penal Colony*.

The scene brings to mind not only Kafka and his fiction. The narrator's Romanian torturers, whom he calls "teachers" in a verbal slip, refer to their device as the "accelerator". This is reminiscent of various tortures utilized during the worst of the Stalin years being referred to as the "conveyor belt" or "physical methods" or "wet work" by their security-police practitioners (Cheka, OGPU, NKVD, MVD and KGB in its history of official designations in the USSR, with counterparts in each of the Soviet satellite states of Central and Eastern Europe). In the USSR's rhetorical vocabulary a conveyor belt as metaphor is homage to an everyday tool of the working class in whose name torture is being conducted as necessary to the building of socialism. A fictional treatment of this subject much closer to Vilikovský's lifetime and experience than Kafka's story is the Czech Pavel Kohout's novel, *The Hangwoman,* a black farce set in a special academy in Prague that teaches the philosophy, history, and practice of torture and execution. From these transmuted memories of the recent Central European past, when police interrogations were a pervasive feature of the region's ruling regimes, the narrator moves into the broader reaches of Slovakia's history in the last four chapters of the novella.

Regarding the brutality prevalent during his lifetime, Vilikovský alludes to another phenomenon that plagued Central and Eastern European nations and societies: anti-Semitism. Commencing with the opening sentence of the second chapter, after you have witnessed the narrator's carnal embrace by the Colonel, you the reader are spoken to with kindness and consideration (and yet you are already found unattractive, perhaps even defective, in some respects):

> Dear young friend, I see traces of inner confusion on your face, a certain, I would say, moral quandary. Your sympathies for a young, talented, and keen-witted officer, not entirely dissimilar to yourself — well, my ears did not stick out so much, and as for your nose (are you Jewish?) — are struggling with disgust at the situation, which was a denial of life's conventions and traditional morals, not to mention good taste.[52]

244

Later the narrator mentions that the Slovaks are not especially desirous of expelling or extinguishing their Jewish neighbors — rather they prefer to keep them at hand in order to have someone to kick around.

The foregoing gives the reader an idea of how the novel is constructed and progresses, veering from one digression to the next as it slyly critiques life in this part of the world. But the question arises: Why choose Alfred Redl as a figure for allegorical transformation, a figure who metaphorically presides over the turbulent and demoralizing aspects of the time and place that fascinates the author? The answer is rather obvious. Redl was the 'spy of the century' in Central Europe, at least in that portion of it embraced within the vanished Austro-Hungarian Empire. Given the prominence of intelligence and secret-police organizations in this part of the world throughout the twentieth century, who better to choose as an emblematic, potent but hidden presence than the infamous spy-as-traitor, Colonel Alfred Redl?

The narrator's nickname for Alfredl is "K.u.K.", introduced on the book's first page, where the reader is told to pronounce this as "kook". This also has deep literary resonance. Readers who have ranged through the literature of the twilight years of the Austro-Hungarian Empire will note K.u.K.'s resemblance to Robert Musil's term "Kakania" in *The Man Without Qualities*, a word that elicits near-mythical aspects of that time and place.[53] Musil's coinage is based on the ubiquitous adjectival phrases of the era, *"k.k."* and *"k. und k"*. (pronounced respectively in German as "kah-kah" and "kah-unt-kah"). They stand for "imperial-royal" and "imperial and royal", titles that captured the Habsburg dynasty's shifting status in the two different halves of the Austro-Hungarian Empire. "Kakania" also takes advantage of the German slang word for feces, *Kacke,* and has another resonance in Hungarian — *kakuk* means "cuckoo" and implies a dweller in the realm of "cloud-cuckoo land", akin to the Yiddish *"Luftmensch"*. In Musil's noun and its adjectival form of "kakanisch", with their childish excremental aura, this entity is a brilliant-yet-foggy presence that permeated the hearts and minds of many of its denizens, even after the Dual Monarchy vanished in 1918. Vilikovský's Alfredl as "K.u.K." adds a sinister note to this presence.

After numerous other detours and frivolous verbal excursions throughout the story, Slovakian history and the fable of extended coitus with the cowherdess finally give way to the deferred consummation of the Colonel's seduction of the narrator, who lets us know that we have embarked upon an educational tour that may contain pleasant surprises. Having come full circle, he returns to the embrace of Alfredl (while not totally ignoring "you"):

> ... because it still applies, dear Colonel ... What's that? I know you're a reserve corporal; I'm not talking to *you* ... Dear Colonel, it still applies, as Goethe famously said, that gray is theory and ever green is ... " ... the horse of life!" the Colonel cried out, opening the door on the cabinet, and when he stretched his limbs, he joyfully neighed.[54]

So ends the story of the interrupted embrace, with Alfredl's equine transformation, reminiscent of Apulieus's disappointed and hexed lover from antiquity who was transformed into an ass—it would not be surprising to learn that Vilikovský found Apulieus's *The Golden Ass* a source of amusement as well as of literary inspiration. And there is a sly allusion to E. E. Kisch in this passage as an annoying presence who intrudes into the amatory shenanigans—for Kisch was a reserve corporal in the Austro-Hungarian army at the time of the Redl affair and was certainly intrusive as far as the authorities were concerned. In leading us so far away from the historical Alfred Redl and the chronicler of his crime, Kisch, Vilikovský has managed to land us back in a Central European political and cultural stew that has much in common—ethnic prejudice, hapless leaders, authoritarian states—with the region as Kisch experienced it during his own lifetime, though he imagined all of these problems could and would be addressed by rational solutions (i.e., his idea of socialism).

Vilikovský thoroughly transformed the character and career of Alfred Redl, turning a historical figure into an allegorical one whose presence waxes and wanes as the loosely organized episodes of a surrealistic comedy unfold. His "Alfredl" represents a departure from serious referential usages of the historical Colonel Redl and his ambience, a farcical wringing-dry of the subject. Is it a final departure? Perhaps not. Some of us may live to see new artistic ventures built with this very old material which has been rummaged through for a century. It took the Napoleonic era more than a century to be (almost) exhausted of its artistic uses, and the world of Hitler and Stalin, now vanishing from living memory (and dreams), is bound to have another half-century as fertile fictional ground—the grandchildren and great-grandchildren of its perpetrators and victims will look back at that era's excitements and miseries with a false clarity born of time's winnowing of the true and messy life-stories that comprised it.

Redl's life ended just before the onset of the First World War, one of the two linked wars that are pivotal events of what has been called 'the crisis of modernity'. The extensive influence of these wars still manifests itself through their aftershocks, but each succeeding decade will dampen these shocks until they become imperceptible among the din caused by new crises that await us as we unwittingly create the conditions of their birth. The future always arrives on time, but not quite in the way we had imagined it, as the rapid disintegration of the Warsaw Pact bloc and the subsequent collapse of the Soviet Union show clearly. The recent return of the atmosphere of the years from 1914 through 1948— when anti-Semitism festered and extreme nationalism clashed with 'universalist' socialist ideologies and the latter cannibalized the former in order to make itself palatable to chauvinists—shows this past echoing over and over. And, whatever shape the future takes, playwrights, novelists and film-makers will be tempted to revive older historical events as points of comparison with their current reality, transforming history into art.

Throughout the 20th century the Redl story maintained its purchase on the popular imagination of Central Europeans for several reasons: it was a 'typical twilight of the Habsburgs tale'; it had an exciting (and troubling) denouement; and, most of all, it had actually happened and was believed to have had momentous historical consequences. In contrast, though its 'historical status' can be questioned (on the grounds of its ultimate factual basis and its significance), the Toni Gallows story was also able to capture the attention of artists and their audiences years after its first appearance as a one-page feuilleton. It too was a trenchant late-Habsburg tale, but one focused on society's underlings. Just as the Redl story had a long afterlife in biography and art, the tale of Toni Gallows found artists interested in transforming it one way or the other in order to make it appeal to audiences no longer familiar with Kisch's version of the story. These revivals and altered narratives are the subject of the next chapter.

Chapter 10. The Toni Gallows Story on Film, the Prague Stage Again, and Television

Like the first three Redl films a well-known cinematic adaptation of the Toni Gallows story took place during Kisch's most active years as a journalist. This 1930 film illustrates how the popular medium of cinema was being used to extend the lifetime, modify scenarios through constantly improving technical possibilities of cameras and film, and broaden the audience for stories that had first appeared in writing or on the stage. With regard to later adaptations of the Toni Gallows story, one can also speak of an "afterlife", but this term should be restricted to stage- and television-plays that were produced between the 1960s and the present; they will be discussed after an examination of the 1930 film.

In contrast to re-creations of the Redl story, different standards of comparison and evaluation should be applied to considerations of film and television versions of Kisch's play about Toni Gallows. There is no issue of historical accuracy involved, as there is in the Redl films. However, drift away from Kisch's intentions and his basic framing of the story come into play. A director converting one form of fiction into another has a great deal of freedom in dealing with source material, though the original writer may complain. In his memoirs Kisch recounts the fantasy story of Toni in purgatory and heaven after giving its allegedly factual basis in events he witnessed and people he met as a Prague journalist familiar with the world of prostitutes, pimps, thugs, and the police. But this re-telling of the tale was not published until 1941-42 and was unavailable to readers (and interested film directors) in Europe until 1947, an unpropitious moment for nostalgic returns to the past. As Kisch told the story in his 1920s feuilletons and cabaret-play versions, it begins immediately after Toni's death, followed by the tale of her earthly life as recounted in a fantasy set in the afterlife. These were the versions available to interested parties in 1930, when the first film adaptation of the story was made. Embedded within the play's fantasy framework are passages of monologue and dialogue that convey social criticism of the forces responsible for Toni's seedy milieu and sad life. The earthly episodes that occasion her reflections are elicited by the President of the Court of the Last Judgment, who proves to be a sympathetic listener to Toni's tales of woe, and they were transformed and used in very different ways in the film and television-versions of the story.

Karel Anton, discussed above in connection with the 1931 'dual release' versions of the Redl film, was also the director of *Tonka Šibenice*, which has a special place in the history of Czech cinema, being the first Czech film with sound.[1] After decades of silently disintegrating in studio inventories (or being disposed of as excess), it all but disappeared from the historical record—at present only one copy exists, used as a master for reproduction. The film is now enjoying a revival through film festivals and availability for home viewing. Originally released as a silent film, it was brought back to the studio for the insertion of post-synchronized sound passages and re-released. In the available copy of the film, the sound is almost completely confined to musical accompaniment, used to orchestrate mood and elicit emotional responses in the audience.[2] In two isolated 'head-shot' frames Toni sings short solo songs (the only spoken words in the film) and gives one horrifying shriek toward the film's end. Subtitles for dialogue and placards that register shifts in scenes are still there, the conventional markers of silent films. The sole surviving copy has French inter-titles and subtitles, as adapted for the film's distribution in France at the time. First released in Czechoslovakia, the film had wide distribution throughout Europe, playing under various titles (*Tonka Šibenice, Die Galgentoni, Tonischka, Erlebnis einer Nacht*, and others).

The wholesomely attractive actress Ita Rina plays Tonka, while her co-star in terms of dramatic impact is Josef Rovenský, who plays the condemned man, Prokupek. The rest of the cast, with the exception of countryside dwellers, is professional, its members having had substantial careers on the stage and in silent films. The question of interest to those familiar with Kisch's versions of the story is: how was the material of his play (fantasy-comedy and social critique) treated in the film?

The answer to this is that Anton jettisoned the story of the afterlife (in which the play's comedy resides) and altered the 'Toni backstory' on earth into a tale that bears little resemblance to Kisch's variant versions of the story; yet it makes its own critique of the demi-monde. Anton de-brutalized, sanitized, and sentimentalized the narrative in a way that made it fit into the conventional cinematic mold of romantic fables, while avoiding film-industry taboos about explicit depictions of sexual acts. Yet, the film is entertaining, touching, and well-worth watching from the historical and aesthetic points of view. It implicitly, and at times explicitly, endorses Kisch's social message regarding the evils of prostitution, though this had been far stronger in his 1914 novel, *Der Mädchenhirt*, than it was in his play. The camera-work and framing of shots and scenes are excellent, and there is a pervasive contrast between the dark narrow streets of Prague and the open, sun-soaked countryside.

Anton presents Tonka (Toni) as a respectable country girl whose life took a wrong turn after she moved to Prague. The film begins with her return home to visit her mother. As she sits in an antiquated train with toy-like cars and miniature engine, we see her well-dressed, well-shod, and using her cosmetic kit. She smiles demurely at her companions on the bench seats, all rugged and shabbily dressed farmers and bare-footed peasant women toting the implements of their livelihoods (an axe, a woven basket, etc.). The scene highlights the contrasts between country and city people—not only in appearance but also in presumed moral character, with the countryside winning the implicit 'battle of values'. Once home she is struck by the innocence of farm animals, lavishes gifts on her tearful mother, and encounters her old suitor, Jan. Her mother's concern about her welfare and Jan's ardor to re-establish a romantic relationship produce anxiety and guilt (she is hiding her status as a 'fallen woman'). After a two-months stay, when we see her entranced by the beauties of the countryside and its rhythms of springtime life, Jan proposes to her. Driven by guilt about her life in Prague, she flees home to return to the city. As the film's interjected placards indicate, the director has structured Tonka's life as four episodes in the passage of a single year's seasons.

In summer she is back in her 'elegant' brothel (the clients are well-dressed, clean, middle-class), though drinking heavily and obviously unhappy. On the crucial night when she is recruited to service a condemned man, she is moody, remote from clients and 'the girls', all of whom are envious of her good looks and popularity. She takes on the job from a combination of despair about her lost life in the country and indifference to the present; she may see it as the ultimate good deed that will pay for her sins. As it turns out, differently from Kisch's version, she doesn't have sexual relations with the prisoner, but spends her night in the cell comforting him. She is more like a mother than a wanton woman. She soothes him by letting him play with a wind-up Father Christmas doll retrieved from her pocket, and the morose man is both tearful and thankful as she maternally strokes his hair. He is terrified of spending his last night with only his own thoughts, and Tonka helps him live through this passage with compassion.

Persecution and catcalls from her fellow prostitutes await her when she returns to the brothel; her former clients also reject her. She has become "Tonka the gallows girl", the hanged murderer's "bride" or "widow". Eventually the madam of the establishment demands she leave, and she begins her life on the streets. By a stroke of luck she meets Jan again at a summer carnival, when he is visiting Prague. He proposes to her and they return to her home town. On the evening before the wedding she is delirious with joy, wearing a beautiful silk dress that Jan has given her. But as fate would have it, Jan is in a tavern being toasted on his good luck, when he overhears a traveling salesman who was a patron of the brothel where Tonka was once the star attraction. Soon enough he reveals her urban identity, sending Jan into a funk of rage and humiliation. Fuming, he rushes to her house and throws her to the floor while her mother removes a beautiful shawl Tonka gave her (a sign of maternal rejection), then faints. A crowd of angry peasants, chanting insults, gathers at her home—here the director removes the veil of innocence and communal spirit that has cloaked the simple folk of the countryside so far. They are as vicious and heartless as Tonka's persecutors in Prague. She flees to the city once again.

During the film's brief four minutes of 'Autumn' we see Tonka sitting alone and desolate in a park under a shower of leaves, wandering the streets at night until dawn, dejected and fatigued. These brief scenes are interspersed with cinematography capturing nocturnal views of the city and the maze of streets in which she lives. This part of the movie is a graphically Expressionistic interlude, required only by the seasonal framing of the story. It is an 'aesthetic interim' that allows viewers to infer Tonka's inner state through postures, facial expressions, autumnal scenery, and panoptic views of a misty Prague.

Winter arrives. By now Toni's good looks have been damaged by alcohol and the harshness of life on the streets. Her face is puffy, her eyes baggy, her make-up smeared. On a snowy night she stumbles into a scabrous dive of the type described by Kisch, full of Prague's most unsavory and down-and-out inhabitants. For the price of a drink she is happy to regale her rough companions with the story of the condemned man. Through another coincidence Jan is in Prague and wanders into the saloon. Seeing her being pawed and manhandled he comes to her defense, a brawl breaks out, and she bolts for the street, running under a pair of horses rushing along as they pull a cab. She dies in Jan's arms, clutching her old wedding dress (retrieved from a street vendor to whom she had sold it) and lapsing into semi-consciousness, where her dreams come true in a vision of an idyllic countryside wedding and a reconciliation with her mother.

As the reader can see, the film's narrative is a far cry from Kisch's. The film is effective as a romantic melodrama, with professional touches of cinematic Expressionism in its light-and-shadow-play, a clever swirling montage scene, and, in the final dying-vision scene, a stately tableaux in which figures move hieratically. However, the director has eliminated the gritty vigor and humor of Kisch's monologues and dialogues and the farcical depiction of the afterlife. Tonka has been cleaned up and given a life history that takes her far away from the defiance and vulgarity of

Kisch's Toni Gallows, and there is no real probing of the world of urban prostitution in a socially critical manner. The comical dream-life of a pleasant brothel as a reward in the afterlife has been replaced by Toni's final, delirium-induced vision of wedded bliss in her home town. The Berlin and Prague presentations of the tale on cabaret stages, often rowdy venues, were different in their goals and effects. As usual, film directors do as they wish when they adapt a written story for the screen.

There was interest in re-writing the story as another screen-play for a Czech film in 1938, this time with the assistance of Karel Čapek, who was at the peak of his fame. On account of Čapek's death in late 1938, the Munich agreement, and the 1939 occupation of the Czech lands as a German Protectorate, the project was not completed; its partial resuscitation forty years later, this time in East Germany, is noted below. The politics of the late 1930s through the opening decade of the Cold War were so turbulent, insistent, and overwhelming that art in several media were 'summoned to the flag' (or to support an ideological system), so 'genre stories' and comedies were fewer in number, though always appreciated by world-weary audiences whose lives were being turned topsy-turvy by 'world-historical' events. Conditions were not suitable for reviving the story until the further passage of time.

But, eventually, the Tonka story had a renewal of life on film and television. In 1955 an American movie, *Hold Back Tomorrow*, had its central theme based on *Tonka Šibenice* (with appropriate changes for setting the narrative in the southwestern US), as indicated by its story-line summarized on a film website.[3] It was directed by Hugo Haas, who also wrote the film's screenplay. Over a twenty-year period Haas had a distinguished and busy career as an actor and director in Czech theater and cinema. Jewish, he fled Europe after the Nazi takeover of Czechoslovakia in 1939. He settled in Hollywood, where he re-established his career as a film actor, director, and screenwriter. He was obviously familiar with Kisch's Toni Gallows story and the 1930 film.

As the post-World War II political situation in Europe stabilized on both sides of the east-west dividing line, many of Kisch's books were reissued in both East and West Germany (translations continued as well). In 1960 the large-scale publishing project of assembling, organizing, and commenting on the complete Kisch oeuvre (the *Gesammelte Werke*) began in the German Democratic Republic (DDR). The Aufbau Verlag of East Germany had acquired (or, in a communist state, assumed) the publishing rights to all of Kisch's work.[4] As a separate work for stage and screen, *Galgentoni* was revived in both Germanies and, in 1989, in Czechoslovakia (as both a staged and televised play). These five adaptations of the Toni Gallows story that appeared between 1965 and 2009 are the subject of the following discussions.

In the DDR, where a general revival (and official promotion) of Kisch's work was under way, a broadcast of the story as a television play took place in September, 1965. The success of this effort to maintain interest in Kisch can be seen in the fact that in 1978 his 1925 book, *Der rasende Reporter*, led the 'literary bestseller' list in East Germany, slightly ahead of Tolstoy's *War and Peace*.[5] The second revival of the play, also televised in a 1978 DDR broadcast, may have contributed to this surge of enthusiasm for his work. Interest in Kisch in West Germany remained high too, indicated by the creation of an annual journalism prize awarded in his name, with an endowment established in 1977. Whether or not they were competing with their rivals in the eastern half of Germany, it appears that West German admirers of Kisch's writing were not going to allow his reputation to be monopolized by the DDR's literary establishment, who often presented him to the world as an "outstanding communist journalist". As the present book makes clear, he was more than that.

The first television play, a black-and-white production, was broadcast by the DDR's newly established television agency, *Deutscher Fernsehfunk*.[6] According to the German national film and television archives, no copy of this 1965 production has survived. It had a Czech director (Rudolf Vedral) and a cast of nine actors and actresses who played their roles using the German names and the earthly and afterlife settings of the 1922 and 1927 versions of the play. The description of the play in documentary sources (television listings and reviews) indicates that the troupe put on Kisch's play as it was performed in the 1920s. It was in fact a 'filmed play', similar to those seen on American and English television during the 1950s and 1960s. It had musical accompaniment and would have used standard, stylized stage sets. The camera did not roam through city streets or the countryside, as in 'filmed-on location' productions (e.g., the 1930 film and a 1972 West German television play discussed below). A television listing service described the upcoming play and noted how Kisch contrasted bourgeois sanctimony and hypocrisy with the rough exterior and compassionate heart of a 'real Berliner' (Toni), indicating reliance on the Hamburg-Berlin script.[7] The *Nationalzeitung*'s reviewer ("S-R") wrote that beneath the jokes and depictions of religious pretense and false piety, there was an ironic handling of social and political relations that yielded *"eine pralle Tragikomödie von 'grausamster Romantik in grauester Realistik'"* ("an intense tragicomedy of very brutal romanticism set within the most dismal realism").[8] In the *Tribüne* the reviewer, Ehrentraud Novotný, praised the high-spirited glee of the actress playing Toni (Marianne Wünschler).[9] The 1965 reviewers' perception of the play and their reactions to it are almost identical with the positive critical responses of the 1920s, as cited by Glosiková and Poláček. There were no complaints of flimsy dramatic structure or thinly-sketched ancillary characters. Whether or not the cast used the very broad Berlin accent of Kisch's 1922 text is unknown.

Although there are no surviving recordings of this television performance, the director's interview of Friedrich Kisch, the youngest brother of Egon, followed the broadcast of the play and has been preserved.[10] In it Friedrich responds to a reading of passages from *Marktplatz der Sensationen* in which Kisch describes his descents into Prague's demimonde with an affirmation that he clearly remembers this aspect of his brother's days as a journalist for *Bohemia*. When queried about Kisch's other efforts as a dramatist he remarks briefly on *Die gestohlene Stadt* and the Redl play. Asked if Kisch should be considered a Czech or German "stirrer" (provocateur), Friedrich replied that, although Egon considered himself as "belonging to the German cultural world", he disdained nationalism in all its forms.

A second revival of *Galgentoni* in the DDR was mounted in 1978 as a 'dinner-theater play' in Karl-Marx-Stadt (formerly, and once again, Chemnitz). A performance of the play was videotaped (in color) and is available for viewing.[11] The director, actors, and supporting technicians created a credible replica of the 1920s cabaret atmosphere, starting with a half-hour of music, comical songs, patter, and commentary on the difficulties of theater-life, as told to the surrounding audience by two actors (Wolfgang Sörgel and Matthias Günther) feigning to be waiters strolling among the tables; later they assume roles in the play, which runs to an hour in length. Staging props are minimal yet clever. Of all the later adaptations of the story, this performance is probably the most authentic presentation of Kisch's play as he conceived it (i.e., the closest a contemporary viewer can come to experiencing the play as it was performed during the 1920s). A few liberties with Kisch's script have been taken: omission of the verbal jousting between the clerical staffs of heaven and hell in the court of judgment ("Purgatory"), including their grousing about smoking rules at the Purgatory scene's opening; some lines of commentary-type dialogue are moved from one part of a scene to another; and the Czech slang and referemces to Prague locales used by Tonka in the 1926 text have been reduced. With these modifications, the 1926 script was used. This returns the action to Prague, and the audience is instructed beforehand to note that the protagonist is "Tonka Šibenice, now known as Galgentoni". Hamburg and Berlin touches and references from Kisch's alternate versions are nowhere in sight or sound.

As to directorial additions, there are several brief song-and-dance routines that fit smoothly into the progress of the dialogues as Toni tells her life story. The lead actress (Amy Stöger) gives a performance that effectively conveys Kisch's intended melange of rambunctious comedy and pathetic reflections on the heroine's earthly fate. The 'weighing of the souls' is imaginatively staged with a simple prop, and Toni's Prague police-file is comically immense. The High Judge is gruffer and less dignified in appearance than one might imagine, but Sörgel artfully fits this new characterization in mien and manner. The rest of the cast is adept and lively. The musical passages consist of gypsy- and tango-like dance tunes, with the sound of violins and mandolin punctuated by rhythmic bursts and squawks from a tuba and bass-drum—an authentic German cabaret style of music. Heaven as Koutsky's brothel is depicted as merry, naughty, and noisy. At the play's end the camera pulls away from a table with a 'menu' displaying Kisch's writing credits and then pans over another placard stating *"Nach einer Erzählung von Karel Čapek"* ("from a re-telling by Karel Čapek"), alluding to the eight pages of script notes the Czech writer made in 1938, which were to be used in another Tonka film that was never made. In spite of this credit and the minor alterations of the 1926 text, the play as performed is unmistakably Kisch's work. The middle-class appearance of the audience and restaurant (filmed as background elements of the play) and the lack of any socialist-art framing remarks during the prelude of conversation between the waiters give no hint that we are in the East Germany that was a political and ideological bogeyman in the Western imagination. One might think oneself out for a pleasant evening in New York or California. The television listing of the program summarizes the narrative of the play, commends the strong characterization of Toni by Stöger, and remarks on the suavity of its opening prelude, with the actor-waiters serving the patrons wine as they banter and sing.[12]

On the other side of the rather permeable 'iron curtain' a 1972 adaptation of the Toni story was directed by the prolific Michael Kehlmann (father of the novelist Daniel Kehlmann), yielding a polished 90-minute television film (*Galgentoni)* that exhibits the typical departures film artists made in order to fill out Kisch's lean narrative.[13] Kehlmann's film has all the earmarks of a thoroughly professional production, including a talented cast (many of whom had long, distinguished careers) and high-quality cinematography — it could have been released in cinemas as well as shown on television. The older side streets of Munich are a plausible stand-in for the streets of Prague as they appeared at the end of the nineteenth century.

Toni is played by the attractive and stylish Czech actress, Jitka Frantova. Her 'backstory' in this version takes place entirely in the 'classy brothel' (the "Salon Diamant") where she works; there is no hint of a nice country girl who took a wrong turn when she came to the big city, as in the 1930 film, though Toni, who is illiterate, has a bordello employee write a kindly (and misleading) letter to her mother. While viewers of the cabaret play in the 1920s saw simplified sets, the bordello depicted in the 1972 television play conforms to Kisch's descriptions of the more elegant establishments he wrote about (e.g., Goldschmied's in Prague or the Viennese bordellos frequented by Archduke Viktor Salvator in the Redl play). The film's opening scene creates the milieu—a well-furnished bordello during the morning hours when the salon room is being tidied up and the last customer tumbles out onto the street after engaging in some banter with a piano player who is a composer and improviser. The pianist has a wry sense of humor and comes to play an unexpected role at the film's end.

All of the original story's characters, both central and peripheral, are amplified and given individual touches that are not in Kisch's play. Toni, for instance, has a love of colorful women's hats, which plays a role in the film's final 'fantasy scene'. Like Karel Anton in 1930, Kehlmann has dropped Kisch's framing of the story as a series of dialogues in the afterlife. The role of the police official who recruits a prostitute to service the killer Prokupek is expanded and comically enhanced. 'Kommisar Flixner' takes the rough edge off Kisch's prototype for the role, the Chief Inspector known as 'old Lederer', by dispensing sage advice as a means of softening his authority as a police official, while he has a romantic relationship with the brothel's madam (is this a token of 'official corruption' or an indicator of a natural, human behavior—the latter, it seems). Toni's inamorata in Kisch's version, Blondie Mirko, is a man of the streets who dresses in a flashy thug's style. Kehlmann replaces him with a comically confused young man who imagines that he might someday marry Toni, army Lieutenant Molnar. And the custodial chores are performed by Aloysia, a haggard 'retired prostitute' who is kept on to work as the bordello's housekeeper and factotum—she is the counterpart of the character 'Olga Petřiková' in Kisch's play. Kehlman adheres to Kisch's story that Toni volunteers for the task of having sex with the the killer out of sympathy for this downtrodden woman who was first assigned to the job.

The crux of the play, the prison scene with Toni servicing Prokupek, also has comic elements foreign to the original grisly treatment. While obese, obsessed with food, and childlike in his appearance and conversation, Prokupek is not the ugly, menacing, and foul-mouthed character sketched by Kisch. He and Toni establish grounds for friendly banter before having sex. All the while the nosy prison guards are treated comically as they eavesdrop and spy on the pair in the cell. While the scene is very different from Kisch's and Anton's handling of this material, its aftermath is not—upon returning to the Salon Diamant, Toni is exposed to vituperative and hypocritical rejection by her fellow prostitutes and former clients, just as in the original story.

Rather than the harsh street-walking life that Toni has been exiled to in Kisch and Anton, Kehlmann shows us only the steady unraveling of Toni's position as the star attraction of the bordello. This ends in her ejection by the Madam, leading to a closing scene that obliquely refers to otherworldly matters. The brothel's pianist ('the composer') proves to be a wry angel who has a sympathetic dialogue with Toni as he magically collects her hats in a whirlwind—they were thrown out of the windows of the brothel with contempt by the other girls. He then demonstrates his clumsy powers of flight, and Toni, in an elevated mood, walks off into an undefined future. Here the 'afterlife' component of Kisch's story and play—central to its framing and comedy—is reduced to a comical grace note

Kehlmann reduced a broader urban social world in which hierarchies exist and people jostle for position and exert power over one another (implied in Kisch by its mirror-image in the brothel and even in Purgatory and Heaven) into the cozier, but no less Hobbesian, domain of the bordello. His social critique of the whole situation is embedded in a witty, comical approach to the story, and both the vulgar and pathetic elements of Kisch's Toni have been suppressed in order to create a charming period piece.

Nearly three decades later an inventive Czech writer, Miloš Macourek, came back to the Toni Gallows story in a way that pared down its essence to a dialogue between the deceased and her guardian angel, with a few off-stage lines for the voice of God. In 1989 his Toni Gallows play, *Racajda*, was shown on Czech television.[14] The play's title itself shows Macourek's familiarity with Kisch's 1926 text of the story, referring to Toni's favorite sentimental love song, played on the gramophone at Koutsky's brothel. With Macourek's involvement the play underwent further modifications and has been replayed (and once again, shown as a television play) numerous times on Czech stages as a 'two-woman show', with the added staging device of having the theater audience vote on whether or not to admit Toni to heaven at the play's end.[15] The revived and transformed play has been performed under its shortened old name, *Tonka Šibenice*, at several Czech theaters in Prague and elsewhere during the years between 2011[16] and 2018.[17] Future performances seem likely, given its popularity in Prague, the ease of its staging, and its low production costs (two actresses, a simple 'one-scene does all' set, and some pre-recorded musical accompaniment played at appropriate moments).

While eliminating all of Kisch's auxiliary characters, both earthly and heavenly, Macourek does bring viewers back to Kisch's comical idea of life beyond the grave, as in the 1920s play. The play opens with Tonka lying in her white death-shroud, in animated suspension until she is aroused by a bell-ringing guardian angel who summons her by name. Tonka's spirit is not in Purgatory but some undefined way-station on the posthumous path to heaven or hell. The guardian angel will be her interlocutor as Tonka explains her life, and the audience will decide her ultimate fate. There is one stage prop, a flimsy life-size puppet with a paper-bag head — this is used to help Tonka describe various events in her earthly life, similar to the way hand-puppets or drawings are used by a psychologist trying to elicit information from a traumatized child. The angel's early attempt to learn the source of her nickname is evaded by Tonka, who agrees to tell the tale later when she gets some cognac (this follows Kisch's narrative).

Like earlier film and television directors, Macourek has given Tonka a deeper 'backstory' than Kisch, with many of its elements taken from typical life-incidents that result in a young woman becoming a prostitute: a broken home; the early death of her mother; a father who acts as a procurer, offering the teen-age Tonka to a sexually eager friend; the father's desertion of Tonka and her mistreated brother; the drift into prostitution with the help of an older woman who finds her clients, both acceptable and perverted ones as well. At the play's outset Tonka tells a pathetic-comical story about a judge named Motejlek who is depressed by his discovery that his wife is having affairs with his colleagues on the University's law faculty—he dies from sorrow and alcoholism, avenging himself by leaving his fortune to prostitutes. This is a transformed version of a story about a "Professor Unger" in Kisch's memoirs.[18]

Macourek intersperses Tonka's biography with other digressions, having her repeat comical tales she has heard about Adam and Eve, the snake, and the apple in the Garden of Eden, and the marital problems of Cain and Abel. By the play's mid-point we are back to Kisch's version, with Tonka ensconced in Mrs. Koutky's brothel, where she is the popular "blue Tonka"; her favorite client, Blondie Mirko, is mentioned as well, but with the distinctive detail of wearing a flower in his trouser's fly. This is followed by the story of her sexually servicing the condemned killer Prokupek and the derision she encounters upon her return to Koutsky's. As in Kisch she moves to an inferior brothel and is soon forced to become a street-walker. Other details of her grim life and milieu have been invented by Macourek, such as the pathetic fate of a young girl forced to sell drugs by Tonka's vicious landlady.

At this point there is a passage that is quite new, the story of her relationship with a client (Karel) who becomes a boyfriend who treats her well, in return for which takes care of his family; unfortunately he is killed in a steamship explosion on the Vltava. This episode is based on material and events described in Kisch's novel, *Der Mädchenhirt*. The narrative returns to Tonka's stressful life on the streets and is punctuated by the story of her brawl with another old prostitute competing for the favor of a prospective client (this is the episode of the fight with "Stuttering Betty" in Kisch's play). As in Kisch, these colorful episodes comprise her Prague police file. At the play's ending Tonka ruminates on life's injustices and God's role in allowing such things to happen. After instructions on correct flying motions she receives wings and flies off into ethereal darkness, with her destination to be decided by the audience.

One can see from the above summary that Macourek wove together materials from Kisch's play, a story from his novel, and tales from other works written over four decades in which he described the world of dives and prostitution in Prague. He manages to do this through a cast reduced to two actresses, Tonka and her guardian angel, who replaces the fatherly Chief Judge of the divine Purgatorial court in the 1926 play. In spite of these changes *Racajda* (*Tonka Šibenice*) is more faithful to the spirit of Kisch's play than either the 1930 film or the 1972 West German television play. Because its simple construction allows it to be performed in small venues with a mere suggestion of scenery, it extends the story's performance possibilities beyond what might be achieved in mounting the play as a revival with Kisch's full cast and setting.

A note of interest here is that Czech website information and poster advertisements for the play state that it is "the true story of a Prague prostitute". This claim rests on what might be called a 'continuation of an urban legend' that Fritz Hofmann, Kisch's well-disposed East German biographer, attempted to discredit, as discussed above in Chapters 6 and 7. It seems that Czech audiences will remain in the dark about this, being unaware that Tonka's reality has been contested by writers and researchers who have delved into the matter. Nonetheless, at the present moment the story (or legend) of Tonka Šibenice is alive and well in Prague, one century after appearing as a light-hearted feuilleton.

The artistic license that writers, screenwriters, and filmmakers extended to themselves when adapting the story of Tonka Šibenice for viewing by successive generations is far more acceptable than similar artistic transformations taken with the Redl story, which, in the final analysis, has an important series of historical events at it core. However, in terms of authenticity, 'freshness', and a realistic depiction of the Prague demi-monde (representative of numerous cities of the era), it is again better to go back to Kisch, due to his direct experience and familiarity with this world of struggle, humiliation, misery, and occasional happiness based on the enjoyment of 'the small pleasures of small people'. His writing about this world is vivid and seldom sentimental or moralizing. He expected readers and viewers to arrive at the correct moral, and even political, conclusions through their exposure to rigorous factual writing, enhanced by his literary capabilities; his own political beliefs were usually implicit rather than openly argued.

Kisch's Toni Gallows story fits into a long series of pieces that exposed the harsher side of life in Prague, but, driven by the imperatives of the cabaret stage, it also introduces both vulgar and surrealistic comedy into its narrative, setting it apart from his more sociological and polemical writing. Toni as a colorful eccentric also takes her place in a series of such portrait-sketches made by Kisch over the years. Taking the most recent revival and adaptations of the story into account, it is obvious that it is not too embedded in its time and place (Kisch's youthful years in Prague) to be of interest only to antiquarians and historians of the period. More generally one can say that the 'expiration date' of fascination with the late Habsburg years has not yet arrived. Societies divided by wealth, class, and power are still prevalent, so Toni's world, illustrative of such social fissures, remains an incentive to modernize the tale, just as her own 'defiant individualism' (reminiscent of John Osborne's protagonists, including his Colonel Redl) makes for compelling drama and raucous comedy.

Chapter 11. Transformations: History, Historical Fiction, and Fantasy

Historians are guided by the record of facts that represent salient events from the time-period they are examining. This is not the same as 'sticking to the facts and only the facts', which would yield a chronicle-style list of major historical events with no further explanatory context. Historians select and consider facts, or interrelated series of facts, on the basis of their presumed historical importance. For instance, starting in 2013 and based on the publishing viability of centennials, there were numerous revisionist histories (and even 'counterfactual' ones) that addressed the causes and consequences of World War I, which ushered in three-and-a-half decades of extreme political turbulence and rapid cultural change (some historians refer to the 1914–1945 years as 'Europe's second Thirty-Years War'). When sketching the immediate pre-war atmosphere in Austria-Hungary, historians often discuss the negative social and political effects of the Redl case, integrating his story into a larger picture of public demoralization and anxiety. Some of that war's causes and effects are still with us, such as the ethno-nationalistic conflicts that immediately preceded and followed the war and that re-emerged in the 1990s and remain prominent in the 2010s.

Self-interests, group-interests, prejudices, and the extraneous aims ('building nationalism', 'building socialism', 'exalting capitalism triumphant', etc.) of narratives that attempt to link facts together and explain them also play a role in what topics historians consider and how they write about the past. Evidence to support such explanatory narratives comes from many sources: official documents; newspaper accounts; interviews of participants in noteworthy events; personal letters between private individuals caught up in history like small boats in a storm; memoirs of the high and mighty or administrators of various policies; and diaries of the 'common man' or front-line conscript in a war or the 'common woman' on the home front of a society in crisis. The real goal of many a memoir is nothing more complicated than a plea to posterity for attention and remembrance: "I was here and did this or that or witnessed this or that—here is my recollection, please don't let the memory of my existence or these events be effaced by the passage of time"; or something close to that. Regardless of this motive, many such works deserve reading, even cherishing, and are of value to political and social historians, as they lead readers from abstraction and generalization to concrete examples.

The social status and point of view of the memoirist or diarist has a great influence on the outcome—look at the differences among Kisch's on-the-scene-notes from the first offensive against Serbia and the miseries of the winter war of 1914–1915 in Galicia, the recollections of Conrad von Hötzendorf, and the official post-war Austrian military histories of the same events. From the point of view of rifleman Kisch, an account with the look, smell, and sound of chaos and high-level confusion and dereliction emerges, while the Field Marshall tells us all about why his mobilization and campaign plans were good, why they misfired, and who was responsible for their failure (not him, of course). Official reports and histories are often expert at minimizing mistakes and diffusing responsibility. Competing accounts are needed for a rounded historical picture in which interactions between different levels of reality are illustrated and explicated, as difficult as this task is.

Historians keep trying to do that explication by sorting and prioritizing the weight and value of competing accounts (a kind of evidentiary triage). Writers of popular histories give us highly readable narratives with an emphasis on leading personalities, heroes and villains, 'key' decisions, and unlikely or surprising conjunctions of events, all bundled up in a way that often flatters the collective egotism of a group or nation (e.g., America as 'benign, disinterested savior' in the two world wars, or the USSR as the 'liberator' of Europe in the second of those wars; or England as the 'defiant and lonely outpost against Nazism', and so on). Academic historians dig deeper and, when they can maintain professional standards of objectivity, are less certain of fully rational or emollient explanations of events and their significance. By dismissing nationalistic myths and legends they often irritate the collective ego, as they should do.

The Redl espionage scandal of 1913 resulted in competing accounts of what really happened, what its consequences were, and who was responsible for the events themselves and their presentation (and deliberate misrepresentation) to an interested public. Newspapers filled in the gaps and near-vacuum of official information with their own speculations. Kisch was one of the speculating journalists in May and June of 1913, but after the war he made a serious attempt to learn as much as he could about Redl's career as a spy, the events of his final day, and the inconsistencies and evasions of the self-exculpatory versions provided by the General Staff. He also assessed the impact of these events on the opening campaigns of World War I in Serbia and Galicia, where the Austro-Hungarian army's losses of men and equipment were disastrous. Like many journalists he was writing 'the first draft of history' when it came to reporting on current events and those in the recent past, memories of which were fresh and often raw. His 1924 book on the Redl affair, with all its flaws (many of which were not exposed for another four decades), gave what came to be accepted as the 'standard version' of what had happened.

Kisch's pre-World War I journalism had been dedicated, for the most part, to chronicling the lives of common men and women ('the little people') of late-Habsburg Prague.[1] With regard to writing about an Empire on its unknowing verge of extinction, his Prague pieces place him in a position that both departs from and overlaps with the literary writing of some of his most famous compatriots (e.g., Musil, Roth, and Kafka). Concerning these last three the literary critic and essayist James Wood wrote, "Roth is the great elegist of that Empire; Robert Musil its great analyst; Kafka its dark allegorist."[2] Each of these men is in a different intellectual and emotional relationship with the object of his contemplations. Though not exalted to the same level of literary attainment as these three writers, Kisch can be considered as the 'exemplary chronicler of everyday life' and the explorer of society's underlying power structures in the late Dual Monarchy and its successor states. Many writers of the late Habsburg Empire who lived in its successor states yearned for the vanished world of their youth. This nostalgia was tinged with hostility toward its object—the Emperor and his (and their) Empire as a symbol of a 'timeless' benevolent system that through inattention and frivolity proved incapable of preserving itself. Kisch was not prone to such ambivalent nostalgia, though, in his final years he did experience yearning (and the grief that follows loss) for his family and friends who had once been part of the vital milieu of his youth.

The new conditions of the post-1918 world and Kisch's political commitment to international communism meant that, while he continued to write about the same kind of people, he reported on their lives in Germany, and, from 1925 through the 1940s, throughout the wider world. Prague was in his past, but it kept a grip on his imagination. His writing about the Redl case was an exception to this rule because it dealt not with everyday social and economic matters but with a high affair of state. Kisch was drawn to the Redl case as a writer who was fascinated by criminals and crime ('society's outsiders' and their deeds). But his understanding of the world inclined him to perceive Redl's crime as one that had its roots in the Habsburg system of rule (or, to its critics, misrule) and its underlying ideology, thus his 1924 book's sharp closing rhetorical flourish, which indicted nationalism and class politics as the most important causes of why and how the case had been mishandled by Austria's political and military establishments.

Such were the fruits of Kisch as a journalist, a man known for his investigative enterprise and vivid writing style. When he retold the story of Redl's fatal day in the form of a cabaret play, he started to depart from the record of facts and connections between them in order to create a work that would entertain while also informing. But, with every little fictional invention used to heighten drama and move the action along, much of this latter goal turned out to be misinforming, though not as egregiously and meretriciously as the General Staff had done. As history *Die Hetzjagd* has to be viewed with extreme caution and more than a little skepticism. Once it is viewed as historical fiction, the standard of truthfulness becomes less rigorous (but not totally irrelevant).

By the time the story moved onto film this standard became even weaker. Viewers of the Redl films will learn that once upon a time there was a well-known high-ranking army officer who betrayed his country, and that he *may* have been blackmailed by Russian intelligence agents who had discovered his homosexuality. If viewers pay attention they might also intuit that at the time of these events there was, in Austrian military and political circles, a desire to punish Serbia, with an attendant anxiety over the possibility of such action leading to a war with Russia. Twenty-first century audiences attending showings of old films will, of course, be unburdened by the intense views of the villain and his deeds that Kisch's contemporaries had when they entered the cinema or cabaret theater. Viewers of Szabó's Redl film will also see something of the strife between the Empire's two master nationalities, Germans and Magyars.

All of this is true as far as it goes, but it doesn't go very far in explaining either Redl, the role of the General Staff in Austro-Hungarian political and social life, or the background of pressing internal and international crises that influenced leadership judgments at the time of Redl's detection, arrest and coerced suicide. The films provide diluted yet tendentious narratives of the history of the Redl affair, and almost all of the details meant to enliven their narratives are the inventions of screenwriters and directors. They make for interesting or even excellent cinematic art and character studies, but they yield very poor history. The real-life Alfred Viktor Redl remains something of a cipher when it comes to his character (though his motives seem clear enough), and, although the record of his deeds remains incomplete, filling it in is the job of interested historians, not artists who are driven by values and goals that have little to do with accurate historical representation.

A broader view of the period's history requires one to examine Redl the respected career military man and Redl the spy in a social and cultural context of the late Habsburg years, when the Dual Monarchy was constantly responding to internal stresses and looming foreign-policy crises. In spite of the unpromising general picture, Austro-Hungarian culture thrived at all levels: traditional high-art, art directed toward a large middle-class audience, and disruptive new art that abandoned old models and experimented with approaches that were spread across a spectrum of engagement with society and politics (aestheticism, expressionism, brutal realism, art with a socialist message.)[3] The First World War exacerbated all of the competing ideas and forces of the previous three decades, and the ideas and forces continued unabated throughout the interwar years. This was a period when artists were constantly reconsidering recent history and its accompanying 'mentalities' that had led to the catastrophic war. They mined this era for topics and themes and used their selected material to express their own ideas of significance. Artistic treatments of the Redl case fit into this mold of reappraisal. Kisch's career as a journalist with a left-wing perspective about what was important in life was also part of his era's competition between traditional and modern ideas in general and political ideologies in particular; he was both a participant in and observer of these tempestuous times, a product and a symptom.

The above considerations do not apply to Kisch's conversion of a newspaper feuilleton into a fantasy-comedy cabaret play like *Die Himmelfahrt der Tonka Šibenice*. Although there was also an implicit social critique in the play, its verbal assaults expressed in Prague-German and occasional Czech street slang and colorful idioms predominate, somewhat undercutting the grisly story of a prostitute sexually servicing a ruthless murderer and the pathos of its heroine's life on earth. It is comedy with a dark underside, but comedy prevails, initiated in the first scene's portrait of a rambunctious woman of the streets who thinks heaven is her due reward for enduring decades of earthly misery, and punctuated at play's end by the idea of heaven as a classy brothel. The film version of the story, though artistically satisfying, ignored both the gritty and comical aspects of the play in order to construct a typical romantic melodrama that appealed to the new 'mass audience'. The later returns to the story in the 1970s and 2000s emphasized its raucous comedy.

Unlike the Redl play the story of Toni Gallows does not put historical veracity at stake. However, there may have been a violation of the contemporary reader's and viewer's trust that Kisch had based the story on a real woman whom he had encountered, rather than an urban legend that he embellished. His 1980s biographer, Fritz Hofmann, offered evidence that the story of the condemned man's last request, fulfilled by a prostitute, cannot be verified. Kisch's remarks on the factual basis of the play did not emerge until his memoirs were published in 1941/42, when it would have been extremely difficult to check his recollections on this point. With regard to his play's heroine, maybe part or all of the events in Prague's underworld described in his memoirs happened. Or maybe they didn't, yet the story itself might provide the reader and viewer with an accurate picture of what Prague's demi-monde was like during Kisch's years as a reporter for *Bohemia* (1906-1913). In this case we are dealing more with the subject of 'sociology into art' rather than 'history into art', and the accuracy of Kisch's view of the milieu he depicted might stand the test of time and be confirmed by historical research.

As to the Redl case, however, the transformation of history into art outlived Kisch. Like the earlier films, Antel's 1955 film was full of romantic and melodramatic fiction, and it was especially careful not to tar the reputations of men in power in 1913. In contrast, an objective historian's look at their performance in that year and during World War I will find many turning points where they made bad decisions for bad reasons. Nervous about Antel's 1955 film before it was released, conservative groups in post-World War II Austria were still defending the honor of Conrad and the old army, regardless of how much evidence had accumulated about his and their failures of commission and omission. Thirty years later Szabó's film was a willful (but explainable in terms of his own experience) distortion of the Redl case that presents a very Hungarian view of long-ago events, so partisan and present-oriented that the reality of those events has been lost in a sea of nonsensical directorial inventions (and yet, it is 'a great movie'). In his *Oberst Redl* we are getting a Redl displaced in time and space, a man who is no longer emblematic of the twilight-of-the-Habsburg years but of Hungary during the period from 1945 through the early 1960s, Szabó's formative years as an artist. Here we have moved from historical fiction to historical fantasy.

The story migrated even farther afield. John Osborne's 1965 play based on the Redl scandal was reasonably accurate in depicting Viennese manners, mores, and attitudes. These aspects of the play are credible re-creations of a time and place, though all of the details of Redl's actual life and his (conjectural) interior life have been invented (or taken, surreptitiously, from Robert Asprey's 1959 biography of Redl). But the real time and place of interest to Osborne was post-World War II England (and London in particular), for which 1913 Vienna was a theatrical stand-in. And, as to Vienna, Osborne's depiction of Austrian society was only a background for the matter of real interest to him, the portrait of an individual who is a defiant 'outsider' who has clawed his way to the top and whose individuality is being constantly assailed by his peers and 'insiders' of wealth, power, and connections (Osborne's idealized self-portrait). His play sheds no light on history, other than the unremarkable generalizations that Viennese society was hierarchical, obsessed with appearances, and anti-Semitic.

Pavel Vilikovský's 1989 novella, *Ever Green Is ...* , uses Colonel Alfred Redl as an allegorical figure ("Alfredl", alternatively, "K.u.K.") around whom a surrealistic, farcical, post-modern novella is built, a digressive tale that obliquely comes to grips with the sinister forces in Central and Eastern Europe that dominated political and cultural life during a long period from the 1930s through the author's adulthood, right up to the moment of the collapse of the communist state in Czechoslovakia. But it does this by purely literary means. Vilikovský's deployment of verbal gags, ironical authorial interjections, real and legendary historical digressions, marginalia, and spurious footnotes contains a great deal of accurate regional history, well-known to its Czech and Slovak readers. While this historical background and the persona of Redl had elicited anger, resentment, depression, and histrionic rhetoric in the earlier artistic depictions of the Redl case, Vilikovský treats these matters with Olympian whimsy and disdain.

Vilikovsky's treatment of the Redl story also illustrates something about the transformation of memory and emotion over time: whether or not particular historical events were truly significant, the strong emotional currents that push their interpretation one way or another are destined to ebb someday. Events become too remote to arouse a strong reaction—that is the real lesson of Nietzsche's (oft-misquoted) aphorism that "a joke is an epitaph on the death of a feeling". In contemplating Redl and his world, going from the 'raging' political animus of Kisch through the psychological intensities and interior dramas of Asprey, Osborne, and Szabó to arrive at the bracing, cold humor of Vilikovský will show you exactly what Nietzsche meant. (Although, it must be said, the anxieties surrounding present cultural issues can also retroactively interact with older artistic material, either elevating or tarnishing it.[4]) To those advancing chauvinist politics in the new nation of Slovakia, Vilikovský's style of humor was offensive and 'alien' (inexcusable even as a fresh, postmodernist perspective on history, because it detached literary skill from nationalist and 'literature of dissent' agendas and mocked those agendas as well). To critics inclined toward evaluations *within* the standards of postmodernist writing and criticism (opposed in general to 'politically useful writing'), his 'joke about history' will offer cold comfort and perhaps be misunderstood as an effort of pure aestheticism. Vilikovksý was far too aware of his surroundings to take that path, so he buried his acidic observations of his own society within a welter of clever wordplay and fabulous events.

The Redl story still intrigues historians of the World War I era, and, as long as the trope of Redl as 'spy of the century' engages a popular audience in Austria, Germany, and other lands of Central Europe, it will provide a basis for further artistic treatments. The Tonka Šibenice story has a more limited audience, primarily Czech, yet it is resonant enough of the late-Habsburg period in Prague that it too may continue to attract new audiences for either revivals or adaptations, as the prolonged success of its most recent adaptation as a two-woman show illustrates. One might add that in Germany the version of the story set in Hamburg and Berlin fits well into a topical grouping of other more powerful depictions of modern urban demi-mondes and vice districts (the best-known of which is Alfred Döblin's *Berlin Alexanderplatz*, a novel with a long afterlife in German film and television adaptations, a powerful example being Rainer Fassbinder's re-creation of the story).

Whether historians still consider Redl to be 'the spy of the century' is questionable, given spectacular cases of treason in high places that have characterized the intelligence services of Great Britain, the USSR, the USA, Germany, Japan and other nations during the latter half of the twentieth century. But historical treatments of the Redl case offer readers a window into a place and time that is still of intrinsic interest as a model of what multinational and multi-cultural polities and societies were and might be. Present-day Americans and Europeans might encounter the Redl story in any of its numerous artistic incarnations. If they are intrigued by the story and wish to learn more, it is necessary to read what biographers and historians have written about the man and the espionage scandal and their place in the broader history of Austria-Hungary during the last fifty years of its existence. Reading Kisch's 1924 book is the first step on that path of self-education, though some of the knowledge it offers is incorrect and some of its conclusions are questionable. Seeing an artistically polished and dramatically compelling film or play about such events can lead viewers in two directions, one undesirable, the other commendable: either they will be satisfied with a work of art as it takes them far afield from the truth while delivering emotional satisfaction, or their curiosity will be piqued and they will turn to reading the works of professional historians who will bring them back to a reality in which certain things happened, though the meaning (historical significance) of what happened must often remain provisional.

Notes

1. Introducing Egon Erwin Kisch, the Raging Reporter

1. Kisch acknowledged the publicity value of the nickname but wasn't happy with it, noting that "raging reporter" was a book's title, not an intentional self-description. Various writers translate *der rasende Reporter* as "the roving reporter" or "the demon reporter".

2. American and British readers unfamiliar with Kisch can find a comparable approach to his international reportage in the "Inside" series of books of socio-political reporting by John Gunther (*Inside Europe, Inside the USA*, etc.), published between 1936 and 1972.

3. Scott Spector, *Prague Territories: National Conflict and Cultural Innovation in Franz Kafka's Fin de Siècle*, 48-60.

4. See www.unz.com/print/author/KischEgonErwin (accessed 05/24/18). A list of eight magazine articles and eight reviews of Kisch's work published in American magazines between 1929 and 1941.

5. Markus G. Patka, *Egon Erwin Kisch: Stationen im Leben eines streitbaren Autors*, 460-475. This list of articles about Kisch between 1933 and 1948 includes more than 200 Australian newspaper and magazine pieces published during his four months there in 1934-1935.

6. When the ban was lifted in 1969 *Australian Landfall* was reprinted in Australia. A. T. Yarwood's Foreword explains the local politics behind the ban and sketches Kisch's foes and supporters.

7. Peter Monteath, "The Kisch Visit Revisited", 76-80. On Tom Fitzgerald, who wrote about Kisch's Australian adventure under the pseudonym "Julian Smith".

8. Julie Wells, "Writers and Fascism: The Kisch Case", 67-83.

9. Egon Erwin Kisch, (Trans. Stewart Farrar), "The Three Cows", published as a two-penny paper booklet in London in 1939.

10. East Germany's National Defense Department Press published this posthumous collection of Kisch's reporting about the Spanish Civil War in a series named *Kämpfende Kunst* (Combative Art). The jacket's rhetorical denunciation of West Germany exemplifies the propaganda uses to which Kisch's work was being put in the communist half of the divided nation.

11. Kisch (Trans. Edith Bone), *Tales from Seven Ghettos*, 200-209.

12. Kisch (Trans. Harold Segel), In Segel, *Egon Erwin Kisch, The Raging Reporter: A Bio-Anthology*, 365-372.

13. *Marktplatz der Sensationen* was first published by El Libro Libre, the German exile community's press in Mexico City; it is a rare book. It was reissued by Globus in Vienna in 1947, with several new chapters.

14. Favorable reviews of *Sensation Fair*: a brief notice in the Nov. 29, 1941 issue of *The New Yorker*; an enthusiastic essay-review in the Dec. 13, 1941 issue of *The Saturday Review*; the Jan. 6, 1942 issue of *New Masses*; and, a brief notice in the February 1942 issue of *Free World* magazine.

15. Kisch (Trans. Guy Endore), *Sensation Fair*, 299-322. The final re-telling of the Redl story by Kisch. See Kisch, *Marktplatz der Sensationen* (1947), 287-306 for the German version of this chapter.

16. The 1948 translation included eleven of twelve chapters from *Geschichten aus sieben Ghettos*, plus seven post-1934 pieces.

17. Kisch In Segel, *Kisch Bio-Anthology*, 162–203.

18. Patka, *Kisch: Stationen*, 409–533. Patka's Bibliography includes: all first editions and reissues of Kisch's books in German and in translation; Introductions by Kisch to the works of other writers or anthologies; all known Kisch pieces published in newspapers and magazines, including short notices, interviews of Kisch, and transcripts of speeches and radio talks (more than 200 newspapers and journals published writing by Kisch); secondary literature, comprising books and articles about Kisch; reviews of Kisch's books, plays, and films based on his work. Each of the foregoing is subdivided into three periods: 1905–March, 1933; March, 1933–April, 1948; April, 1948–1997. These periods cover Kisch's first publication until the time of his arrest by the Nazis; his period of exile and postwar return to Prague; posthumously published work by and about Kisch up until 1997.

19. Patka In Patka (Ed.) *Der rasende Reporter Egon Erwin Kisch: Eine Biographie in Bildern*, 273–287. This essay, "Facette rasender Zeit", is the book's Afterword.

20. Patka (Trans. Heidi Zogbaum), "Afterword: The Writer behind the Reporter's Mask". In Heidi Zogbaum, *Kisch in Australia: The Untold Story*, 139–157.

21. Sheila Skaff, "Ambivalence and Cigarettes: Egon Erwin Kisch's 'At Ford's Place in Detroit,' with a Translation of the Text", 119–131.

22. See: http://www.podiumcafe.com/book-corner/2015/2/1/7960457/elliptical-treadmill-by-egon-erwin-kisch for Davis's translation (accessed 05/24/18). See: Kisch, *Der rasende Reporter*, 241–245 ("Elliptische Tretmühle") for the original article.

23. Joseph Roth, "The Twelfth Berlin Six-Day Races", In Roth (Trans.M. Hofmann), *What I Saw*, 161–166.

24. Segel, *Kisch Bio-Anthology*, xii–xiii. See also Segel, *The Vienna Coffeehouse Wits 1890–1938*, 5–6, 29–35 for an expansive discussion of *Kleinkunst*.

25. Kisch, *Sensation Fair*, 327. The column's title was *Prager Streifzüge*, perhaps better translated as "Prague Raids or Excursions" rather than "Roaming" or "Rambles".

26. Segel, *Kisch Bio-Anthology*, 15–16.

27. Patka, *Kisch Stationen*, 520–521. List of reviews and commentaries on Kisch's novel.

28. Karl Hans Strobl, "Ein Roman vom unterirdischen Prag" (A Novel of Underworld Prague). In Vera Schneider, *Wachposten und Grenzgänger. Deutschsprachige Autoren in Prag und die öffentliche Herstellung naionaler Identität*, 274–278. An adulatory review of Kisch's novel, published in *Bohemia* on July 30, 1914.

29. Spector, *Prague Territories*, 177–180.

30. Kisch In Segel, *Kisch Bio-Anthology*, 143–157.

31. Max Hastings, *Catastrophe 1914: Europe Goes To War*, 145–147, 150, 152, 154–156, 428, 511.

32. Patka, *Kisch Stationen*, 276–292. On Kisch's relationships with Roth and Musil during the interwar years.

33. Segel, *Kisch Bio-Anthology*, 22–27. On Kisch's Red Guard activities. See also: Patka, *Kisch Stationen*, 48–58.

34. Patka, *Kisch Stationen*, 56. Re. Kisch joining the (German-)Austrian Communist Party (*KP(D)Ö*) in 1919. For Kisch's 1922 Czech CP membership, See: www.radio.cz/en/section/czechs/egon-erwin-kisch-the-raging-reporter-1

(accessed 05/24/18) See also: Patka (Ed.), *Kisch Biographie in Bildern*, 96, 256 for photographs of his 1925 German and 1946 Czech CP party cards.

35. For Australia, See: Julian Smith, *On The Pacific Front: The Adventures of Egon Kisch in Australia*, 167-174, and Zogbaum, *Kisch in Australia*, 47-49. For the US, See: Patka, *Kisch Biographie in Bildern*, 206.

36. Istvan Deak, *Germany's Left-Wing Intellectuals*, 249-251. See also: Patka, *Kisch Stationen*, 432 for Kisch's articles in *Die Weltbühne*.

37. Patka, *Kisch Stationen*, 523-24. A list of 21 newspaper and magazine reviews of *Der rasende Reporter* and 26 contemporary commentaries on the book.

38. Publisher's endpapers in 1927's *Zaren, Popen, Bolschewiken* show that *Der rasende Reporter* was in its 15th printing at the time. The first printing ran to 10,000 copies.

39. Kisch ed., *Klassischer Journalismus*, 1-5 ("*Vorrede*").

40. Kisch, *GW (1993) Vol.10*, 91-104 ("John Reed, Ein Reporter auf der Barrikade"). *GW* refers to the 1992-1993 edition of the Kisch *Gesammelte Werke* in 12 volumes.

41. Kisch, *GW (1993) Vol. 10*, 397-400.

42. Keith Williams, "The Will to Objectivity", 95.

43. John Willet, *Art and Politics in the Weimar Period: The New Sobriety 1919-1933*, 108-109, 111. An often-reproduced photo-montage of Kisch as a giant bio-mechanical device sweeping up data is on p. 108.

44. Terrence O'Keeffe, "The Long Hangover: Private and Public Memory in the Former Communist Lands", 688-89. Re. Maxim Leo's discussion of Kisch in the DDR context.

45. Michael Horowitz, *Ein Leben für die Zeitung: Der rasende Reporter Egon Erwin Kisch*, 69. "Mom" approximates Kisch's salutation "Mutterl", a word used by Kafka to refer to Prague as a "little mother with claws". "Egonek" was Kisch's nickname from childhood.

46. Kisch In Segel, *Kisch Bio-Anthology*, 91-92. Kisch's remarks on reportage ("A Dangerous Literary Genre"). See also: Kisch, *Der rasende Reporter*, vii-viii. (*Vorwort*) and *GW (1993) Vol. 10*, 5-12 for two pieces on classical journalism and the 'social mission' of reportage.

47. Dieter Schlenstedt, *Egon Erwin Kisch: Leben und Werk*, 82-94 ("Entwicklung der Reportagetheorie Egon Erwin Kischs").

48. Fritz Hofmann, *Egon Erwin Kisch: Der Rasende Reporter*, 190-218. Adjacent chapters discuss 'the raging reporter' and the first 'genuine reportages', a designation Hofmann reserves for Kisch's post-1924 writing, especially the books based on his worldwide travels.

49. Segel, *Kisch Bio-Anthology*, 69-80.

50. Patka, *Kisch Stationen*, 91-111("Fragmente einer Reportagetheorie und literarisches Leben in der Weimarer Republik").

51. Spector, *Prague Territories*, 53-60. Re. Kisch's "false modesty" about the extent to which his personal experience and knowledge informed his reportage.

52. Monteath, "Kisch Visit Revisited", 69-70.

53. Theodor Balk (Trans. S.D. Kogan), "Egon Erwin Kisch and his Reportage", 57-70. From a Comintern-funded journal's 1935 issue containing numerous tributes to Kisch on the occasion of his 50th birthday.

54. Julian Smith ed., *Newspaper Reporting and Modern Reportage*, 3-14. A pamphlet that includes Smith's praise of Kisch, a definition of reportage, translated excerpts from a Kisch piece illustrating his humor and skepticism, and the

Minutes and other documents related to the foundational meeting of the Australian Writers' League.

55. Peter Steiner, *The Deserts of Bohemia: Czech Fiction and Its Social Context*. 94–150. "The Past Perfect Hero", which also glosses Milan Kundera's caustic depiction of the role of the "Fučik youth cult" in his novel, *The Joke*.

56. Over a period of five decades the following prominent anthologies of reportage written in English appeared: *The Orwell Reader* (1956); J. Carey, ed., *The Faber Book of Reportage* (1987); I. Jack, I ed., *The Granta Book of Reportage* (2006); and R. Silvers ed., *The New York Review Abroad: Fifty Years of International Reportage* (2013). All of them are silent about Kisch as founder or exemplar of reportage.

57. Kisch In Segel, *Kisch Bio-Anthology*, 285–301 ("In the Dungeons of Spandau: From the First Days of the Third Reich").

58. Kisch, "Unmasking Gustav Regler", 12–13.

59. Patka, *Kisch Stationen*, 375–376. Re. negative responses to Kisch's Regler article by American and German liberals and leftists who were anti-Stalinists.

60. Zogbaum, *Kisch in Australia,* 129–37.

61. Jonathan Miles, *The Dangerous Otto Katz*, 244–251.

62. Patka, *Kisch Stationen*, 33, 386–389. Re. the festivities ("Eine Woche Geburtstag") and the era's eminent leftists in Mexican exile who took roles in the play.

63. Patka ed., *Kisch Biographie in Bildern*, 239–244. Photograph Nr. 254 shows the friends who took roles in the 1945 performance of *Die Hetzjagd* in Mexico City.

64. R. W. Seton-Watson ("Scotus Viator"), *Racial Problems in Hungary*, passim. A controversial book on Hungarian chauvinism and oppression of ethnic minorities ("races" or nationalities) as reported in 1908.

65. Hugh Seton-Watson, *The Sick Heart of Modern Europe: The Problem of the Danubian Lands*, passim. A 1975 anticipation of how ethno-nationalistic rivalries would emerge in Central and Eastern Europe if the Soviet bloc dissolved.

66. Joseph Rothschild, *Eastern Central Europe between the Two World Wars*, passim. In the author's country-by-country survey he gives a full account of Central and Eastern European ethnic rivalries, irredentism, and emergence of autocrats in the successor states to the Dual Monarchy during the interwar period.

67. Joseph Rothschild and Nancy Wingfield, *Return to Diversity: A Political History of East Central Europe since World War II, passim*. Updating the preceding citation for the years from 1945 through the 2000s.

68. Patka, *Kisch Stationen*, 394. Quoting Kisch on his sense of loss and isolation on account of the deaths of almost all of his pre-WWII friends and family in Berlin and Prague. See also Patka ed., *Kisch Biographie in Bildern*, 254, 258.

69. Erhard Schütz, "Moral aus der Geschichte—Zur Wahrheit des Egon Erwin Kisch", 38–47.

70. Patka, *Kisch Stationen*, 407. Re. an attempt by the security services organizing the case against Slánský to retrospectively brand Kisch as a 'Trotskyite' in Mexico.

71. Miles, *The Dangerous Otto Katz*, 271.

72. Spector, *Prague Territories*, 49, 51–52. To illustrate Kisch's youthful identification with older German-liberal values, Spector translated some of his poetry and a passage from a short-story ("novella").

2. Notes on the Plays: Sources and Translation

1. Kisch, *Hetzjagd durch die Zeit*, 33–76, 200–234. The 1926 texts of *Die Hetzjagd* and *Die Himmelfahrt der Tonka Šibenice*.
2. Kisch, *Abenteuer in fünf Kontinenten* (1936), 74–87. Post-WWII editions of this book have very different contents.
3. Kisch, *GW (1993) Vol. 9*, 390–396; 499fn390. The 1921 "Tonka Šibenice in the Afterlife" feuilleton and source information.
4. Kisch, *GW (1993) Vol. 12*, 105–123; 462. The 1922 text of the play and source information.
5. Kisch, *Wagnisse in aller Welt*, 71–100. The 1927 'Hamburg-Berlin' version of Kisch's play about Toni Gallows. With a 1927 copyright date, the book was publishee as the "second volume of the yearly series for 1929".
6. An example of Kisch's attention to details, even when he only lightly edited a piece, is the amount Meseritzer paid in advance for a fawning obituary—in 1922 it is 500 marks (at the outset of runaway inflation), while it is adjusted to 60 (re-stabilized) marks in 1927.
7. Kisch, *Der Fall des Generalstabschefs Redl*, 19–20.
8. Kisch, *GW (1993) Vol. 12*, 112.
9. Kisch, *GW (1992) Vol. 1*, 531–555; 656; 660–661. The 1926 text of the "Tonka" version of the play; Afterword remarks on variant texts and performance history; footnotes clarifying slang and translating Czech and Latin words and phrases into German.
10. Spector, *Prague Territories*, 77.
11. Kisch, *GW (1992) Vol. 1*, 660fn537. The editors' translation of this phrase.

3. The Pursuit

1. Kisch uses the era's ubiquitous Austro-Hungarian acronym, "k.u.k.", for "Imperial and Royal" (*kaiserlich und königlich*). For some usages it was shortened to "k.k." In his 2005 review of the Redl espionage case John Schindler reports that his Italian intelligence handlers referred to Redl as "K.K.". Historically "k.u.k." points to the different statuses of the Emperor in the Austrian and Hungarian halves of the Empire, a result of the Compromise (*Ausgleich*) of 1867. In the Austrian lands Franz Joseph was Emperor, in the Hungarian lands he was King, with Hungarians claiming that their alliance with the Habsburg dynasts was by virtue of a personal connection that had to be confirmed by the Hungarian Assembly. Both halves of the Dual Monarchy were in fact "empires" in the sense of being multinational states. See p. 243 of the present book for a discussion of the connotations of the acronym and its relationship to Robert Musil's term "Kakania".
2. As noted in my discussion of the play, Archduke Viktor Salvator is an invented character, a composite of several members of the Habsburg family who were known for public displays of frivolous sexual indiscretion and, in some cases, distasteful or exhibitionistic behavior. The position of Inspector General of Troops had been in abeyance until, in the wake of the Redl scandal, Franz Joseph assigned it to Archduke Franz Ferdinand, who viewed it as an opportunity to "clean up" the officer corps and the General Staff.
3. Franz Xaver Joseph Conrad Baron von Hötzendorf was one of the most important figures of the final two decades of the Dual Monarchy. He was even-

tually ennobled to Count and attained the highest rank of full Field Marshal. Born into a middle-class family of civil servants and military men in 1852, he became a career officer in the army in 1871. As a teacher at the War College he developed a loyal following of younger officers. He was Chief of the General Staff between 1906 and 1911, when he was replaced by General Blasius von Schemua, an eccentric pan-Germanist who proved so ineffective that the Emperor and Franz Ferdinand pushed Conrad back into the position in late 1912. During the 1890s General Beck-Rzykowsky transformed the role of Chief of the General Staff into a politically significant and powerful position, making it the military–executive arm of the Emperor and bypassing the control of the War Ministry. This was a source of bitter political struggles during Conrad's tenure. Conrad was deemed to be a "military intellectual", having written serious studies of earlier military campaigns and strategies as well as current specialized infantry field manuals. By nature a pessimist and fatalist, he was a devotee of Schopenhauer, believing that all life was struggle. His reforms of the peacetime army (more realistic field exercises, less drill and parade-ground time, and better treatment of enlisted men and conscripts) were rational and admired. Throughout his career he advocated pre-emptive wars against Serbia and Italy, believing they could be localized without bringing in any of the Great Powers such as Russia or France. He favored using the joint army to bring the Hungarians to heel (an idea with which Archduke Franz Ferdinand agreed). After the Redl case broke Franz Ferdinand turned against Conrad once and for all, but, given the tense international situation in 1913, Conrad was kept on. When WWI broke out his mobilization plans proved disastrous and he became a 'headquarters general', remote from the carnage of the active fronts and the demoralizing effects of poorly planned and led campaigns on his troops. Like many of his Allied counterparts, he was committed to the 'spirit of the offensive', exemplified by the infantry charge that would end in using bayonets, not understanding that this approach would prove to be near-suicidal in the face of machine-gun and improved artillery fire that inflicted immense casualties. Removed as Chief of the General Staff in 1917, he was given command of an army group in the South Tyrol on the Italian front, where he led inconclusive campaigns with high casualty rates. Lawrence Sondhaus's biography, *Franz Conrad von Hötzendorf: Architect of the Apocalypse* (2000), is the best source of information about him in English.

4. Kisch was slightly off as to the deputy-chief's name, which was Franz (Baron) Höfer von Feldsturm. During WWI he became a Lieutenant Field Marshal, working at the War Ministry.

5. Readers may be confused by Redl's title while he was on assignment in Prague. He was not Chief of the General Staff, but the General Staff Chief of an Army Corps. When a General Staff officer held this monitoring, instructional, and liaison position with a higher-level formation (e.g., regiment, brigade, division, or army corps) he was the General Staff Chief of that formation. As Deák notes, even a Captain in this position could overrule a decision made by the unit's commander, usually a Colonel or General. See Fn 3 above for the position of Chief of the General Staff.

6. Kisch's name for the character modeled on Colonel August Urbanski von Ostrymiecz, who was forced into "retirement for medical reasons" in late April, 1914 in response to pressure from Franz Ferdinand. The Successor held him responsible for the mistakes and cover-up of the Redl affair. Franz Ferdinand

would have gone after Conrad with similar determination, but he and the Emperor realized that in the unstable international situation of 1913-1914 it would have been difficult to dismiss Conrad and find an equally competent and respected replacement. Despite his strong coterie of supporters within the army, Conrad also had enemies in the War Ministry, the Reichsrat, and at court, as well as rivals like General Oskar Potiorek, who hoped to replace him. After the Successor's assassination at Sarajevo, Urbanski, a favorite of Conrad, was reinstated, serving as an infantry general during WWI and attaining the rank of Lieutenant Field Marshal. Under his real name he plays a major role in Kisch's 1924 book about the Redl case.

7. The German spelling for Wenzel Vorlíček, who served the government of the Czechoslovakian First Republic after the end of WWI.

8. A pseudonym for Stefan Horinka, Redl's protégé and lover.

9. Kisch's fictitious name for Horinka's (Hromadka's) fiancé. In his 1985 book about the Redl scandal, the Austrian journalist Georg Markus, recorded her real name as Marie Dobias (nicknamed 'Mitzi') and quoted correspondence between her and Horinka.

10. Kisch used the name Baroness Daubek here to indicate a woman of high status. Whether Conrad knew the real Baroness Daubek, the wife of a Czech nobleman and a public figure in her own right, is unknown to the present author. Some reports on the Redl case propose that Conrad's actual dinner companion was Gina von Reininghaus, his beloved, whom he (a widower) eventually married after a politically tricky divorce.

11. Kisch notes in his 1924 book that this musician was well-known because he once had an amorous relationship with a Belgian princess.

12. The two detectives are unnamed in Kisch's 1924 book. In the Redl play they are Strebinger and Steidl, but in his memoirs he recalls the former as Ebinger, as does Robert Asprey in his biography of Redl. Later researchers discovered that neither Strebinger/Ebinger nor Steidl were the actual names of the (three) policemen involved in catching Redl.

13. Lest the reader imagine Kisch has invented a misogynistic tract, he is referring to a well-known book by Paul Möbius, *Über den physiologischen Schwachsinn des Weibes* (On the Physiology of Mental Deficiencies in Women), published in 1901. Within two years this was followed by the better-known 'philosophical' diatribe, *Geschlecht und Charakter: Eine prinzipielle Untersuchung* (Sex and Character: A Fundamental Inquiry), written by Otto Weininger, who was assailed by Möbius for plagiarism. Weininger's book was frankly, and at times hysterically, misogynistic and anti-Semitic. Its author, a young Jewish aesthete and pseudo-scientist, committed suicide at the age of twenty-three and became the object of a reverential cult, to which many outstanding Viennese thinkers and writers belonged, indicating strains of deep ethnic and patriarchal prejudice that characterized Austrian intellectual life of the late Habsburg years and the following decades. See: William M. Johnston, *The Austrian Mind*, 158-162, for a succinct sketch of Weininger and his ideas.

14. The German word for this bond was *Kaution*. The following summarizes István Deák's description in *Beyond Nationalism* (pp. 139-42). The bond was considered a form of insurance by the high command, who thought that professional officers of modest family means who married might be tempted to engage in outside work or peculation in order to support a family. It was also designed to prevent officers from marrying socially inappropriate women

(i.e., those from families of modest means or questionable backgrounds). There was also a limit on the percentage of married officers within regiments. The sum required at this time was 60,000 crowns for a lieutenant (about 30 times a year's pay), dropping down to half that amount for more senior officers such as majors and above. The *Kaution* was waived for colonels and generals. A note in Schindler (2005, 488) contradicts these latter observations, stating that in 1908, at age 42, then-Lieutenant Colonel Urbankis had to post a 50,000 crown bond in order to marry. The army itself administered payments from the escrow account enabling the officer to maintain a respectable family existence. A wealthy officer or one who married a woman whose family would post the bond had no problems in securing approval to marry. This restriction accounted for the phenomenon of the middle-aged officer who retired as a bachelor when eligible for his pension. Many of these men in their late 40s and early 50s married women twenty to thirty years younger, pairings often encountered in novels of the period. Note that Redl fitted into this category, to which so many career officers belonged that an officer's bachelorhood raised no suspicions of homosexuality. For those of modest means the general idea was 'career first, marriage second'. Since this often led to sexual relations with the 'soubrettes' of the era and with prostitutes, it also accounted for a fairly high incidence of venereal disease among this group of men, which did not bar advancement if it was judged by military physicians to be not disabling (this too applied to Redl, and there is a line in the play where Archduke Viktor Salvator alludes to a bout of venereal disease contracted when he was a young officer). Asprey and Gunther Rothenberg (the pre-eminent historian of Franz Joseph's army) also explain how the *Kaution* worked and what its effects were. See also: Johnston, *The Austrian Mind*, 49–50 for how the *Kaution* concept was applied to press and book censorship.

15. Admission into the War College was a stepping-stone to more rapid promotions and increased the likelihood of assignment to the General Staff.

16. The Kladrub stables in Bohemia were famous for breeding and training a handsome, sturdy, gray-coated breed of horses, nicknamed 'Old Kladrubs'. They were used to pull Habsburg ceremonial carriages. The current managers of the stable doubt they ever bred horses suitable for a cavalry officer (personal communication to the author). In any event, playgoers knew them as 'very expensive horses'. They were bred and trained according to an old protocol, similar to the more famous Lippizaners.

17. Having consulted with native Austrians and Germans, I have not been able to find out what "*Hofnix*" means; it is archaic slang. A guess, based on its two elements, is that it means something like "we're not at Court now", indicating that one may converse and deport oneself in a relaxed fashion. Franz Joseph's Court was known for its rigid protocol and hewing to all possible formalities. For the 'frivolous Viennese' attendance at court functions was a chore, not a pleasure. In the play Viktor Salvator is the last person in the world who needs encouragement to let his hair down.

4. Kisch and the Redl Case: Reportage into Melodrama

1. Kisch, *Marktplatz der Sensationen* (1947), 287–306 ("Wie ich erfuhr dass Redl ein Spion war" or "How I discovered that Redl was a spy"). See also: Kisch, *Sensation Fair*, 299–320 for G. Endore's translation of this chapter.

2. Robert Asprey, *The Panther's Feast*, 262. Asprey's translation of the May 26th article in the *Neue Freie Presse*.
3. Kisch, *Sensation Fair*, 318. See Kisch (unsigned), *GW (1993) 12*, 401. "Falsche Gerüchte"(the text of the 'false rumor story' concocted by Kisch and his editor). See also: Johnston, *The Austrian Mind*, 48–49, 55 for how bureaucratic rules invited this kind of official gaffe and their consequences in the Redl case.
4. Patka, *Kisch Stationen*, 36–39. Re. Kisch's 1913 articles, also citing early reports about rumors of Redl's espionage in Vienna's *Die Zeit* and *Arbeiter Zeitung*.
5. John Sadler and Sylvie Fisch, *Redl: Spy of the Century*, 3–4. In their "Prelude" Sadler and Fisch cite articles from Vienna's *Neueste Wiener Tagblatt* (May 26, 1913) and *Die Zeit* (May 27, 1913) that challenged details of the cover-up story fabricated by the General Staff about Redl's death.
6. Kisch (unsigned), *GW (1993) 12*, 398–439. The 17 Kisch articles about the Redl case in *Bohemia*.
7. Asprey, *Panther's Feast*, 266. English translation of notice in the *Militärische Rundschau*. A reproduction of the original German text of this notice is in Georg Markus, *Der Fall Redl*, 239.
8. *Ibid.*, 297–303. Bibliographical notes on ministerial archives and file folders (boxes) containing information on Redl and the investigations of the espionage case.
9. *Ibid.*, 306. Re. information from "Tristan Busch" on Russian intelligence files on the Redl case that allegedly vanished in or after 1915. See also: John Schindler, "Redl—Spy of the Century?", 490, 504fn7 for biographical information on "Tristan Busch" (A. Stütz) and an evaluation of his (doubtful) reliability as a source.
10. Kisch In Segel, *Kisch Bio-Anthology*, 166–177. The passages from Kisch's 1924 book covering the events of May 24–25, 1913. See also: Kisch, *Sensation Fair*, 304–315 for Redl's final day as recollected by Kisch in his memoirs, differing in some details from his 1924 account. See also: Asprey, *Panther's Feast*, 240–259, for his account of Redl's final day.
11. Asprey, *Panther's Feast*, 298. List of archival files on five high-profile espionage trials in which Redl was an investigator and witness for the prosecution.
12. *Ibid.*, 176–180. Testimonials to Redl's intelligence and character, (including notes from his military personnel files). The remarks of Theodore Körner von Siegringen (President of Austria when Asprey interviewed him) about Redl as an affable man with a broad knowledge of politics, diplomacy, and human nature are at variance with Kisch's dismissive attitude about Redl's personality and intellect.
13. Kisch In Segel, *Kisch Bio-Anthology*, 203.
14. Markus, *Der Fall Redl*, 98–99, 210. Re. Horinka's fiancé.
15. *Ibid.*, 269.
16. Asprey, *Panther's Feast*, 290, 306.
17. Timothy Snyder, *The Red Prince: The Secret Lives of a Habsburg Archduke*, 36–38. Re. Habsburg eminences known for their inappropriate behavior and sexual peccadilloes.
18. Kisch In Segel, *Kisch Bio-Anthology*, 162.
19. Gunther E. Rothenberg, *The Army of Francis Joseph*, 259fn93 ("An excellent book, obviously resting on documents in the KA [*Kriegsarchiv*], is Robert Asprey, *The Panther's Feast* (London, 1959). The author, however, seems to overestimate the effects of Redl's treason.")

20. Ian Armour, "Review: Markus *Der Fall Redl*", 186–189. In this comparison Asprey comes off better than Markus.

21. István Deák, *Beyond Nationalism: A Social and Political History of the Habsburg Officer Corps, 1848–1918*, 144–145.

22. Patka, *Kisch Stationen*, 35–36; 36fn26. Re. Poláček, in 1966, finding no such newspaper report on the football game about which Kisch wrote in his 1924 book and 1941/42 memoirs.

23. Horowitz, *Ein Leben für die Zeitung*, 33–36. "Enthüllung einer Enthüllung" or "Unmasking of an Unmasking", a chapter on deliberate misinformation in Kisch's 1924 book.

24. Sadler and Fisch, *Spy of the Century*, 5–6.

25. No cipher 'Opernball 13' is on the envelope or in the text of the letter addressed to Nikon Nizetas, as shown in the same photograph reproduced in the following books: Ronge (1933); Asprey (1959); Markus (1985); and Moritz and Leidinger (2012).

26. Markus, *Der Fall Redl*, 202–203, 216–224. See also: Moritz and Leidinger, *Oberst Redl*, 93, citing a source based on an "authentic police report" that has variant spellings of two of the detectives' names: Macher and Wolny.

27. *Ibid.*, 207. In the preceding citation Moritz and Leidinger identify the postal clerk as Betty Hanold. Markus identifies her as Betty Österreicher, who was 19 years old in 1913; presumably one of the two surnames was her maiden name.

28. (Generalmajor) Max Ronge, *Zwölf Jahre Kundschaftsdienst: Kriegs– und Industrie-Spionage*, 78–86. A chapter discussing the Redl case and its significance for events in 1914–15, "Die Verräter im eigenen Lager: Wölkering und Redl"(The traitors in their lairs: Wölkering und Redl). The book's publication date is 1933 (copyright of 1930) and a "note on the present situation" by the author is dated "Fall, 1932".

29. Tristan Busch, *Entlarvter Geheimdienst: Secretinismus*, 37–60. The chapter on Redl and Batjuschin, "Verbrüderung der Verräter" (The Traitors Fraternize). See Busch (Trans. Ireland), *Secret Service Unmasked*, 30–48, for the English translation.

30. Schindler, "Redl—Spy of the Century?", 483–507.

31. *Ibid*, 489–490.

32. Markus, *Der Fall Redl*, 74–75.

33. Samuel R. Williamson Jr., *Austria-Hungary and the Origins of the First World War*, 145–156. See also: F. R. Bridge, *The Habsburg Monarchy among the Great Powers, 1815–1918*, 288–344 for details reflecting the waverings and inherent weaknesses of Austria-Hungary's diplomacy in the years immediately before WWI.

34. Kisch In Segel, *Kisch Bio-Anthology*, 187–189. On Redl's damage to Austria's espionage program in Russia and the consequences of his actions for WWI.

35. Rothenberg, *Army of Francis Joseph*, 172–177. Re. the inadequacies of the army in the face of a major war in 1914.

36. Holger Herwig, *The First World War: Germany and Austria 1914-1918*, 14–16; 52–53; 53–57; 65. On: Austria-Hungary's lack of preparation for a major war; lack of any meaningful co-ordination between the German and Austro-Hungarian armies; the fatal flaws of Conrad's mobilization plan and his remiss leadership during the disastrous opening battles of the war; the impact of Redl's treachery on the war.

37. Geoffrey Wawro, *A Mad Catastrophe: The Outbreak of World War I and the Collapse of the Habsburg Empire*, 83–90. Re. the Redl case and its impact on operations. Wawro's version of the Redl case is replete with mistakes, though these are irrelevant when it comes to its likely consequences in 1914-1915. The tenor of his book is thoroughly negative about the pre-war Austro-Hungarian polity, as is his assessment of the Empire's army.
38. Schindler, *Fall of the Double Eagle*, 29; 83–90. Re. Austria's lack of preparation for a war and its military incompetence; on the Redl case and its consequences for the Galician front in 1914.
39. Hannes Leidinger (Trans. Inge Fink), "The Case of Alfred Redl and the Situation of Austro-Hungarian Military Intelligence on the Eve of World War I", 35–52.
40. Herwig, *The First World War*, 53–57. On Conrad's decisions leading to the events glossed in Fn 36 above and his refusal to accept responsibility for the failure of his ill-conceived plans.
41. Lawrence Sondhaus, *Franz Conrad von Hötzendorf: Architect of the Apocalypse*, vii–viii; 237–244. On the posthumous cult of Conrad as brilliant commander and "great German warrior", with dissenting views.

5. The Ascension of Toni Gallows to Heaven

1. *Prager Tagblatt* was a German-language daily paper. Kisch 'interned' there in 1906 before moving to *Bohemia* where he worked until mid-June, 1913. The other newspapers mentioned in the play are *Pražský Ilustrovaný Kurýr* and *Tribuna*, both Czech.
2. The detective-inspector named here was a well-known police official who worked in Prague from the early 1870s up until his retirement in 1909. Kisch sketched him in a piece published in 1912's *Aus Prager Gassen und Nächten*, translated by Harold Segel as "The Chief of the Prague Detectives" (*Kisch Bio-Anthology*, 119–122). Kisch encountered "old Lederer" often during his newspaper days covering crime in Prague.
3. Kisch, *GW (1992) Vol. 3*, 13–25. A piece in *Prager Pitaval* about the Wohlschlägers, a family of Prague public executioners dating back several generations.

6. Toni Gallows, a Real Prague Legend: Feuilleton into Comic Fantasy

1. Russell Campbell, *Marked Women: Prostitutes and Prostitution in the Cinema*, 344–346.
2. *Ibid.*, 345.
3. *Ibid.*, 346.
4. Kisch, *GW (1992) Vol. 2*, 292–295 ("Magdalenheim").
5. Kisch In Segel, *Kisch Bio-Anthology*, 111–118.
6. *Ibid.*, 112.
7. Kisch, "*Die Himmelfahrt der Tonka Šibenice*" In: *Prager Tagblatt*, 20.02.21 (46.Jg.Nr 43), 1–3. See also: Kisch, *GW (1993) Vol. 9*, 390–396.
8. Kisch, *GW (1993) Vol. 9*, 396.
9. Deborah Holmes, "The Feuilleton of the Viennese 'Arbeiter Zeitung' 1918-1934: Production Parameters and Personality Problems", 99-117.

10. A reproduction of Kisch's feuilleton in *Rote Fahne*: http://anno.onb.ac.at/cgi-content/anno?aid=drf&datum=19280101&seite=1&zoom=33. Kisch's story is on page 5 of this Sunday (New Year's day) supplement issue, which also has an advertisement for John Reed's *Ten Days That Shook the World* in German translation with an Introduction by Kisch, as well as a humorous piece about taxes written by Mark Twain. (accessed 08/12/18)

11. This is Austria's *Die Rote Fahne*, published in Vienna. Patka's Bibliography in *Kisch Stationen* lists this version of the story as having been published in the 1927 Christmas Day issue of Berlin's *Rote Fahne*. The present author assumes that the piece is identical with the Viennese version. This textually different version of the 1921 feuilleton is not included in the *GW*.

12. Patka, *Kisch Stationen*, 427–428. A list of Kisch's numerous pieces published by the Berlin *Die Rote Fahne* and only one published by the Vienna edition of the paper.

13. Kisch, *Sensation Fair*, 241–266. See also: Kisch, *Marktplatz der Sensationen* (1947), 235–258.

14. Hofmann, *Egon Erwin Kisch*, 172–173. Hofmann's remarks on the lack of evidence for the hanging of a serial killer of women, followed by his account of Vejvara's remarks. Vejvara reported on Prague matters for *Národni listy* (National Gazette). The booklet that accompanies the film version of Tonka Šibenice available from the Czech National Film Archive contains a photograph of a woman named Antonie Pařizková, who is alluded to as the real-life model for Tonka. There is no information on the documentary basis of this claim, leaving the question of whether Toni Gallows had a real prototype unanswered.

15. Kisch, *Sensation Fair*, 114–115; 120; 125–127. In passages portraying his journalistic colleagues, Kisch emphasized their social conservatism, pre-occupations and foibles. He sketches "Papa Vejvara" as an irascible old-hand in the news business who had passionate views on what was newsworthy and who detested editors who truncated his local stories to give space to interesting new phenomena (e.g., Vejvara was infuriated by the amount of reporting on an "X-ray demonstration craze" in Prague and elsewhere).

7. Kisch's Career as Playwright

1. Kisch, *GW (1993) Vol. 12, 7–39. Vom Blütenzweig der Jugend* (From the Blossoming Branch of Youth), a collection of 49 poems.

2. Kisch, *GW (1993) Vol. 12, 41–87. Der freche Franz und Andere Geschichten* (Cheeky Frank and Other Stories), a set of six short stories.

3. Spector, *Prague Territories*, 51–53.

4. Kisch, *Sensation Fair*, 63. Kisch overlooked the vibrant classical musical life and the abundant popular music venues of Prague and other major cities in the Dual Monarchy.

5. Kisch, *Die Abenteuer in Prag*, 83–88 ("Neues deutsches Theater!"). An earlier version of this piece had been published in 1913's *Prager Kinder* as "Theaterjubiläum".

6. Segel, *Kisch Bio–Anthology*, 28–29.

7. Kisch, *Sensation Fair*, 65.

8. As an avid reader of Kraus's 'one-man magazine', *Die Fackel* (The Torch), Kafka took Kraus's sarcasm in stride. In his diaries and letters he wrote that

Kraus was in the same problematic situation as other German and Austrian Jews, whose Western-European-oriented cultural choices and writing in German were becoming "increasingly impossible" due to pervasive anti-Semitism and the attendant identity crisis of Jews. They were left with several options, each of which had serious drawbacks and threatened individual integrity: assimilation, conversion, Zionism, or total detachment from the community in the interest of artistic independence, an idealized aesthetic position of many influential modernists, whether Jewish or not (e.g., James Joyce). Kafka agonized over this, never arriving at a satisfactory solution before his premature death, as is amply documented and discussed in Rainer Stach's three-volume Kafla biography.

9. Patka, *Kisch Stationen*, 80–81. The list of Kisch's plays and known or attributed co-written plays. The latter are: *Die Reise um Europa in 365 Tagen, Die Schwestern Teige*, and *Die Tragödie von Mayerling*, a lost play allegedly co-written with a member of the Habsburg family.
10. Patka, *Kisch Stationen*, 92.
11. Schlenstedt, *Egon Erwin Kisch*, 29–31.
12. Hofmann, *Egon Erwin Kisch*, 170–174. Re. Kisch's circle of Czech friends in the arts and the early Czech performance of his plays. Hofmann notes that Kisch wished to have *Die gestohlene Stadt* (published in Berlin, 1922) republished and promoted but couldn't find a willing publisher.
13. *Ibid.*, 190.
14. *Ibid.*, 187–189. Re. the Redl story as it appeared in book form and on the stage in 1924.
15. Kisch, *GW (1993) Vol. 10*, 210–215. Published in the monthly periodical *Schünemann's Monatsheft* (9) in 1928, "Mein Leben für die Zeitung" (My Life for the Newspaper) briefly surveys the development of newspaper reporting in the 1800s, then gives Kisch's account of highlights of his 1906–1913 years as a reporter in Prague.
16. Horowitz, *Ein Leben für die Zeitung*, 38.
17. Kisch, *Sensation Fair*, 241–245. In a section dubbed "The dives of Prague" Kisch tells of how he met 'Toni Gallows' and several of her fellow prostitutes; this leads into the prose re-telling of Toni's imagined ascension to heaven.
18. Klaus Haupt, *Egon Erwin Kisch (1885–1948): Der rasende Reporter aus dem Prager "Haus zu den goldenen Bären"*, 26–27. Though cursory, this short work sheds interesting sidelights on Kisch's character not mentioned elsewhere (including his many flings with various women).
19. Patka, *Kisch Stationen*, 79–91.
20. William Grange, *Cultural Chronicle of the Weimar Republic*, xii, 79Fn9.
21. *Ibid.*, 34–35.
22. Segel, *Kisch Bio-Anthology*, 29.
23. Viera Glosiková, "Egon Erwin Kischs Dramatische Arbeiten I", *Philologica Pragensia 28* (1985): 177–192.
24. Glosiková, "Dramatische Arbeiten Egon Erwin Kischs II", *Philologica Pragensia 29* (1986): 14–27.
25. Glosiková, "Dramatische Arbeiten I", 177–179. Re. Kisch and E. A. Longen's attempts to establish 'revolutionary theater'.
26. Patka ed., *Biographie in Bildern*, 78–80.
27. Glosiková, "Dramatische Arbeiten I", 185–187. Re. the cabaret play *Pasaci, pasaci*.

28. Kisch (Trans. J. Poláček), *GW (1993) Vol. 12*, 323–328.
29. Kisch, *GW (1993) Vol. 9*, 374–379. *Prager Tagblatt* version of the "Kde Wacht am Rhein" story.
30. Kisch, *Der rasende Reporter*, 19–42. In this longer treatment "Kde Wacht am Rhein" becomes "Scene V – Der entdeutschte Rhein" or "the Rhine de-Germanized".
31. Glosiková, "Dramatische Arbeiten I", 188–192. Re. the play co-written with Hašek.
32. Kisch, *GW (1992) Vol. 1*, 557–653.
33. Glosiková, "Dramatische Arbeiten II", 14–15. Re. *Castans Panoptikum*.
34. Kisch, *Der rasende Reporter*, 62–77.
35. Kisch, *GW (1993) Vol. 11*, 289–293.
36. Glosiková, "Dramatische Arbeiten II", 15–16. Re. the *Piccaver* play.
37. Kisch, *Hetzjagd durch die Zeit*, 342–359.
38. Kisch, *GW (1993) Vol. 12*, 311–322.
39. Glosiková, "Dramatische Arbeiten II", 18–20. Re. *Die Mutter des Mörders*.
40. Kisch, *Der rasende Reporter*, 306–317.
41. Kisch, *Sensation Fair*, 159–171.
42. Kisch, *GW (1993) Vol. 12*, 289–310.
43. Kisch In Segel, *Kisch Bio-Anthology*, 127–140. Segel's translation of passages from *Die Abenteuer in Prag* as, "On Pubs and Their Guests: Dramaturgy of the Flea Theater". Segel notes that Angelo Maria Ripellino also wrote about the improbable character Ferda Mestek in his book, *Magic Prague (Praga Magica*, 1973).
44. Glosiková, "Dramatische Arbeiten II", 24–26. Re. the play about Ferda Mestek.
45. *Ibid.*, 22–23. Re. reviews of *Die gestohlene Stadt.*
46. *Ibid.*, 20–24. Re. *Die gestohlene Stadt.*
47. Kisch, *GW (1993) Vol. 9*, 397–404. The *Käsebier* story as it appeared in *Prager Tagblatt.*
48. Kisch, *Prager Pitaval*, 219–223.
49. Kisch, *GW (1993) Vol. 9*, 390–396. The Tonka Šibenice feuilleton as published in *Prager Tagblatt.*
50. Glosiková, "Dramatische Arbeiten I", 179–185. Re. the Tonka play.
51. Glosiková, "Dramatische Arbeiten II", 17–18. Re. *Die Hetzjagd.*
52. Kisch, *GW (1993) Vols. 9–12*. These volumes have Introductions, Afterwords, and bibliographical and text footnotes written or co-written by Poláček.
53. Kisch, *GW (1993) Vol. 11*, 283–478 and *Vol. 12*, 289–342.
54. Poláček, Josef. "Egon Erwin Kisch und das Theater in Berlin", 243–261.
55. *Ibid.*, 245–252. Re. the Toni Gallows play and the four variant long versions of the story; he does not include the feuilleton versions.
56. Kisch, *GW (1993) 12*, 105–123; 462. The text of the Toni Gallows play as published in Berlin in 1922; source information on this, noting that the weekly's end-pages have an advertisement for the play as it was being performed at *Rakete* in Berlin, starring Rosa Valetti.
57. Kisch, *Wagnisse in aller Welt*, 71–100.
58. Kisch, *Marktplatz der Sensationen* (1947), 235–258. The Toni Gallows chapter. See also: Kisch, *Sensation Fair*, 241–266 for the English translation of this chapter.
59. Poláček, "Kisch Theater in Berlin", 250–251. Re. the "local accent problem" in different mountings of the *Galgentoni* play.

60. *Ibid.,* 248–249. Re. Kisch's newspaper interview about *Galgentoni.* See *GW (1993) Vol. 11,* 481–482 for the full interview.
61. Glosiková, "Dramatische Arbeiten II", 24.
62. Poláček, "Kisch Theater in Berlin", 252–255. Re. *Die gestohlene Stadt.*
63. *Ibid.,* 255–257. Re. *Die Hetzjagd.*
64. Marjorie Perloff, *Edge of Irony,* 1–18.
65. Kisch, In Segel, *Kisch Bio-Anthology,* 93–100. "Germans and Czechs", Segel's translation of a chapter from Kisch's memoirs.
66. Derek Sayer, *The Coasts of Bohemia: A Czech History,* 84–88; 306fn14. Re. the changing demographic profile of various Bohemian and Moravian towns and cities between ca. 1850 and 1910; a footnote on Kisch's piece.
67. Gary Cohen, *The Politics of Ethnic Survival. Germans in Prague, 1861–1914 (2nd Ed.),* 41–104. As to how this quandary applied to Czech Jews writing in Czech, See also: Avigdor Dagan, "The Czech Jewish Symbiosis of Prague: The Langer Brothers", 191–192. For panoptic, critical surveys of the positions, prospects and aspirations of Jews in the Dual Monarchy, See Robert Wistrich's *The Jews of Vienna in the Age of Franz Joseph* and *Laboratory for World Destruction: Germans and Jews in Central Europe.*
68. Thomas Ort, *Art and Life in Modernist Prague,* 215–216fn16. Re. the indignant Czech reaction to a clumsy effort by Werfel to mediate between Czechs and Germans in the realm of cultural discourse.
69. Spector, *Prague Territories,* 49.
70. Patka, *Kisch Stationen,* 410–413. Portion of the Bibliography listing 12 Kisch books and one book–chapter translated into Czech and published between 1928 and 1939.
71. Kisch, *GW (1993) Vol. 11,* 283–426. Poláček's 'back-translations' into German of 54 articles Kisch wrote in Czech for *Lidové noviny* during 1922–1925.
72. O'Keeffe, "Role Reversal—Shabbos Goy in the Mirror", *passim.*
73. Ort, *Art and Life,* 3–17. Definition and description of this generation.
74. *Ibid.,* 129–132. Re. the communist allegiances of the *Devětsil* group members, especially of its prominent spokesman, Karel Teige.
75. Max von der Grun, "Die Entdeckung eines Autors", 1–5.

8. Theatrical Context: German Playwrights and Weimar Comedy and Cabaret

1. Grange, *Comedy in the Weimar Republic: A Chronicle of Incongruous Laughter,* 1–12. A summary history of German comedy on the stage from the late middle ages up through the mid-19th century.
2. Grange discusses premieres of popular works in translation written by foreign playwrights. From France: Marcel Achard and Marcel Pagnol. From England: George Bernard Shaw and Noel Coward. From the US: Broadway-hit writers Avery Hopwood, Arthur Hopkins, and Ben Hecht (like Kisch, a well-known journalist).
3. Patka, *Kisch Stationen,* 80; 516–517. Re. the play's short run in Teplitz-Schönau; a list of 65 unsigned and four signed reviews of the play during 1925-26, indicating a substantial amount of critical interest (in either the play or its author).
4. Grange, *Comedy in the Weimar Republic,* 9.
5. *Ibid.,* 115–16. Re. the failures of Brecht's *Happy End* and *Mann ist Mann,* quoting a thoroughly negative review of the latter by Alfred Kerr, the dean of Berlin reviewers.

6. *Ibid.,* 112, 118–119. Re. *The Captain of Köpenick.*
7. Segel, *Kisch Bio-Anthology*, 29.
8. Grange, *Cultural Chronicle*, 130.
9. Kisch, *Sensation Fair*, 54–55. Kisch's disavowal of his volume of adolescent verse, also noting the influence of "The Eleven Executioners" on his youthful outlook.
10. Segel, *Turn-Of-The-Century Cabaret. Paris, Barcelona, Berlin, Munich, Vienna, Cracow, Moscow, St. Petersburg, Zurich*, 143–182.
11. Wedekind played acoustic guitar to accompany his cabaret songs. The genre of 'crime ballads' was noted by Kisch at the start of his memoirs, where he discusses the impression made on him as a child by a local knife-grinder balladeer, nicknamed 'Blind Methodius'.
12. Segel, *Turn-Of-The-Century Cabaret*, 155–160.
13. Polaček, "Kisch Theater in Berlin", 246.
14. Hofmann, *Egon Erwin Kisch*, 190–202. In this chapter ("Der rasende Reporter") Hofmann chronicles the rapid tempo of Kisch's life during 1924–1925 and the wonder of readers at his kaleidoscopic range of subjects from disparate locations.
15. Kisch, *Briefe an den Bruder Paul und die Mutter 1905–1936*, 215–216. In a November 1924 letter to his mother Kisch writes he is "bogged down in work" in Berlin. He asks her to pick up his royalties in Prague for two of his plays that Longen is putting on, complains about a "stagnation crisis" in publishing and that he's not making enough from *Der rasende Reporter* though it's a big success. He worries about the upcoming release of his Redl book, and after that his "big book about Prague" (*Hetzjagd durch die Zeit*) in the coming months. He remarks that he's going to Leipzig to seek a deal with a publisher, asks questions about the approaching Christmas holidays and several family members, and relays the greetings of a Berlin friend to his mother.
16. Patka (ed.), *Biographie in Bildern*, 90, 92. Citations from Musil's positive review of *Der rasende Reporter* and Roth's equally glowing review of *Hetzjagd durch die Zeit.*

9. Afterlife of the Redl Story: Films, on the English Stage, a Slovak Novel

1. Kisch, *Sensation Fair*, 322–325. Kisch complains about plagiarized versions of his Galgentoni and Redl stories (and other works) on film, on the stage, and in books, including a 1937 American espionage anthology that recapitulated his 1924 book without citing him. Though not identified, this was Richard Wilmer Rowan's *The Story of Secret Service.*
2. Frederic Morton, *Thunder at Twilight*, 219.
3. https://de.wikipedia.org/wiki/Oberst_Redl_(1925) See: under *Hintergrund*: "Originally released on February 20, 1925 in Vienna. On the 27th of February 1925 the Berlin Police Department issued a ruling prohibiting its viewing by minors. (Nr. 09912)." (accessed 09/13/18)
4. Eva Offenthaler's biographical sketch of Löwenstein is in a May, 2011 entry of a German film-history website: "Biographie des Monats. Ein Vertreter des frühen österreichischen Films: Hans Otto Löwenstein". The relevant passage falls under the sub-heading "Von "der Bar-Maid" zu "Oberst Redl", where the author writes: "[Walter] Reisch also wrote the screenplay for the 1925 'Oberst

Redl', a very successful film in Germany, with music composed by Robert Stolz. Johannes [sic] Schober had a special showing of the film put on for the police command at the end of 1924. Army officers who had collaborated on the film were subjected to a disciplinary inquiry." Johann Schober was Vienna's Police Commissioner at the time of Redl's apprehension in 1913, noted in Kisch's 1924 book. During the 1920s he held the Austrian Chancellorship twice and was Foreign Minister for a brief period. He is the acknowledged founder of Interpol. He also played a role in censoring performances of Kisch's *Galgentoni* play. See Patka, *Kisch Stationen*, 82, re. a Viennese police directive about the play written (or signed) by Schober. See film website at: https://www.oeaw.ac.at/fileadmin/Institute/INZ/Bio_Archiv/bio_2011_05. htm (accessed 06/13/17)

5. Sadler and Fisch, *Spy of the Century*, 90. Contradicting the credit cited in the preceding footnote, the authors write that the retired military man, Hans Seeliger, wrote the screenplay for this film. Seeliger's brother, Emil, was part of the prosecutor's team in the Hekailo-Wieckowski-Acht espionage affair, later expressing reservations about Redl's vacillating behavior during the investigation of the case. See also: Fn. 8 below.

6. http://www.filmportal.de/film/oberst-redl_3406b0cdf4a2498b81ea97cf3a 2ff9eb (accessed 06/05/17).

7. The author obtained a DVD copy of the film from the Austrian Film Archive. The sole surviving fragile nitrate copy of the film was transferred to a more durable medium during 2017-2018.

8. See: https://www.imdb.com/title/tt0431952/ (accessed 09/13/18) Re. Hans Otto (Löwenstein) and Hans Seeliger as screenwriters.

9. https://www.viennale.at/de/film/oberst-redl-0 (accessed 09/13/18): "Die Pressevorberichte hoben vor allem die Authentizität der Verfilmung hervor: 'Der Film ist, abgesehen von seinem von Anfang bis zu Ende mit überzeugender Glaubwürdigkeit durchgeführten Inhalt, auch darstellerisch und technisch von einer das gewohnte Maß weit überragenden Qualität.' ..."

10. The film's missing sequences have to do with a narrative thread featuring another old friend of Redl's, Lieutenant Heszky, and his girlfriend, Fifi; their eventual role in the film's narrative is unclear due to the missing segments.

11. https://www.imdb.com/title/tt0884032/?ref_=nv_sr_6 (accessed 09/13/18).

12. Bernadette Kester (Trans. Hans Veenkamp), *Film Front Weimar: Representations of the First World War in German Films of the Weimar Period*, 75–79. Kester notes that in Germany the film was advertised as "Ein Beitrag zur Kriegsschuldlüge" (A Contribution to the War-Guilt Lie), pointing out that "gegen" (against) rather than "zur" makes more sense.

13. Robert Dassanowski, *Screening Transcendence: Film under Austrofascism and the Hollywood Hope 1933-1938*, 53. Dassanowski notes that Neufeld's stalled career in Austria revived due to the success of *Die Brandstifter Europas*.

14. Eva Urbanová et al. eds. (Trans. Karolina Vočadlodá), *Český hraný film II – 1930-1945* ("Czech Featured Film II"), 25–27. The anthology cites Kisch and E. A. Longen as "sources" of the story, Benno Vigny and Alfred Schirokauer as screenwriters of the German version, and Karel Tobis and Ruda Jurist for the Czech version.

15. While the Czech film anthology cited in the precedomg footnote gives one German and one Czech title for the film, it was also released under other titles. See: Patka (ed), *Kisch Biographie in Bildern*, 44, for a reproduction of a poster

advertising the film as *Die Affäre des Obersten Redl*, with Longen playing Redl (implying the Czech version was also dubbed or sub-titled in German).

16. Sadler and Fisch, *Spy of the Century*, 127–131. Based on the authors' perusal of letters between Horinka and his fiancé, they portray them as greedy leeches fattening off their "Uncle Redl", yielding a very different portrait of the woman in Horinka's life than Kisch created in his Redl play.

17. Markus, *Der Fall Redl*, 273.

18. Requests to download the film must be made to the Czech National Film Archive.

19. Horowitz, *Ein Leben fur die Zeitung*, 160.

20. *Der Spiegel Feb. 23, 1955*, 38-40. A review of *Spionage* in the German weekly news magazine, titled: "Redl—O du mein Österreich*, with the following sections: "Ein Dementi wurde erfunden"; "Hast du einen Revolver?"; and, "Das Ministerium hatte Bedenken" (Redl—Oh thou my [beloved] Austria: An official denial is fabricated; 'Do you have a pistol?'; and, The Ministry had second thoughts). The reviewer described the punitive 1925 official rulings on co-operation of military men with filmmakers and on regulating the export of films that might damage Austria's prestige, comparing this to the 1955 government's attempts to influence Antel by requesting him to ensure that *Spionage* made it clear that Redl was a unique exception to the traditions of honorable service in the k.u.k. army and to end the film with a patriotic march. The review briefly discusses the "Spannocchi affair" examined in detail by Georg Markus. See http://www.spiegel.de/spiegel/print/d-31969309.html for the on-line article (accessed 06/05/17). *An Austrian patriotic song—like Szabós use of "The Radetzky March" in his 1985 film, Antel opened and closed his film with a patriotic hymn, "Gott erhalte Franz den Kaiser".

21. Markus, *Der Fall Redl*, 274–275. Re. General Bornemann (who had known Redl) commenting on the accuracy of Balser's portrait of his personality and mannerisms. Also included here is General Regler's remark that the film did not affect the world's high opinion of the k.u.k army (which, retrospectively, seems delusional). Markus also noted that General Gustav Auffenberg-Komarow was listed in the film's credits as an "adviser on military matters". He was the stepson of Austria's War Minister and WWI general of the same name, who was involved in political scandals and field-command controversies in 1914–1915.

22. See https://www.youtube.com/watch?v=sT0r-F8ME for a 51-minute documentary film featured on Austrian television in 2013, titled "Leidenschaft und Verrat: Oberst Redl—Der Jahrhundertspion" (Passion and Treason: Colonel Redl—The Spy of the Century). (accessed 06/05/17) It has interviews of historians and descendants of Colonel Urbanski and uses contemporary actors (including one playing Kisch) and footage from *Spionage* to recreate scenes from 1913.

23. Luc Gilleman, *John Osborne Vituperative Artist*, 141.

24. John Heilpern, *John Osborne: The Many Lives of the Angry Young Man*, 268–269.

25. John Osborne, *Plays Three: Luther, A Patriot for Me, and Inadmissible Evidence* (1998).

26. Heilpern, *John Osborne*, 14–26; 303–315. Heilpern's characterization of Osborne as "a patrtiot for us" (i.e., Englishmen); his chapter on the Redl play.

27. Gilleman, *John Osborne*, 141–149. "A Patriot for Me (1965) Society and the Hidden Self".

28. Gilleman, *John Osborne*, 141; 249fn2. Re. Osborne's indebtedness to Asprey's book for the basic outline of the Redl story, as told in the second volume of Osborne's autobiography, *Almost a Gentleman*; a note on Osborne's dismissing the book as a "bad biography". Despite this dismissive opinion, Osborne took many characters, scenes, and the content of dialogues from Asprey's book.

29. Osborne's appropriations of Asprey's material include characters (with name changes) and specific episodes in Asprey's book. For instance, Asprey's Russian intelligence handlers, identified as Batjuschin and Pavlov became Osborne's Oblensky and Stanitsin, and Asprey's scene in which they confer with their female agent, "Countess Kobiakov", is used by Osborne, with the agent now called "Counterss Delyanoff". There are five or six more characters Osborne took from Asprey and as many scenes or episodes.

30. There is a "restored" 1985 version of the film in which all of the dialogue is in Hungarian and which contains several scenes cut from the film as it was distributed and shown in Europe, the UK, the US, and elsewhere.

31. Peter Robinson and David Hames, "Ezredes Redl/Oberst Redl", In Hames (Ed.), *The Cinema of Central Europe*, 203–212.

32. Ibid., 203.

33. Ibid., 205.

34. Leidinger, "Redl—Austro-Hungarian Military Intelligence", 35–37. A discussion of the spy-mania of 1913-1915. See also: Kisch In Segel, *Kisch Bio-Anthology*, 166, noting that the postal-intercept operation in Vienna that snared Redl also yielded large numbers of investigations, contributing to the spy-mania.

35. William C. Fuller, *The Foe Within*, 156–183; 168, 219–220. Re. the Russian spy mania; re. Russian theories of who betrayed Redl.

36. Kisch, *Marktplatz der Sensationen* (1947), 290. See also: Kisch, *Sensation Fair*, 303 for the English translation of this passage.

37. Osborne, *A Patriot for Me*, 113.

38. Schindler, "Redl—Spy of the Century?", 492. Re. the reminiscences of an Italian military intelligence officer about Redl's spying on behalf of Italy.

39. Gilleman, *John Osborne*, 155.

40. Alan Sked, *The Decline and Fall of the Habsburg Empire*, 44–52. See also: Sked, *Metternich and Austria*, 123–177.

41. Armour, "Colonel Redl: Fact and Fantasy", 182–183.

42. Schindler, "Redl—Spy of the Century?", 507fn55.

43. Pavel Vilikovský (Trans. Charles Sabatos), *Ever Green Is…*, 192fn111. The translation by Sabatos is outstanding (free-flowing and idiomatic), as are his Introduction and footnotes.

44. Ibid., 13.

45. Rothschild, *Eastern Central Europe*, 117–121.

46. Vilikovský, *Ever Green Is…*, 95–96.

47. Rothschild, *Eastern Central Europe*, 88–90.

48. Charles Sabatos, "Czechs, Sex, Spies and Torture", 173–192. See also: Rajendra A. Chitnis, *Literature in Post-Communist Russia and Eastern Europe*, 25–38 and Robert Murrary Davis, *The Literature of Post-Communist Slovenia, Slovakia, Hungary and Romania*, 131–133, re. Slovak critical reactions to postmodernism, which novelists used to escape obligatory nationalism, the requirements of 'socialist realism', and the moral obligations of the 'literature of dissent'. See also: Shari Cohen, *Politics without a Past*, 4–7; 33–43; 115–117, re. the fluidity of

post-1992 Slovak 'national identity construction' in an era of political opportunism.

49. Vilikovský, *Ever Green Is...*, 38.

50. Stanislav J. Kirschbaum, *A History of Slovakia, passim.* Surveying a thousand years of history, the author's conclusion is that the main achievement of Slovak society is to have survived assaults on its integrity as an ethno-linguistic entity.

51. Vilikovský, *Ever Green Is...*, 22–23. As a grace-note to this historical fantasy the narrator calls Hanussen (the protagonist of one of Szabó's films) Hitler's "personal physician". Rather, Hanussen insinuated himself into Berlin Nazi circles as a clairvoyant who predicted great things for Hitler.

52. *Ibid.*, 18.

53. Robert Musil (Trans. Burton Pike), *The Man without Qualities Vol. 1, Part I*, 26–31. "Kakania" is a fascinating chapter in Musil's masterwork that not only elucidates the subtle differences between "k. k." and "k. & k.", but also sketches the Austrian mentality about such matters. Musil's writing about Kakania is wry, sometimes ironical, and tinged with rue over its demise. Given what happened after 1918, especially in the 1930s, nostalgia for a less "rigorous" and hysterical way of life was warranted. At the outset of his sketch Musil also depicts an 'alternate reality' to the vanished Habsburg Empire—a sort of 'super–America' of the near future in which everything is streamlined, efficient, time-managed, and productive, and where people feel free to "reinvent" themselves at a moment's notice. This is a portrait of a land and people with no deep roots in the past. With this he created a foil of everything that Kakania (Austria-Hungary) ever was or could be under the Habsburgs.

54. Vilikovský, *Ever Green Is...*, 111.

10. The Toni Gallows Story on Film, the Prague Stage Again, and Television

1. See https://www.imdb.com/title/tt0021484/ for a short plot summary, cast listings, etc. See: https://www.filmcomment.com/blog/tonka-of-the-gallows/ for an enthusiastic review of the film on a cinema blog website, written by Farran Smith Nehme, in response to viewing the film at a 2017 New York film festival. (both accessed 09/19/18).

2. The film's score has piano and orchestral renditions of music by Boccherini, Beethoven, and Smetana (from *Ma Vlast*). The booklet accompanying the Czech National Film Archive's copy of the film notes that much more dialogue in Czech was post-synchronized and the score featured music by Czech composers only in the Czech version of the film, of which no copies survive. It also contains a plot-summary, a critical evaluation, contemporary (1930) reviews of the film, historical information on the transition from silent to sound films, and an appraisal of Karel Anton's film career.

3. https://www.imdb.com/title/tt0048174/?ref_=fn_al_tt_1 has a plot summary of the film. Instead of a prostitute, a down-and-out waitress agrees to sexually service the condemned man on the eve of his execution—an appropriate change in a story relocated to the American Southwest (accessed 09/19/18).

4. Personal communication to the author: "Aufbau has a general agreement for the representation of Egon Erwin Kisch's works since 1989." This implies that

in the DDR, no such agreement was sought, therefore allowing other publishers to reprint Kisch's works without legal restraint during the 1945–1989 years.

5. Schütz, "Moral aus der Geschichte", 38.
6. https://www.imdb.com/title/tt2645068/?ref_=nv_sr_1?ref_=nv_sr_1 has basic information on the film. (accessed 02/28/19)
7. *Fernseh Dienst, Heft 38/65* S. 21 (11.9.1965). Television listing with cast, other credits, and a plot summary.
8. Reviewer "S-R","Urberliner Geschichten". In *Nationalzeitung*, 23.9.65. A review of two television plays: Kisch's *Galgentoni* and Werner Bernhardy's *Eisenjustavs dollste Fuhre*.
9. Novotný, Ehrentraud, "Mit der Droschke nach Paris". In *Tribüne*, 23.9.65. Another newspaper reviewer's reaction to the two television plays in the preceding citation, with remarks on the interview of Friedrich (Bedřich) Kisch.
10. The interview, a surviving 'trailer' to the 1965 television play, is six minutes long.
11. Video copies of the 1965 interview and 1978 performance are available (at cost) by applying to the appropriate department of the *deutsche Rundfunk Archiv* (dRAMitschnitt).
12. *Fernseh Dienst, Heft 44/1978, S. 24* (Sonntag 29.10.1978).
13. See https://www.youtube.com/watch?v=MgEy8Hx2_8g for the televised play. (accessed 02/28/19) The credits cite Michael Kehlmann as scenarist and Ludvik Aškenazy as screenwriter, based on his adaptation of a "reportage by Egon Erwin Kisch".
14. See: https://www.imdb.com/title/tt4305252/?ref_=nm_flmg_wr_22 for basic information on the 1989 television play. (accessed 05/01/19)
15. Information on the following website notes that the 2013 audience voted on Tonka's fate (heaven or hell) at the play's end. (accessed 05/02/19) https://translate.google.com/translate?hl=en&sl=cs&u=http://kampa.vps2.vnetu.cz/divadla-kampa/repertoir/vecerni-program/item/337-tonka-siben ice&prev=search.
16. The play as it was performed at the Kampa Theater in Prague in 2011 can be viewed at: https://www.ceskatelevize.cz/ivysilani/10000000034-divadlo-ka mpa/211251000300014-tonka-sibenice/diskuse (accessed 05/02/19)
17. Information on the 2018 season of the play at Prague's Karel Hacker Theater is at: https://www.praha8.cz/Tonka-Sibenice-v-Divadle-Karla-Hackera-1.html (accessed 05/02/19)
18. Kisch, *Marklatz der Sensationen* (1947), 236. See *Sensation Fair*, 242, for the translation of this passage, in which Professor Unger (Ungarski), who is devastated by his wife's orgies with his colleagues, drinks himself to death at the pub "Battalion" In his will he leaves his assets to fund a farewell drinking party in his honor, to which the 90 of pub's regular customers are invited.

11. Transformations: History, Historical Fiction, and Fantasy

1. Kisch's writing about late-Habsburg Prague and its demi-monde is concentrated in Vols. 1–3 of the *GW (1992)* and his memoirs. Numerous other Prague-based feuilletons, reportages, and essays written between 1920 and 1947 are dispersed throughout other *GW* volumes
2. James Wood, *The Irresponsible Self*, 142.

3. Excellent cultural surveys that relate trends in the arts, sciences, and philosophy to the political life (including nationalist ferment and the growth of anti-Semitism) of the Dual Monarchy exist, e.g.: William Johnston's *The Austrian Mind*, Carl Schorske's *Fin-De-Siècle Vienna*, and Allan Janik and Stephen Toulmin's *Wittgenstein's Vienna*. These supplement the broad picture of Austria-Hungary's political history as presented in such well-known works as A. J. P. Taylor's *The Habsburg Monarchy, 1809-1918*.

4. Gilleman Op. cit. 127. Gilleman remarked on how social changes reverse earlier positive critical responses to a work of art: "Feelings and attitudes, however, carry the stamp of time as well and are harder to account for or modernize." His example is Osborne's successful play, *Inadmissible Evidence*. By the 1990s its "message" seemed to be evidence of deep and objectionable male chauvinism (or misogyny) in Osborne's writing. There is an irony here. The objectionable protagonist in *Inadmissible Evidence* was an invented character into whom Osborne poured a good deal of himself. The truthfulness of its portrait of a certain kind of man, praised at the time of its debut, made it objectionable several decades later, a sign of how 'political correctness' can warp critical judgment, yielding anachronistic commentary. On the other hand, with respect to the Redl story, these strictures may not apply. Although he was a real man whose career is well-documented, historians and artists know little of how Redl felt about anything beyond his sexual affairs, leaving his character a suitable vessel for constant re-creation; his closeted yet active homosexual life is open to a wide variety of artistic and psychological interpretations.

Bibliographical Note on earlier Kisch editions and the Kisch *Gesammelte Werke*

For many of the citations from and references to Kisch's books in the present work I have used first editions. Where necessary, I have cited the later edition (1992–1993) of the Kisch *Gesammelte Werke* (*GW*). In most instances the texts will be identical because the *GW* usually took its texts from first editions. However, there are several often-reissued books that Kisch altered through rewriting and additions over the years, and for these the editors of the *GW* used the later, augmented versions (e.g., his war diary, his memoirs, and his 1945 book about Mexico). Kisch's memoirs (*Marktplatz der Sensationen*) were originally published in 1942 by El Libro Libre, a German exile press in Mexico City. This was preceded by an English translation (*Sensation Fair*), released in New York in late 1941, which lacks a small amount of material that is in the German version. Copies of the Mexican edition are rare, so for citations and references I use the 1947 Globus version published in Vienna, to which Kisch had already added some new chapters.

The *GW* was first issued as a series of single volumes between 1960 and 1985 by Aufbau Verlag in (East) Berlin and Weimar. Each of its volumes contains several books or editorially organized collections of newspaper and magazine pieces. All of its volumes were reprinted several times during those years, indicating a considerable level of demand for Kisch's writing in both East and West Germany. The series ran to eleven books, though they are numbered Volume (*Band*) I through X. Volume II, Kisch's Prague writings, comprised two volumes published a year apart (II/1 and II/2). *GW* volumes were not published in an order that matches their series numbers, with Volumes III, IV, and VII coming out several years before both parts of Volume II.

After this major effort to bring out as much of Kisch's writing as possible, the editors reissued the series in a new edition in twelve volumes in 1992–1993. This edition has a different numbering scheme. Volumes I and II/1 are now Volumes 1 and 2, while

Volume II/2, becomes Volume 3, leading to Volumes III through X becoming Volumes 4–11. Volume 12 of this reissued series is new and contains numerous works not published in the earlier series: Kisch's youthful poetry volume and collection of short stories; variant versions of some works published in the older series (e.g., the first 'Hamburg-Berlin' version of the play about Toni Gallows); articles 'back-translated' from Czech and other languages into German, including the texts of three one-act plays; a large number of unsigned pieces published in *Bohemia* during the years 1906–1913, including all of Kisch's reporting on the Redl espionage case in May and June, 1913; and, transcripts of interviews and speeches. The general indices in the older Volume X have been moved to the new Volume 12, with the exception of the name index (*Personenregister*), which does not appear in the reissued series. Due to differences in page-formatting and typeface-size the pagination of the two series is not identical in all of the volumes, but it is easy to match up the location of pieces by comparing the general index of articles (*Inhaltsverzeichnis*) in the two editions.

The editors of the 1992–1993 series made no textual changes in Kisch's works as published between 1960 and 1985, but they did rewrite several Afterwords (*Nachbemerkungen*). In both editions the first eight books (seven Volumes in the 1960–1985 edition) cite Kisch's old friend, the political activist and writer, Bodo Uhse, and Kisch's wife, Gisela Lyner Kisch, as editors. Uhse wrote a long introductory essay on Kisch's life and work for Volume I of the original series. Gisela Kisch died in 1962 and Uhse in 1963, therefore the editorial credits cited in the series up to 1973 probably refer to an overall plan of publication which they had worked out. Presumably they wrote only the earliest of the Afterwords that appear in the first eight books of the original series. For Volumes VIII-X in the old series (Volumes 9-11 in the 1992–1993 edition) and the new Volume 12 the editors were Fritz Hofmann and Josef Poláček. Up through Volume VII of the old series each volume has an Afterword and Footnotes that identify people, places, and things and also translate the many foreign words and phrases Kisch used into German. From Volume VIII onward each volume also has a set of Bibliographical Footnotes regarding original publication source data (newspapers, magazines, dates, etc.) and remarks about variant versions of pieces. The reissued series of 1992-1993 follows this addition to the format, starting with Volume 9. In Volume VIII of the earlier series the new editors mention the original editors' intention of continuing the series with a variety of Kisch materials, including transcripts of talks, Introductions to works by other writers, interviews, and essays about Kisch. However, in the meantime the later editors had uncovered hundreds of articles from newspapers and magazines that Kisch had not gathered into collections, thus yielding two volumes titled *Mein Leben für die Zeitung* ("My Life for the Newspapers"), broken down into the years 1906–1925 and 1926–1947.

The stated policy of the editors was not to include every variant version of pieces that Kisch rewrote (including dropping and adding passages) and published more than once in reissued books or different collections of his journalism throughout the years. If they judged changes to be minor, they included the piece in the first collection where it appeared and ignored or edited out later appearances (e.g., they removed passages from 1920's *Die Abenteuer in Prag* that had appeared in 1913's *Prager Kinder*). They also moved pieces around on a topical basis. The texts of the two plays translated in the present work originally appeared in 1926's *Hetzjagd durch die Zeit*. The editors placed these in 1960's Volume I, which contained Kisch's novel, his major plays (but none of his 'one-acters'), and his 1930 augmented and revised war diary (thereby omitting the diary's earlier version, 1922's *Soldat im Prager Korps*). Therefore the Redl and Toni Gallows plays do not appear in *Hetzjagd durch die Zeit* as published in the *GW*.

Kisch's small 1924 book on the Redl case was not printed as a separate work in the series because he had included it verbatim as a long chapter in 1931's *Prager Pitaval*, where it appears in the *GW*. In the new Volume 12 the editors relented on some of the earlier principles of selection, thereby including the 1922 variant of the play about Toni Gallows (*Galgentoni* in 1922, *Tonka Šibenice* in 1926), but they did not find enough changes in a later version of the play (*Galgentoni* again) to include it in their edition of his book *Wagnisse in aller Welt*, in which it appeared in 1927.

After his return to Prague in 1946 Kisch planned to revise and expand several of his books into second volumes. He wrote some new pieces for these and wanted to include other pieces he had written during his exile years (1933–1945), but he did not live long enough to carry out his plans. The editors of the *GW* took Kisch's wishes into account by adding chapters to their versions of several books. The books most affected by these enhancements, whether actually attached to the original text or published under the heading "*Nachlese*" (literary estate) in later volumes were his memoirs, his book on Mexico, and *Geschichten aus Sieben Ghettos*. This new material was sorted out by the editors from post-1933 pieces published in various works and from the large number of hitherto unpublished and/or ungathered pieces found in Kisch's literary estate, owned by the Kisch archive in Prague. Of these hitherto unpublished works (in German or Czech) some were handwritten manuscripts, others typewritten, with cross-outs, re-writes, and marginal notes.

One of Kisch's books does not appear in the *GW*. This is 1936's *Abenteuer in fünf Kontinenten*, which came out in identically formatted editions in Moscow and Paris (both presses were run by the Comintern). The *GW* editors presumably made this decision because all of its pieces appeared in other collections of Kisch re-portage or as chapters of books. However, the chapter on the Redl case, though its title is identical with his 1924 Redl book, is different in extent and style. It is a sort of 1921 'working draft' for the later book (and play, as well) and is more telegraphic in its writing than the book. The post-World War II reissues of *Abenteuer in fünf Kontinenten* dropped some of the 1936 material and added many more of Kisch's reportages to the book. Rather than thematic, it is a miscellany of reportages previously published elsewhere. Kisch probably made the selections based on their appeal to postwar reading audiences, most of whom had not been able to read his work in Germany during the Nazi years. I should note here that in 1978 the Aufbau Verlag published a companion volume to the *GW* series, *Briefe an den Bruder Paul und an die Mutter, 1905–1936* ("Letters to his Brother Paul and his Mother, 1905–1936"), also edited by Josef Poláček and Fritz Hofmann. It contains other Kisch pieces (e.g., a series of both admiring and critical sketches of Karl Kraus) and commentaries on them.

A final difference between some of Kisch's works in their early or reissued printings and the way they appear in both versions of the *GW* is the lack of illustrations in the latter. Several of Kisch's books had been printed in first editions with line-drawings, more finished sketches, or photographs, none of which are in the *GW*. The same applies to feuilletons, some of which were accompanied by cartoon-style sketches in the newspapers or magazines in which they first appeared. Not all of these illustrations are carried over into translations of Kisch's books — this depended on editorial discretion in London, Paris, or elsewhere.

Regarding the five Kisch books that were translated into English, the above notes about later editions and *GW* additions to the texts point to the fact that 1941's *Sensation Fair* covers about two-thirds of the writing Kisch planned for a revision of his memoirs, and the same relative proportion applies to 1948's *Tales from Seven Ghettos*. The remaining one-third of each of these books is still only available in German in post-1945 editions or in the *GW*. The other three books translated into English, *Changing Asia*, *Secret China*, and *Australian Landfall* do not differ appreciably in their contents from the original German texts, though the 1969 reprint of his Australian book has a new Foreword explaining the politics of Kisch's supporters and foes during his visit there. As noted in the present book, Harold Segel's 1997 Kisch *Bio-Anthology* effectively adds a sixth book of Kisch in English, with its selection of reportages and essays from over four decades of writing. A few magazine articles or book chapters translated into English during the late 1920s, early 1930s, and 2000s, plus my own translations of his two most popular cabaret plays, increase this total by a slight amount.

The Kisch bibliography is complicated and not yet completely unraveled. For instance, the present author has no idea of how many liberties were taken with respect to editorial cuts and chapter reorganizations by editors and translators responsible for bringing Kisch out in seven or eight European languages (and some of his journalism in Chinese). Another problem for the Czech archivists striving for completion is the detective work involved in locating newspaper and magazine pieces by Kisch that first appeared in languages other than German or Czech. Kisch may have written some of these himself (he was capable of putting together a short piece in English or French), or translators may have brought them over into their native languages from manuscripts they received from Kisch. Besides the *GW*, especially the general indices of Volume X of the original series and Volume 12 of the 1992-93 reissue, the best place to examine the scope of Kisch's writing in both German and in translation is the immense Bibliography in Marcus Patka's 1997 biography. Both the *GW* editors and Patka deserve praise for their persistence and achievements in the effort to document this large body of writing, most of which is intrinsically interesting on a topical and stylistic basis, and all of which is historically interesting on account of Kisch's status as the outstanding figure of German reportage during the interwar era.

Bibliography

Armour, Ian D. "Colonel Redl: Fact and Fantasy." *Intelligence and National Security* 2(1) (1987): 170–183.

——, "Review of: Georg Markus, *Der Fall Redl.*" *Intelligence and National Security* 2(4) (1987): 186–89.

Asprey, Robert B. *The Panther's Feast.* New York: G. P. Putnam's Sons, 1959.

Balk, Theodor. "Egon Erwin Kisch and his Reportage—On the 50th Year of a Noted Revolutionary Reporter." Translated by S. D. Kogan. *International Literature* 4 (1935): 57–70.

Bridge, F. R. *The Habsburg Monarchy among the Great Powers, 1815–1918.* New York, Oxford, Munich: Berg, 1990.

Busch, Tristan. *Entlarvter Geheimdienst: Secretinismus.* Zurich: Pegasus, 1946.

——,*Secret Service Unmasked.* Translated by Anthony V. Ireland. London: Hutchinson and Co. Ltd., 1950.

Campbell, Russell. *Marked Women: Prostitutes and Prostitution in the Cinema.* Madison, WI: The University of Wisconsin Press, 2005.

Carey, John, ed. *The Faber Book of Reportage.* London: Faber and Faber, 1987.

Chitnis, Rajendra A. *Literature in Post-Communist Russia and Eastern Europe: The Russian, Czech and Slovak Fiction of the Changes, 1988–1998.* New York: Routledge, 2005.

Cohen, Gary B. *The Politics of Ethnic Survival: Germans in Prague, 1861–1914 (2nd Ed. Revised).* West Lafayette, IN: Purdue University Press. 2006.

Cohen, Shari. *Politics without a Past: The Absence of History in Postcommunist Nationalism.* Durham, NC: Duke University Press, 1999.

Dassanowski, Robert. *Screening Transcendence: Film under Austrofascism and the Hollywood Hope 1933–1938.* Bloomington, IN: Indiana University Press. 2018.

Dagan, Avigdor. "The Czech Jewish Symbiosis of Prague: The Langer Brothers." *Cross Currents* 10 (1991): 180-193.

Davis, Graham. http://www.podiumcafe.com/book-corner/2015/2/1/7960457/elliptical-treadmill-by-egon-erwin-kisch

Davis, Robert Murrary. *The Literature of Post-Communist Slovenia, Slovakia, Hungary, and Romania: A Study.* Jefferson, NC: McFarland and Co. Inc., 2008.

Deak, Istvan (Deák, István). *Weimar Germany's Left-Wing Intellectuals: A Political History of the Weltbühne and its Circle.* Berkeley and Los Angeles: University of California Press, 1968.

——,*Beyond Nationalism: A Social and Political History of the Habsburg Officer Corps, 1848-1918.* New York: Oxford University Press, 1992.

Der Spiegel. "*Redl—O du mein Österreich*" (Feb. 23, 1955): 38-40.

Fuchik (Fučik), Julius. *(Reportage:) Notes from the Gallows.* New York: New Century Publishers, 1948.

Fuller, William C. Jr. *The Foe Within: Fantasies of Treason and the End of Imperial Russia.* Ithaca, NY and London: Cornell University Press, 2006.

Gilleman, Luc. *John Osborne, Vituperative Artist: A Reading of His Life and Plays.* London: Routledge, 2001.

Glosíková, Viera. Egon Erwin Kischs Dramatische Arbeiten I". *Philologica Pragensia (časopis pro moderní filologii)* 28 (67) no. 4, (1985): 177-192.

——, "Dramatische Arbeiten Egon Erwin Kischs II". *Philologica Pragensia (časopis pro moderní filologii)* 29 (68) no. 1 (1986): 14-27.

Grange, William. *Comedy in the Weimar Republic. A Chronicle of Incongruous Laughter.* Westport, CT and London: Greenwood Press, 1996.

——,*Cultural Chronicle of the Weimar Republic.* Lanham, MD and Plymouth, UK: Scarecrow Press, 2008.

Hames, Peter, ed. *The Cinema of Central Europe.* London: Wallflower Press, 2005.

Hastings, Max. *Catastrophe 1914: Europe Goes To War.* New York: Alfred A. Knopf, 2013.

Haupt, Klaus. *Egon Erwin Kisch (1885–1948): Der rasende Reporter aus dem Prager "Haus zu den goldenen Bären".* Berlin: Hentrich & Hentrich, 2008.

Heilpern, John. *John Osborne: The Many Lives of the Angry Young Man.* New York: Alfred Knopf, 2007.

Herwig, Holger H. *The First World War: Germany and Austria 1914–1918 (2nd Edition).* New York: Bloomsbury Academic Press, 2014.

Hofmann, Fritz. *Egon Erwin Kisch, Der rasende Reporter: Biografie.* Berlin: Verlag Neues Leben, 1988.

Holmes, Deborah. "The Feuilleton of the Viennese 'Arbeiter Zeitung' 1918-1934: Production Parameters and Personality Problems." *Austrian Studies* 14 (2006): 99-117.

Horowitz, Michael. *Ein Leben für die Zeitung: Der rasende Reporter Egon Erwin Kisch.* Wien: Verlag ORAC, 1985.

Jack, Ian, ed. *The Granta Book of Reportage.* London: Granta Publications, 2006.

Janik, Allan and Stephen Toulmin. *Wittgenstein's Vienna*. New York: Simon and Schuster (Touchstone), 1973.

Johnston, William M. *The Austrian Mind: An Intellectual and Social History 1848–1938*. Berkeley, Los Angeles and London: University of California Press, 1983.

Keegan, John. *The First World War*. New York: Alfred A. Knopf, 1999.

Kester, Bernadette. *Film Front Weimar: Representations of the First World War in German Films of the Weimar Period (1919–1933)*. Translated by Hans Veenkamp. Amsterdam: Amsterdam University Press, 2003.

Kirschbaum, Stanislav J. *A History of Slovakia: The Struggle for Survival*. New York: Palgrave Macmillan, 1995.

Kisch, Egon Erwin. *Die Abenteuer in Prag*. Wien, Prag and Leipzig: Ed. Strache Verlag, 1920.

———, *Soldat im Prager Korps*. Leipzig and Prag (University of Michigan Libraries Reprint): Verlag der K. Andréschen Buchhandlung, 1922.

———, *Klassischer Journalismus: Die Meisterwerke der Zeitung Gesammelt und Herausgegeben von Egon Erwin Kisch*. Berlin: Rudolf Kammerer Verlag, 1923.

———, *Der Fall des Generalstabschefs Redl*. Berlin: Verlag Die Schmiede, 1924.

———, *Der rasende Reporter*. Berlin: Erich Reiss Verlag, 1925.

———, *Hetzjagd durch die Zeit*. Berlin: Erich Reiss Verlag, 1926.

———, *Zaren, Popen, Bolschewiken*. Berlin: Erich Reiss Verlag, 1927.

———, *Wagnisse in aller Welt (Second Ed.)*. Berlin: Universum Bücherei für Alle, 1929.

———, *Egon Erwin Kisch Beehrt Sich Darzubieten: Paradies Ameika*. Berlin: Erich Reiss Verlag, 1930.

———, *Schreib das auf, Kisch! Das Kriegtagebuich von Egon Erwin Kisch*. Berlin: Erich Reiss Verlag, 1930.

———, *Prager Pitaval*. Berlin: Erich Reiss Verlag, 1931.

———, *Geschichten aus sieben Ghettos*. Amsterdam: Verllag Allert de Lange, 1934.

———, *Changing Asia*. Translated by Rita Reil. New York: Alfred A. Knopf, 1935.

———, *Secret China*. Translated by Michael Davidson. London: John Lane The Bodley Head Ltd., 1935.

———, *Abenteuer in funf Kontinenten*. Paris: Éditions du Carrefour, 1936.

———, *Landung in Australien*. Amsterdam: Verlag Allert de Lange, 1937.

——, *Australian Landfall*. Translated by John Fisher, Irene Fitzgerald and Kevin Fitzgerald. London: Martin Secker and Warburg, 1937.

——, *The Three Cows* (Key Books No. 8). Translated by Stewart Farrar. London: Fore Publications Ltd, 1939.

——, *Sensation Fair*. Translated by Guy Endore. New York: Modern Age Books, 1941.

——, *Marktplatz der Sensationen*. Ciudad de México: El Libro Libre, 1942.

——, "Unmasking Gustav Regler." *New Masses* (March 1942): 12–13.

——, *Marktplatz der Sensationen*. Wien: Globus Verlag, 1947.

——, *Tales From Seven Ghettos*. Translated by Edith Bone. London: Robert Anscombe & Co. Ltd., 1948.

——, *Unter Spaniens Himmel*. Berlin: Verlag des Ministeriums für Nationale Verteidigung, 1961.

——, *Australian Landfall*. Translated by John Fisher, Irene Fitzgerald and Kevin Fitzgerald. Sydney: Australasian Book Society, 1969.

Kundera, Milan. *The Joke*. Translated by Aaron Asher. New York: Harper Collins, 1992.

Leo, Maxim. *Red Love: The Story of an East German Family*. Translated by Shaun Whiteside. London: Pushkin Press, 2013.

Leidinger, Hannes. "The Case of Alfred Redl and the Situation of Austro-Hungarian Military Intelligence on the Eve of World War I." Translated by Inge Fink. In *1914: Austria-Hungary, the Origins and the First Year of World War I*. Edited by Günter Bischof and Ferdinand Karlhofer. New Orleans: University of New Orleans Press, 2014.

Márai, Sándor. *Embers*. Translated by Carol Brown Janeway. New York: Alfred A. Knopf, 2002.

Markus, Georg. *Der Fall Redl. Mit unveröffentlichten Geheimdokumenten zur folgenschwer-sten Spionage-Affäre des Jahrhunderts*. Wien: Amalthea Verlag, 1984.

Miles, Jonathan. *The Dangerous Otto Katz: The Many Lives of a Soviet Spy*. New York: Bloomsbury USA, 2010.

Monteath, Peter. "The Kisch Visit Revisited." *Journal of Australian Studies* 16 (1992): 69-81.

Moritz, Verena and Hannes Leidinger. *Oberst Redl: Der Spionagefall, Der Skandal, Die Fakten*. St. Pölten, Salzburg and Wien: Residenz Verlag. 2012.

Morton, Frederic. *Thunder at Twilight. Vienna 1913/1914*. New York: Charles Scribner's Sons (Macmillan). 1989.

Musil, Robert. *The Man without Qualities Vol. 1: Part I – A Sort of Introduction.* Translated by Sophie Wilkins. New York: Alfred A. Knopf Inc., 1995.

———, *The Confusions of Young Törless.* Translated by Shaun Whiteside. New York: Penguin Putnam, Inc. 2001.

O'Keeffe, Terrence. "The Long Hangover: Private and Public Memory in the Former Communist Lands." *Slavic and East European Journal* 58, 4 (2014): 686-696.

———,"Research Note: Egon Erwin Kisch – Supplementing and Correcting the Biographical Record." *Labour History* 110 (May 2016): 161-171.

———,"Role Reversal–Shabbos Goy in the Mirror: E. E. Kisch's 'Jack Oplatka's Mass'." *Journal of Austrian Studies* 53 (In press 2020).

Ort, Thomas. *Art and Life in Modernist Prague: Karel Čapek and His Generation, 1911-1938.* New York: Palgrave Macmillan, 2016.

Orwell, George. *The Orwell Reader: Fiction, Essays, and Reportage by George Orwell.* New York: Harcourt Brace Jovanovich, 1956.

Osborne, John. *Almost a Gentleman. An Autobiography Volume II: 1955-1966.* London: Faber and Faber, 1992.

———,*Plays Three: Luther, A Patriot for Me, and Inadmissible Evidence.* London: Faber and Faber, 1998.

Patka, Marcus G. *Egon Erwin Kisch: Stationen im Leben eines streitbaren Autors* (Literatur in der Geschichte, Geschichte in der Literatur Band 41) Wien, Köln und Weimar: Böhlau, 1997.

———, Ed. *Der rasende Reporter Egon Erwin Kisch: Eine Biographie in Bildern.* Berlin: Aufbau Verlag, 1998.

———, Afterword: "The Writer behind the Reporter's Mask" Translated by Heidi Zogbaum. In Heidi Zogbaum, *Kisch in Australia: The Untold Story.* Carlton North, Victoria: Scribe Publications Pty Ltd, 2004.

Perloff, Marjorie. *Edge of Irony: Modernism in the Shadow of the Habsburg Empire.* Chicago and London: University of Chicago Press, 2016.

Poláček, Josef. "Egon Erwin Kisch und das Theater in Berlin". In *Berlin und der Prager Kreis.* Edited by Margarita Pazi and Hanns Dieter Zimmermann. Würzburg: Königshausen & Neumann, 1991.

Ronge, (Generalmajor) Max. *Zwölf Jahre Kundschaftsdients: Kriegs- und Industrie-Spionage.* Zürich, Leipzig and Wien: Almathea Verlag, 1933.

Roth, Joseph. *The Radetzky March.* Translated by Joachim Neugroschel. New York: Everyman's Library, Alfred A. Knopf, 1996.

———, *What I Saw: Reports from Berlin, 1920-1933.* Translated by Michael Hofmann. New York: W. W. Norton & Company, 2002.

Rothenberg, Gunther E. *The Army of Francis Joseph*. West Lafayette, IN: Purdue University Press, 1976.

Rothschild, Joseph. *Eastern Central Europe between the Two World Wars*. Seattle: University of Washington Press,1974.

Rothschild, Joseph and Nancy M. Wingfield. *Return to Diversity: A Political History of East Central Europe Since World War II (4th Ed.)*. New York and Oxford: Oxford University Press, 2008.

Sabatos, Charles. "Czechs, Sex, Spies and Torture: Slovak Identity as Translation in Vilikovský's *Ever Green Is ...*" *Comparative Literature Studies*, 40, 2 (2003): 173-192.

Sadler, John and Silvie Fisch. *Spy of the Century: Alfred Redl and the Betrayal of Austria-Hungary*. South Yorkshire: Pen and Sword Books Ltd., 2016.

Sayer, Derek. *The Coasts of Bohemia: A Czech History*. Princeton, NJ: Princeton University Press, 1998.

Schindler, John R. "Redl—Spy of the Century?" *International Journal of Intelligence and Counterintelligene* 18 (2005): 483-507.

———, *Fall of the Double Eagle: The Battle for Galicia and the Demise of Austria-Hungary*. Lincoln, NE: Potomac Books (University of Nebraska Press), 2015.

Schlenstedt, Dieter. *Egon Erwin Kisch: Leben und Werk (2nd Ed)*. Berlin: Volkseigener Verlag Volk und Wissen, 1967.

Schneider, Vera. *Wachposten und Grenzgänger: Deutschsprachige Autoren in Prag und die öffentliche Herstellung nationaler Identität*. Würzburg: Könighausen & Neumann, 2009.

Schnitzler, Arthur. *The Road to the Open*. Translated by Horace Samuel. Evanston, IL: Northwestern University Press, 1991.

———, *Bachelors—Stories and Novellas*. Translated by Margret Schaefer. Chicago: Ivan R. Dee, 2006.

Schorske, Carl E. *Fin-De-Siècle Vienna: Politics and Culture*. New York: Random House Vintage Books Edition, 1981.

Schütz, Erhard. "Moral aus der Geschichte—Zur Wahrheit des Egon Erwin Kisch." In Ludwig Arnold, ed. *Text + Kritik: Zeitschrift für Literatur—Egon Erwin Kisch* 67 (Juli 1980): 38–47. München

Segel, Harold B. *Turn-Of-The-Century Cabaret: Paris, Barcelona, Berlin, Munich, Vienna, Cracow, Moscow, St. Petersburg, Zurich*. New York: Columbia University Press, 1987.

———, *The Vienna Coffeehouse Wits 1890–1938*. West Lafayette IN: Purdue University Press, 1993.

———, *Egon Erwin Kisch, The Raging Reporter: A Bio-Anthology*. West Lafayette, IN: Purdue University Press, 1997.

———, *The Columbia Guide to the Literatures of Eastern Europe Since 1945*. New York: Columbia University Press, 2003.

Seton-Watson, Hugh. *The Sick Heart of Modern Europe: The Problem of the Danubian Lands*. Seattle and London: University of Washington Press, 1975.

Seton-Watson, R. W. ("Scotus Viator"). *Racial Problems in Hung*ary. London: Archibald Constable & Co. Ltd., 1908.

Silvers, Robert B., ed. *The New York Review Abroad: Fifty Years of International Reportage*. New York: The New York Review of Books, 2013.

Skaff, Sheila. "Ambivalence and Cigarettes: Egon Erwin Kisch's 'At Ford's Place in Detroit,' with a Translation of the Text." *Michigan Historical Review* 29, 1 (Spring, 2003): 119-131.

Sked, Alan. *The Decline and Fall of the Habsburg Empire* 1815-1918. London and New York: Longman, 1989.

———, *Metternich and Austria: An Evaluation*. New York: Palgrave Macmillan, 2008.

Slater, Ken. "Egon Kisch: A Biographical Outline." *Labour History* Nr. 36 (May, 1979): 94-103.

Smith, Julian. *Newspaper Reporting and Modern Reportage: A Lecture to the Writers' League by Julian Smith—With Notable Examples from the Works of Egon Erwin Kisch*. Sydney: Australian Writers' League, 1935.

———, *On the Pacific Front: The Adventures of Egon Kisch in Australia*. Sydney: Australian Book Services Limited, 1936.

Snyder, Timothy. *The Red Prince: The Secret Lives of a Habsburg Archduke*. New York: Basic Books, 2008.

Sondhaus, Lawrence. *Franz Conrad von Hötzendorf: Architect of the Apocalypse*. Boston: Brill, 2000.

Spector, Scott. *Prague Territories: National Conflict and Cultural Innovation in Franz Kafka's Fin de Siècle*. Berkeley, Los Angeles and London: University of California Press, 2000.

Steiner, Peter. *The Deserts of Bohemia: Czech Fiction and Its Social Context*. Ithaca, NY: Cornell University Press, 2000.

Taylor, A.J.P. *The Habsburg Monarchy, 1809–1918. A History of the Austrian Empire and Austria–Hungary*. Chicago: University of Chicago Press, 1976.

Urbanová, Eva, Blažena Urgošiková, and Vladimir Opěla, eds. *Český hraný film II – 1930–1945* (Czech featured film II). Translated by Karolina Vočadlodá. Národní filmový archive. Praha,1998.

Vilikovský, Pavel. *Ever Green Is ...—Selected Prose*. Translated by Charles Sabatos. Evanston, IL: Northwestern University Press, 2002.

Von der Grün, Max. "Die Entdeckung eines Autors." In Ludwig Arnold, ed. *Text + Kritik: Zeitschrift für Literatur – Egon Erwin Kisch* 67 (Juli 1980): 1-5.

Wagner, Rudolf G. *Inside a Service Trade: Studies in Contemporary Chinese Prose*. Cambridge MA: Harvard University Press, 1992.

Wawro, Geoffrey. *A Mad Catastrophe: The Outbreak of World War I and the Collapse of the Habsburg Empire*. New York: Basic Books, 2015.

Wedekind, Frank. *Four Major Plays*. Translated by Carl R. Mueller. Hanover, NH: Smith and Kraus Inc., 2000.

Wells, Julie. "Writers and Fascism: The Kisch Case." In *Workers and Intellectuals: Essays on Twentieth Century Australia from Ten Urban Hunters and Gatherers*. Edited by Richard Niles and Barry York. London: Edward Blackwood, 1992.

Willett, John. *Art and Politics in the Weimar Period: The New Sobriety 1917–1933*. New York: Pantheon Books, 1978.

Williams, Keith. "The Will to Objectivity: Egon Erwin Kisch's *Der rasende Reporter*." *The Modern Language Review* 85(1) (Jan, 1990): 92-106.

Williamson, Samuel R. Jr. *Austria-Hungary and the Origins of the First World War*.Houndsmills, Basingstoke, Hampshire and London: Macmillan Education Ltd, 1991.

Wistrich, Robert S. *The Jews of Vienna in the Age of Franz Joseph*. New York: Oxford University Press, 1989.

——, *Laboratory for World Destruction: Germans and Jews in Central Europe*. Lincoln, NE: University of Nebraska Press, 2007.

Wood, James. *The Irresonsible Self: On Laughter and the Novel*. New York: Picador, 2004.

Zogbaum, Heidi. *Kisch in Australia: The Untold Story*. Carlton North, Victoria: Scribe Publications Pty Ltd, 2004.

Zweig, Stefan. *The World of Yesterday: An Autobiography*. Translated by Harry Zohn. Lincoln, NE: University of Nebraska Press, 1964.

Index

A

Antel, Franz, 207, 220–222, 271, 292fn20

Anton, Karel (Karl), 213–219, 250–252, 259, 260, 294fn2

Armour, Ian, 102, 235, 284fn20, 293fn41

Arnold, Franz, 199

Asprey, Robert, 86, 87, 99, 102–106, 207, 210, 224–227, 235, 272, 273, 281fn12, 282fn14, 284fn20, 293fn28–29

Auffenberg-Komarow, Gustav (General), 292fn20

B

Bach, Ernst, 199

Balser, Ewald, 221, 292fn21

Batjuschin, Nikolai, 104, 284fn29, 293fn29

Beck-Rzykowski, Friedrich, 280fn3

Bone, Edith, 17

Bornemann (General), 292fn20

Brandauer, Klaus-Maria, 227

Brod, Max, 162, 163

Burian, Vlasta, 168, 171, 172, 179, 183

Busch, Tristan (Artur Stütz), 210, 283fn9

C

Campbell, Russel, 141

Čapek, Karel, 162, 182, 191, 254, 258

Ceauşescu, Elena, 243

Conrad von Hötzendorf (Count, Field Marshal), 12, 43, 45, 90–91, 92, 94–99, 106–108, 187–188, 209, 213, 216, 221, 222, 233, 266, 271, 279–280fn3, 281fn6, 281fn10, 284–285fn36, 285fn40, 285fn41

D

Daubek (Baroness), 72–74, 281fn10

Die Elf Scharfrichter (cabaret troupe), 201

Deak, Istvan (Deák, István), 24, 102, 280fn5, 281fn14

Dobias, Marie, 96, 281fn9, as 'Franzi Mittringer", 45, as "Mitzi", 281fn9

E

Eichmann, Adolf, 239

Endore, Guy, 154

F

Fisch, Sylvie, 84, 102

Frantova, Jitka. 258

Franz Ferdinand, Archduke, 279–280fn3, 280fn6

Franz Joseph I, Emperor, 67, 231, 279fn1, 282fn14, 282fn17

Frederick the Great, 179, 186

Fučik, Julius, 30, 278fn55

G

Gayer (Police Chief), 90

Giesl von Gieslingen, Arthur, 87, 91, 92

Gilleman, Luc, 9, 224, 234, 296fn4

Glosiková, Viera, 9, 150, 151, 164, 170, 174, 176, 178–183, 186, 188, 256

Goethe, Johann Wolfgang, 175, 237, 246

Goldschmied's, 176, 177, 259

Goldstücker, Eduard, 166

Grange, William, 9, 169, 197–201, 289fn2

Günther, Matthias, 257

H

Haas, Hugo, 254

Habsburg, Archduke Wilhelm, 100

Habsburg, Archduke Ludwig, 100

Habsburg, Emperor Karl I, 176

Hames, Peter, 227, 228

Hanold (Österreicher), Betty, 284fn27

Hašek, Jaroslav, 162, 164, 166, 172, 173, 184

Heilpern, John, 224, 292fn26

Hekailo-Wieckowski-Acht (e-spionage case), 93, 216, 235, 291fn5

Heine, Heinrich, 202

Herwig, Holger, 107

Hitler, Adolf, 187, 188, 192, 202, 220, 242, 247, 294fn51

Hofmann, Fritz, 30, 157, 158, 164–167, 183, 204, 263, 271, 277fn48, 286fn14, 290fn14, 298, 301

Hofmann, Michael, 19

Holmes, Deborah, 152

Höfer, Anton, 45

Horinka, Stefan, 85, 87–88, 90, 96, 97, 99, 213, 217, 220, 281fn7, 281fn8, 283, 292, as "Stefan Hromodka", 87, 99, as "Stephan Dolan", 213, 215, 217, as "Zeno von Baumgarten", 221

J

Janik, Allan, 296fn3

Jandrić, Cedomil, 105, 229

Johnston, William, 281fn13

K

Kafka, Franz, 20, 41, 163, 191, 194, 243–244, 267, 277fn44, 287fn8

Käsebier, 179, 181, 186

Katz, Otto (André Simone), 32, 34, 278fn60

Kehlmann, Michael, 258-260, 295fn13

Kester, Bernadette, 211

Kisch, Egon Erwin, army service, 23–24, Australian trip, 15–16, biographies of, 13 (Harold Segel), 17–18 (Marcus Patka), 19, (Dieter Schlenstedt; Fritz Hofmann), 166 (Klaus Haupt; Michael Horowitz), biographical sketch, 19–25, 31–34, *Bohemia*, 21, 83–85, 94, 141, 142, 158, 189, 256, 271, 298, Central Asia, 14, China, 14–15, Communism 17, 24, 28–29, 31–32, 164–165, in English translation, 14–18, on film, *Der Mädchenhirt* (Pasak holek), 22, 141–142, 161, 172, 251, 262, *Die Brandstifter Europas*, 221, *Der Fall des Generalstabschef Oberst Redl*, 38, 83, 213, *Galgentoni*, 39, 141, 142, 152, 163, 168, 184, 186, 188, 203, 250, 255, 257, 258, 288fn59, 289fn60, 290fn1, 291fn4, 295fn8, 299, 300, *Oberst Redl*, 7, 41, 102, 207, 211, 223, 225–228, 235, 271, 284fn26, 290fn4, 292fn22, *Tonka Šibenice*, 38, 39, 111, 141, 145, 150–152, 154, 158, 165, 166, 171, 181, 182, 200, 203, 250, 254, 257, 261, 263, 270, 273, 279fn1, 286fn14, 288fn49, 299, Judaism, 13, 17, 155, *Lidové noviny* 176, 179, 190, Mexico, 16, 31-32, 192, 204, 275, 278fn62: fn69, 297, 300, *Prager Tagblatt*, 20, 24, 37, 144, 152, 166, 172, 181, 285fn1, reportage, 25–31, school, 20, Spain, 11, 16, 31, 275fn10

Kisch, Ernestine, 20

Kisch, Friedrich, 256

Kisch, Gisela Lyner, 31, 298

Kisch, Paul 290fn15, 300, 301

Kohout, Pavel, 244

Kraus, Karl, 23, 163, 286fn8, 301

Kundera, Milan, 30, 278fn55

L

Laikov (Russian Colonel), 217

Langer, František, 162, 289fn67

Langer, Jiří, 289fn67

Lederer (Detective Inspector), 130, 259, 285fn2

Leidinger, Hannes, 102, 107

Leo, Maxim, 29, 277fn44

Longen, Emil Artur, 141, 162, 163, 165, 166, 168, 170–174, 179, 181, 182, 183, 190, 193, 203, 213, 220, 288fn25, 290fn15

Longenová, Xena, 150, 171, 174, 178, 179, 182, 183, 185

Loos, Theodor, 213, 214

M

Macha, Michael, 103, 104

Marchenko, Mitrofan, 104

Markus, Georg, 86, 102, 103, 219, 281fn9, 292fn20

Macourek, Miloš, 260–263

Mestek de Podskal, Ferda, 179

Monteath, Peter, 30

Moritz, Verena, 102

Möbius, Paul, 281fn13

Mueller-Stahl, Armin, 227

Musil, Robert, 23, 196, 204, 245, 267, 276fn32, 279fn1, 294fn51

N

Neufeld, Eugen, 211

Neufeld, Max, 211

Neumann, Angelo, 176–177

Nijinsky, 69

Nizetas, Nikon, 88–90, 103, 216, 284fn25

Novotný, Ehrentraud, 256

O

Osborne, John, 9, 109, 210, 221, 223–227, 231, 234–237, 264, 272, 273, 292fn26, 293fn28–29, 296fn4

Österreicher (Hanold), Betty, 103, 284fn27

Ort, Thomas, 191

Otto (Löwenstein), Hans, 207, 211, 290fn4, 291fn8

P

Poláček, Josef, 103, 170, 172, 176, 178, 180–188, 256, 284fn22, 298, 301

R

Redl, Alfred Viktor (Colonel), detection and suicide, 21, 37, 87, 90–92, 94–96, 101, 104, 196, 209, 216–219, 228, 229, 233, 269, 281fn13, effect on WWI, 99, 101, 105, 108, espionage affair, 7, 35, 93, 105, 209, 215, on film, 269, 291fn4–5, 291fn10

Regler (General), 292fn21

Regler, Gustav, 32

Robinson, David, 227, 228

Ronge, Max, 90, 91, 104, 217, 222

Roop, Vladimir, 105

Roth, Joseph, 23

Rothenberg, Gunther E., 102, 107, 282fn14

Rothschild, Anselm (Maier), 175, 176

Rothschild, Joseph, 239, 240

Rovenský, Josef, 250

S

Sadler, John, 84, 102, 103

Schindler, John, 104, 105, 107, 235, 279fn1, 282fn14

Schlenstedt, Dieter, 30, 100, 150, 151, 164, 165, 187

Schnitzler, Arthur, 169, 193– 197

Schober, Johann, 291fn4

Segel, Harold, 9, 10, 12, 16, 17, 23, 30, 31, 142, 169, 170, 200, 202, 301

Sked, Alan, 235

Slánsky, Rudolf, 34, 278fn70

Smith, Julian (Tom Fitzgerald), 15, 275fn7, 277fn53

Snyder, Timothy, 100

Sörgel, Wolfgang, 257

Spector, Scott, 13, 22, 30, 161, 190

Stach, Rainer, 287fn8

Stalin, Josef, 32, 202, 244, 247

Sternberg, Adalbert, 106

Stöger, Amy, 257, 258

Szabó, István, 7, 109, 218, 221, 223, 225–237, 269, 271–273, 292fn20, 294fn51

T

Toulmin, Stephen, 296fn3

Tucholsky, Kurt, 166

U

Uhse, Bodo, 298

Urbanski, August (Colonel), 90– 92, 94–96, 207, 210, 213, 216, 221, 222, 280fn6, 292fn22, xx as "Ulmanitzky/Umanitzky", 211

ut Hamm, Hanns, 143

V

Valberg, Robert, 207, 210, 211
Valetti, Rosa, 150, 168, 182, 185, 201, 203, 289fn30
Vejvara, Josef, 157, 286fn14–15
Volny, Vinzenz, 103
Vilikovský, Pavel, 9, 109, 236–240, 242–244, 246, 272, 273
Voigt, Wilhelm, 200
von Reininghaus, Gina, 281fn10
von Schemua, Blasius, 280fn3
Vorliček (Worliček), Wenzel, 91, 92, 281fn7

W

Wagner (locksmith), 94, 95, 103, 230
Watzek, Ferdinand, 103
Wawro, Geoffrey, 107, 285fn37
Wedekind, Frank, 169, 193, 194, 196, 197, 202, 290fn11
Weininger, Otto, 281fn13
Wells, Julie, 16
Werfel, Franz, 23, 163, 191, 289fn68
Werner, Oskar, 221
Wilder, Billy, 166, 220
Wünschler, Marianne, 256

Z

Zankevich, Mikhail, 105
Zogbaum, Heidi, 18, 32
Zuckmayer, Carl, 200